# CONFLICT AND CRISES

## *A Foreign Service Story*

Revised

D1257483

**Roy M. Melbourne**

**University Press of America, Inc.**
Lanham • New York • Oxford

Copyright © 1997 by
**University Press of America,® Inc.**
4720 Boston Way
Lanham, Maryland 20706

12 Hid's Copse Rd.
Cummor Hill, Oxford OX2 9JJ

**Library of Congress Cataloging-in-Publication Data**

Melbourne, Roy M.
Conflict and crises : a Foreign Service story / Roy M. Melbourne.--
Rev. ed.
p.  cm.
Includes index.
l.  Melbourne, Roy M.  2.  Diplomats--United States--Biography.  3.
United States--Foreign relations--20th century.  I.  Title.
E748.M5A3   1997  327.73'0092--dc21  97-6262 CIP

ISBN 0-7618-0729-2 ( pbk: alk. ppr.)

For Virginia and our daughters

To Carol and Jody,
Tops in their profession.
With appreciation,

Ray of Virginia
2/01

iii

Acknowledgements

The spirit of the Foreign Service, whose reality made this narrative feasible.

The people cited or unmentioned, whose presence ~~and expertise~~ made this narrative viable.

The Anchor Atlas of World History, Volume II, whose facts within chapter introductions made this narrative traceable.

The late Burton Berry, whose unpublished chronology of Bucharest, in the Lilly Library at Indiana University, made this narrative reliable.

Finally, Pat Towne, whose editing patience and skill made this narrative readable.

# TABLE OF CONTENTS

# PREFACE

O. Henry in a short story says that about the only chance for the truth to be told is in fiction. Forewarned, I have tried to be professional, reasonably honest, and forthcoming. This is the Foreign Service of the United States I knew over a thirty-five year career. Global American interests offered a singular opportunity for a venturesome Service life. I participated in the birth and maturity of an American foreign policy coincident with world war, the cold war, mideast turbulence, and Third World development. Most of my career was dominated by the cold war. There were conflicts and crises.

I witnessed World War II under Japanese house arrest, observed as a reporter from Turkey on Axis Eastern Europe, and viewed with Washington's political eye. In the early cold war I was an involved actor from communized Rumania to Washington with the Tito-Stalin rift, and, during a more sophisticated phase, in Tehran and Baghdad crises. That cold war is history, but the supportive emotions and principles that brought success can serve if ever needed. With the emergence of a continuing challenge, the Third World, I helped guide our policy during Nigeria's crucial civil war and in its conflicts on Capitol Hill.

Throughout, I saw the United States gain friends and allies, encounter complex neutrals, and re-learn the world contained those opposed to its basic values. In building my skills I met all six presidents under whom I served and learned the ways offices operate and how to manage them; helped design and structure the operations of our national security policies, and acquired a perspective through broad training of civilian and military, foreign affairs and national security officers. I came to respect a diverse global humanity for kindred virtues, gained a deeper appreciation for American values, and understood its human faults.

An ancient Greek definition of happiness is the exercise of vital powers along lines of excellence, in a life affording them scope. As applied to my chronicle, it is more than contacts with the famous or an adventurous passage through American and global change. Starting from our American matrix, my odyssey is not restricted as to time and its truths, for experience demonstrates the more life changes the more steady its values shine.

The Foreign Service, I found, was held together by an esprit d'corps, defined as collegial confidence in its mission and that each officer would perform professionally. To me, at its apex was Loy W. Henderson, representing the Service and its standards. In his credo if you disagreed with a policy you had to

vii

speak up, for it was your duty.  Most of my chiefs I admired, and realistically an anonymous few less so.

Participating in stimulating events and working with dedicated people were rewarding.  There were episodes of aiding our country and inevitable occasions of tasting defeat.  Despite its physical and personal hazards, for my temperament I knew the Foreign Service as a deeply satisfying career, for which, at the same time, my family and I paid a price.  Thus, given the realities, in a sense timeless, of this global narrative, there is a story to tell.

With the expiration of the hard copy edition of "Conflict and Crises" this revision gives me the opportunity to add certain episodes worthy of inclusion. The story still stands as a tale of the Foreign Service in my time.

R.M.M.
The Forest at Duke
1996

*The revised edition adds some minor changes, and style changes, but remains a tale of my time.*

*R.M.M.*
*The Forest at Duke*
*1997.*

*The personal changes mark the first curtain.*

*R.M.M.*
*2000*
*The Forest of Duke*

# LIST OF ILLUSTRATIONS

Roy

Lauretta & Roy

Dad

Mother

# CHAPTER ONE

# PRELUDE TO SERVICE: THE UNITED STATES

## April 1913 - August 1937

*The quarter century created formidable changes which the young barely noted. Still, growing populations and cultural strains, combined with economic and political dislocations, were reflected in the great world economic depression, widening international violence, and radical solutions. As a member of a navy family I lived on both coasts, traveled inside America, and enjoyed a memorable European training cruise. I was drawn to the Foreign Service because of its professional code and promise of a stimulating, meaningful career. After strenuous university preparations and competitive examinations, I was successful and assigned as vice consul at the consulate general in Montreal.*

A year before the First Great War my world begins, emerging in a series of little pictures. At four I am aware there is Trouble and my naval officer father is obliged to leave us for an unknown North Sea. He commands a ship, a minesweeper, and he and his engineer officer take me to its launching. I see them in stiff collars and starched white uniforms at a luncheonette, where we sit in a highbacked wooden booth. Hesitatingly I worry we will miss the launching, but the engineer assures me he can haul the ship up the ways for a fresh start. About the time of the launching, I am at a movie with my parents that features a devastating flood. Puzzled, I ask my father what is happening, and he replies that a dam broke. Still persisting, I ask, "What's a dam broke?" To my confusion and the chuckles of others, I still hear Dad's response, "That's me." Early I adjust to changing locales with Mother always there as our stabilizer. We have a winter near the Brooklyn Navy Yard, where Dad, in naval terms, puts a ship in commission, and a summer away from Philadelphia, partly for my mother's health, in a small Delaware town.

During the Trouble our front door has two stars, one for my father and one for my mother's brother. My younger sister and I are cautioned by Mother to eat what we are given or a mysterious Mr. Hoover will be informed. (He is, of course, the Food Administrator.) In the troubled time, people wear foul smelling black bags around their necks to ward off illness.  The illness hits us, and our family of three is helped by a selfless neighbor, for it is the great influenza epidemic.

Next, our Philadelphia neighborhood rejoices at the Armistice, which means my father and uncle and other sailors and soldiers come home.  At the homecoming parade, dressed in an officer's uniform by an indulgent grandmother, I am sure General Pershing has looked at me from his car.

The pictures are clearer when we go by train on a long journey to join my father in San Diego.  I have jumbled impressions of conductors, berths, and Harvey restaurant stops in the desert; San Diego sunny and pleasant with its palm trees; Coronado Island's picturesque tent city; impressive Point Loma, and Babe Ruth hitting a home run in an exhibition game.  In my schoolroom children obediently pledge allegiance to the American flag and to the California Bear.

We move north to Bremerton where we take water trips to Seattle, with its sidewalk steps up from the waterfront, and see impressive vistas of the Cascades interspersed with the heavy fog and rain.  There are political buttons marking a presidential election that a man named Harding wins.  I steal into a local movie theatre by creeping through the back door and inadvertently see "The Birth of a Nation."  I also learn to read in adult style, fascinated by volumes of Civil War history from the navy yard library.

California reappears.  My father drives over smooth, dual concrete lanes, and I glimpse San Francisco Bay with ferries - but no bridges - bound for far-off places.  We are not long there before my father is assigned to San Pedro, the Los Angeles port, with its inviting Point Firman and, again, the sea.  East by train to New York, we see Niagara Falls on a wet, gloomy day.  Once again I am with my father and my New York grandmother.

To my fresh eyes New York has wonderful facets.  On Sunday nights, after visiting my father on duty, Mother promises my sister and me to wake us on the elevated railroad when we cross the extensive theatre district.  Its brilliantly lighted streets and marquees hold our attention.  In winter the shovel-built, block long, snow mounds of Manhattan cut off any view until a child reaches a corner.  In summer from open windows of my grandmother's apartment I can hear the distinctive bell of the distant, open air trolleys, whose high running boards allow the conductors to swing along and collect fares.  An organ grinder, with his capped and jacketed monkey, occasionally passes by playing Italian operatic music.  Across the street two elderly ladies enter their electric car, its chassis an old fashioned coach with carriage lamps, and, after they press its horizontal levers, the machine slowly progresses up the incline.

The apartment has a living room with a crowded curio cabinet including a Chinese lady's tiny slipper and an elaborately carved, multi-layered, ivory cardcase. A secretary-bookcase holds complete sets of short stories by Poe, O. Henry, and De Maupassant; sets of novels by Robert W. Chambers, Booth Tarkington, and Jack London, and P. G. Wodehouse. Mounted on the dining room wall is a large glass-enclosed tarpon, caught off Florida by my great uncle. It draws my particular attention, and my great uncle gives me his elaborate fishing gear, which I never use.

My father has shore duty at the Third Naval District in New York, and we live in Queens, where I am among a group of congenial boys. We are sports mad, for New York is the American sports capital. The newspapers carry exciting tales of 6-day bicycle races, horse races against American champion Zev, jockeys like Earle Sande, and boxing matches at the old Madison Square Garden with Paul Berlenbach and other champions. We boys listen in turn to a radio crystal set, and each announces an inning of the World Series, with pitcher Walter Johnson, to the others. Outside of my boys books, there is a tangible sign of a larger world as the remaining army planes fly over our house bringing home our first around-the-world fliers. I develop an interest in opera and often am glued to my grandmother's victrola, listening to her albums of opera stars. I begin seven years of violin lessons, the last three with the assistant concertmaster of the Philadelphia Orchestra, and my violin accompanies me over the world.

I plunge into the life of boys my age and older. Sandlot ball clubs are endemic, and those friends a few years older manage to emulate a more senior team down to the name (Juniors) and uniforms, playing for one or two baseballs and a few dollars as stakes. Being too small to play, I am an ardent cheerleader. We all become baseball card collectors, and particularly prize Brooklyn Dodger players like Casey Stengel and Dazzy Vance. It makes me proud when a young man selects me several times as his warm-up catcher, and catching becomes my favorite spot, but in high school I pull a shoulder throwing to second base, halting an embryonic career. A popular group game, played in the early evening, is to identify each model of automobile as it passes us on the street. We sit around a small curbside fire, roasting potatoes, in turn volunteering a name.

Life is new impressions and continued movement, and nothing delights me more than when, in a later family transfer to Philadelphia, I am an excited fifteen-year-old cadet on a training ship for youths up to 21, bound for a Western European cruise. On shipboard we have classes in seamanship and navigation, and ashore get a strong impression of foreign living. I promptly kiss the Blarney Stone; discover legendary sites like the Eiffel Tower actually exist; hear an American popular song in French at the Folies Bergere, and witness my first opera, "Faust". I enjoy some of the Olympics, and to the amusement of the natives, parade with friends in wooden shoes through Amsterdam. We sail on Hamburg's Alster lake, and watch a gray dawn at the Brandenburg Gate of Berlin.

A new curiosity is the overly friendly women of the town, and my three same-age pals and I (perhaps looking older in our uniforms) keep score of the approaches. There is little alcohol on board but ample drinking ashore by some of the young fellows. In Hamburg brash Louis Hayward, destined to be a film star, lies on his bunk singing a German drinking song interspersed with draws from a bottle of kummel.

In Hamburg, the ship, aptly named The Albatross, is attached for non-payment of bills. I can now sympathize with our consulate general, coping with our stranded ship and the deluge of messages from parents and prodded congressmen calling for official help. Untroubled, we explore the city from the Hagenbeck Zoo to St. Pauli. The rescue operation goes smoothly and transport money is wired. On the way home I wander in a legendary London with a shipmate, and return on the Aquitania tourist class, where we enjoy observing the behavior of the first class passengers and some pre jet-set celebrities. Since we wear our cadet uniforms the crew knows we are out of our depth in first-class, but tolerates us. In its aftermath the work of the Hamburg consulate general on our behalf arouses my interest in the Foreign Service, and on my return I am pronounced a youth by my parents.

Philadelphia is my first extended residence, where, by luck and despite eight grammar schools, I graduate at seventeen from Germantown High School. By junior year, after the European trip and likely caused by it, I wake up academically, and for this I am grateful to a first mentor, an English teacher. Aside from school sports, I participate in the Footlight Club, on the staff of the school paper, and as sports editor of the class Record Book, where these activities bring me one of our class prized "G-Pin" awards.

Over time, the uniqueness of Philadelphia grew upon me. William Penn's statue stood atop City Hall, and his hat was higher than any city building. Its citizens always gathered for the outstanding New Year's Day Mummer Parade, featuring elaborate costumes, immense streetwide, silken canopies carried by costumed retainers, and interspersed by string bands joyfully playing songs of the day and always, the jaunty perennial, "Golden Slippers." Fairmount Park along the Schuykill River was a lovely natural city area, the largest east of the Mississippi. In those days, Philadelphia had the country's best known ice cream, and for a purely local taste, its scrapple, while the area's collection of colleges and universities was rivalled only by Boston. The Academy of Music housed what Rachmaninoff called "the world's greatest orchestra." Professional baseball, university football, and the annual Army-Navy game drew large crowds. Theater, unhappily, was weak, with little original drama, but it was a try-out stop for Broadway-bound productions and a major center for touring companies. Its Sunday blue laws also fostered the town's sober reputation reflected in city native W.C. Fields's proposed epitaph: "On the whole, I'd rather be in Philadelphia," and a persistent joke, "I went to Philadelphia on Sunday, but it was closed."

With growing interest as school progressed, I gathered information about the Foreign Service from a State Department brochure and library books. Few people knew what it was, confusing the Foreign Service with the Foreign Legion, recently known from Christopher Wren's novels. Also, diplomats were un-American, for everyone knew diplomats were foreigners. Nevertheless, in 1924 a progressive congressional Act combined our separate diplomatic and consular services into the Foreign Service, the first for any country. The material emphasized that candidates were selected nationwide and from diverse universities, and private income and status education did not apply to candidates for this unique organization. The Service mission further appealed to my sense of adventure and travel. Under State Department mandate, the Service operated American foreign policy and advanced our global interests. At home it worked with the State Department's Civil Service, and staffed American embassies and consulates, such as Hamburg, abroad. These reports clarified what had been an aspiration, and made the option of such an exciting career tangible.

My high school grades generally were good, although math was my nemesis, for I worked hard for quite mediocre results, while in science labs I had the wit to choose a clever partner. English classes I supplemented by voracious reading, and out-of-class activities were fun, especially track and cross country. Of track, one episode I cannot fully account for. My final year, in the inter-high mile run we were bunched at the first turn. A runner half a step ahead stumbled and fell, with me among others in the pileup. The race continued, the fallen runners untangled and cleared the track, and I remained alone. Angry, I started running, and almost caught the last runner before the finish. My knees still bear cinder tattoos.

I was not opposed to participating in organizations, for I joined De Molay, a junior organization sponsored by the Masons, and into college headed a Chapter, but I went against the tide regarding the Boy Scouts. I read their manual thoroughly, but was put off by the discipline I sensed in the scout summer camps. With like-minded friends, I preferred camping, retiring when we wanted, rising about 9 a.m., and having a day of swimming (learned at the "Y"), hiking, relaxing, and just doing what we wished. On merit badges I was completely neutral, and have not regretted it.

Like most high schools, vacant periods were given over to study halls. Ours was in the auditorium, and our pit monitor was an obese Mrs. Clyde, whom we irreverently termed "Steamboat." We livened the quiet by passing around the latest issue of Ballyhoo magazine, then a craze. Into the rustling silence an inspired student at the inclined top of the hall would drop a marble that slowly rolled, row by row, in an effect that magnified the sound, ending at the indignant Steamboat's desk. It was impossible to trace the culprit. Traditionally the senior class took a spring trip of some days to Washington, the boys at one hotel and the girls at another. It was a group adventure, the first of its kind for us, as we had a rollicking time amidst the sightseeing. Two of our irrepressibles, when in a class picture at Mount Vernon, noted the slow turning, scanning camera, and from one fringe scooted behind the assemblage to reappear in the photo on the other. It gave us two sets of twins! Then in Washington, at the Corcoran Art Gallery, I spoke with a desk-seated lady, who introduced me to a healthy, fortyish lady whose unusual vitality was apparent. The receptionist mentioned the other woman's paintings, and only later did I recall the artist being introduced as Georgia O'Keeffe.

As soon as we were old enough to have driving licenses, my friends, including my best friend, Ira Lambert, and I drove to New England and Canada, to Chicago's World Fair, and into the south. The travel gave us adventures. In Chicago we four visited a World's Fair cafe serving all you could eat for fifty cents. A master of ceremonies appeared making jokes about fans, followed by a dancer, Sally Rand, who manipulated two huge fans for discreet coverage. It was the publicity event of the Fair and our brush with a bit of Americana. On our trips we all contributed to car maintenance, and, since carburetors were a personal mystery, my jobs were simple, such as changing and pumping tires. Philadelphia to the Jersey beaches was an excursion, and at night we slept beneath the boardwalk in that popular hostel known as The Underwood.

The sea, combined with travel and public service abroad, held its appeal, so after high school I intended to try for the Naval Academy, save my parents college tuition, serve the required time in the Navy, and then shift into the Foreign Service. Unknowingly, it had been done before. My parents matched my optimistic dual plan by sending me to a prep school in Annapolis, where my incapacity in math - not fully plumbed - surfaced, and I flunked. It was back to square one.

Fortunately I heard of an opening on intercoastal freighters through the Panama Canal. My father knew the nature of the job, but kept his counsel, and I went to sea as a wiper, the lowest of the black gang, working stripped to the waist in intense heat; using pneumatic chipping hammers to scrape and in preparing to paint; crouching carefully in small catchbasins under blessedly cool but rapidly turning propeller shafts, or taking 15 minute cleaning stints in unbelievably hot, pressure-on fire boxes. There we walked on boards and donned heavy gloves to grasp wooden broom handles in the searing heat. In cleaning carbon chunks from the walls, we wore scarves over nose and mouth to escape the worst carbon dust, but shaving still resembled scraping wire that had been a beard.

We watched scenes of the Canal from on deck, as our usual work area far below was unendurable in Panama's heat, working Sundays to compensate. We smelled the tropical vegetation, saw frond shacks along the lake, watched ships passing in the opposite direction, and surveyed the bustling activity around the locks as we were raised or lowered. Off the barren, mountainous coasts of Mexico and Lower California, whenever we wipers surfaced, there was a panorama bright in the sunshine.

Noticeably thinner after some months, I learned what manual labor was, and what life was like for many. Afterward I empathized with those living on the margin and understood that they exist on the thin edge of violence. A Greek fireman comes to mind for his insights as one of the most thoughtful men I have known. My two fellow wipers, simply called Chile and Porto Rico, knew me as Boy. Porto Rico once helped cut my fire box time, bearing the additional period himself. I learned that violence could unexpectedly erupt, and there were two episodes. One involved a hammer and a forehead. The target, a large, incredibly strong man who could arm carry a full, regular size oil barrel, handled the aggressor.

There were compensations. Ashore on the Columbia River, I saw the clear, closed end of the most magnificent rainbow, and one night in San Francisco Bay, as I dozed on a wharf watchman's table awaiting my shifting freighter's early morning arrival, I heard and saw the waterborne sounds and lights. I again saw Points Loma and Firman and the steep steps of Seattle.

Transferred to the deck through the offices of a ship's mate and building on my earlier training cruise experience, in standing night watches I sensed the horizon line by steady gazing. Regardless of weather, the running lights were checked hourly and the signal given to the bridge, "The lights are burning bright, sir." Other seaman duties and an in-port small boat handling exam finally gained me an AB (able bodied seaman) rating, but my most interesting time on shipboard was the brief chance to become a candidate, to 'strike for quartermaster.' Learning to steer a freighter close on a set course, my initial preoccupation, is difficult, shown by my ship's early wavering wake, but my sea training was ending.

On my earlier European trip I had seen women treated as commodities. On freighters crewmen rarely were in port long enough to develop natural relationships. They did not wear wedding rings or any rings to avoid snagging on cargo or ship's gear for they could result in serious injuries. One day my ship storekeeper boss and a young water tender invited me to join them for dinner and a popular movie, but first we made a stop. In San Francisco my guides took their unsuspecting greenhorn to an apartment where my boss was greeted by an older woman. She then called two young women, instant companions for both men. After some congenial bantering, regarded by this bemused spectator, the two couples retired. The pleasant-faced older woman in this sort of homey atmosphere offered me a newspaper, interspersing my reading with small talk. Finally my two shipmates reappeared, the women on their arms. Amid cheerful farewells all around (the older woman telling me to take the paper along), we three took off for our dinner and movie. It was a family style, seagoing outing.

Home in Philadelphia after my protracted sea time and freighter lessons, and with dismal economic conditions ashore, I planned to enter a local university, and convinced my folks that the University of Pennsylvania offered the widest scope. Here I began a series of moltings toward a self-sustaining life, but with a retrospective look at my family.

Our name in southern England was Melbourne, or mill stream. In the North and Scotland, it became Milburn. I was influenced equally by each parent, with Dad a pattern for adventure. When he was home, our dinners always ended with cheerful talks. His training nickname was "Happy," and he was quick-witted and always ready with a joke, but professional and tough-minded. We particularly enjoyed the formal, yet relaxed, atmosphere of a ship officers's mess, the chief warrant officers' table set in best style, my father presiding; ample dishes and elaborate silver cutlery, and the white-jacketed Filipino messboys serving. Good training for later official dinners!

Early, my folks agreed that the children would never hear any navy french at home, and later I understood how restrained Dad had been; swear words were never heard at home. His tales of navy life inculcated humor, duty, and professional pride. There was his story of a fleet champion whaleboat crew which dragged an unseen bucket beneath the keel during practice runs to "encourage" better odds in the races. He also told of a Navy Yard captain with a tendency to second-guess Dad's style, who privately said he had proved to be a man. "Well, captain," said unimpressed Dad, "Years ago I had to decide whether to be a man or a monkey, and I made my decision." They had a truce. I remember his World War I story about a sailor who fell overboard in submarine infested waters. The ship could not stop, and the sailor, knowing this, shouted, "So long, fellas. Give 'em hell for me!"

My father's vessel was first in mooring ship during a fleet divisional exercise (a system he helped to perfect), the ship's liberty boats heading ashore while others were still mooring. His captain offered congratulations, but Dad pointed out that as a professional he merely was doing his duty. One had duty in a specific function or location. There was sea duty, a ship billet, and shore duty, a land posting. In short, in a career one did his designated work, his duty.

In Navy style, following a strong hunch, Dad would occasionally place a substantial bet, on which he was generally lucky. During one cruise he had a particularly fortunate strike and sent my mother half the winnings, saying "Enjoy spending it." Practical Mother deposited it just as the pre-depression bank crashes began and lost it all when the bank closed, taking all the depositors' money down with it. On his return, when Dad learned this, he said, "I told you what to do so it is your fault, but I had a heck of a good time with mine." It took some years, but eventually Mother calmed down to retell the story with a grim smile.

Dad was a chief boatswain, a chief warrant officer trained under sail, gaining mate's papers (any tonnage, any ocean) from what became the New York State Merchant Marine Academy. On the training ship he met a Navy lieutenant detailed there, later Admiral William Moffett. Unusual for time and rank, they became good shipmates and he was responsible for Dad choosing the Navy rather than the Merchant Marine. Moffett was impressive; he was the sole captain of a battleship to dock without small craft help. At forty, he learned to fly and became the first chief of the Navy's Bureau of Aeronautics. Accompanied by Dad, I met him when he recommended me for the Naval Academy. His memorial, Moffett Field, California, became a center of naval aviation.

My father gave me some Navy experiences. On my first such trip, from Washington, where the Navy Yard manufactured the great gun barrels for warships, Dad took two such loaded barges escorted by three tugs to Philadelphia for fitting on ships there and I sailed with him. We were in the leading craft and proceeded down the Potomac, over Kettle Bottom Shoals into the Chesapeake, up past the gleaming Naval Academy to the start of the Chesapeake and Delaware Canal. There we overnighted, and with one ship's crew I went to a local dance, where the chief petty officer ordered a stream of twelve beers and a coke. I have never drunk so many cokes! The next day we traversed the canal. Close to the first crossing, the chief, who had done the trip before, had belated thoughts on sounding to lift the drawbridge. Dad quietly remarked we would soon find out. Our rigging slipped under. In a further episode, at the tail end of a hurricane I accompanied Dad to a badly-flooded Washington Navy Yard. We surveyed the flooded machine shop and noticed a sailor swimming toward us. When the sailor saw Dad, he rose chest high from the water, saluted, and resumed swimming!

Every warship after World War I to which my father was assigned won its divisional seamanship trophy, and he was quietly proud of becoming, as the senior chief boatswain, the leading seaman in the Navy. Before the onset of World War II, he retired under a disability, but when asked to return to an assured commander's position, he refused the promotion as he preferred to retain his former rank. In his later retirement, what pleased him most about my career was the efficiency report comment of a respected ambassador who wrote that I was not a yes man. True to himself, when his time came Dad gave Mother some practical carry-on suggestions, honestly prefaced by a life of no regrets.

Dad's lifestyle gave him scope for stories, but my mother, Mae Douglass, took over when he was at sea. She was direct in fostering responsibility and school motivation for her two children and in conveying family values. She saw to it that we attended Sunday schools and churches, mainly Methodist and Presbyterian, with the ministers the sole participants dressed for the occasion. Unruffled by our frequent moves, one on two days notice, Mother discovered new schools, friends, and neighborhoods, and handled the finances, her conservative ways contrasting with my open-handed father. For me, she was a pillar of support when convinced I knew what I was doing. Her annual income taxes were typed in a small looseleaf book and a new accountant was impressed, for although she had no business experience, she had re-evolved double entry bookkeeping simply because it seemed most logical. Often in poor health (Mother suffered severe angina attacks), she refused to accept physical limitations, and personified such directed energy and purpose that her grandchildren came to view her, as one said, as a force of nature. At eighty she took up letter typing, in upper case to compensate for Parkinson's Disease. Later, her voice, always young and reminiscent of her earlier vocal training, startled her nursing home associates at 87 with its quality. My parents were very close and loving. Following his death, Mother invariably used the phrase, "After Dad left," as if he had gone on another cruise.

My sister Lauretta bore a family name, and she and I were contrasts. Lauretta was blonde and I brunette, she was social while I preferred sports. She taught me to dance by tugging on my belt to get me to move in the proper direction and couldn't understand my refusal to attend our high school senior prom. Lauretta studied at a Washington business college for two years and successively was one of its staff, a leading Washington lawyer's secretary, secretary to the chairman of the Maritime Labor Board, and in World War II the supervisor of a large Navy typing pool. In between, she married my old friend, Ira Lambert.

My mother's brother, Charles Malcolm Douglass, named after his Scottish grandfather, was her favorite as well as my boyhood idol. He was handsome, athletic, zestful, and smart, a favorite of our family. He was dropped or expelled from three colleges, and enlisted in the Navy, where he had periods in the brig. Naturally I was intrigued by his maverick personality. He never had an automobile accident despite becoming successively a race car driver and then driver for the Philadelphia fire chief, where he found his career. Fire fighting was his first serious study and my uncle relished its risks. He lived life to the full and was killed at age 39 in a large paper mill fire while showing the men the layout. He was by then deputy chief for the city. I share his middle name.

My maternal grandfather, Elisha Holland Douglass, was a Philadelphia businessman who must have enjoyed domestic challenges. My grandmother Allen, of part-Indian ancestry, left a Catholic convent where she was a novice to marry him. Years later, when I was five, his second wife, Elizabeth Taylor, was read out of meeting by her strict Quaker congregation upon marriage, but always seemed happy with the exchange.

The other grandfather, Jacob Young Melbourne, also from a farm family, was a witty man, a bank officer in New York, and close to my parents. Unusual for the time, he and my theatre-loving grandmother were long amicably divorced. Her English grandfather Lockyer opened the New York office of the Cunard Steam Packet Company, and I regularly saw his comfortable old New York house near the Holland Tunnel. His father, flag captain of the British fleet bearing its army to New Orleans, was an unsuccessful negotiator with pirate Jean Lafitte before the battle. There were others: Quakers named Emry arriving with William Penn, and a Pennsylvania Dutch Snyder.

The only great grandparent I knew, Sarah Priscilla Douglass, was an austere, strong-minded Quaker. Although proud of her brother, Judge Holland of Maryland's Eastern Shore, who left an enviable record with no decisions reversed and never a death penalty, she felt he had compromised his heritage on marriage by becoming an Episcopalian. Her three children also left her faith. As an awed child of six, I regarded her in an upstairs sitting room gently rocking, shawl over shoulders, lace and cameo at her throat, and straight hair pulled into an old-fashioned topknot that highlighted her strong, pale features.

Plumb, the English historian, has it that since the Norman conquest of 1066 A.D. each of us, regardless of origin, averages one million two hundred thousand ancestors, each of whom is equally responsible for our being here. A newspaper obituary of a prominent Frenchman called him a direct descendant of Charlemagne, who flourished in 800 A.D. Given northern Europe's sparse population and the mobility that is history, my future wife would remark, "Who isn't?"

Genealogy is simply a chronicle of aspects of history, with families merely supplying brief actors. Its importance to me is in giving a strong sense of identity to meet with varied cultures and peoples during a transient global life.

Back on a career track, now as a freshman at the University of Pennsylvania, I was alerted that Roland Morris, a prominent international lawyer and former ambassador to Japan, was among the political science faculty. I queried him about the Foreign Service until he discovered I was merely a freshman, and advised me to hold my questions for two years. Subsequently I got to know him, and I found his approach to foreign affairs was representative of a gentlemanly code. He was a delegate to the Washington Arms Conference, where a 5-5-3 ratio for capital ships was established for the United States, Great Britain, and Japan, and where Secretary of State Hughes, the head of our delegation, daily studied the decrypted instructions sent to the Japanese. Morris could not understand how a man of Secretary Hughes' probity could read the Japanese mail and then negotiate with them.

Although I was in the Liberal Arts College and bound for a B.A., I majored and minored in two congenial Wharton Business School subjects, political science and economics. Each semester I took extra credits and previous Foreign Service exams were my curriculum guide. My first friends, also in political science, were A.K. Bowles and Blake Metheny, who knew my family and who later became a senior FBI official and a lawyer. In sports, I was attracted to rowing and was one of the J.V. crew squad. It was a disappointment though, when an unprecedented X-Ray of all students uncovered a treatable lung spot which forced an end to my college athletics. Despite this, I enjoyed dormitory life and occasional long night discussions (friends sleeping around the room), and best of all, became a member and president of an old literary, debating, and dramatic club called the Zelosophic Society.

College friendships centered around Zelo, with its rooms in the student union to which each member had a key. This meant continuous action as members dropped in for congenial talk and a quick evening visit to the Horn & Hardart Automat. We gave two campus plays yearly, such as Barrie's "Dear Brutus", with young women from the Women's College. There were also weekly evening meetings with assorted speakers. One of these, a bachelor English professor, recounted hazards of his profession, such as meeting students at inconvenient times. At a Paris Opera intermission he talked at the bar with an attractive young woman, when two of his students strolled by, greeted him, and took full note. "Perhaps they saved me from a fate worse than death," he mused. LeRoy Smith, a remarkable speaker and wit, an exceptional poet, and a good friend over a lifetime, was the only authentic genius I ever knew. A delightful companion of mine, Bostonian Bob Tucker, a lifelong friend, had determined not to follow family tradition by going to Harvard.  He chose Penn, and at the mail boxes would destroy checks sent by his concerned family.  As an innate businessman he preferred to make his own way.  He also introduced me to Smith, the women's college in Massachusetts, where the grass was greener and where I was attracted to an offbeat, striking girl with whom I was in touch until her graduation.  Among other distinctive young men was Martin Landenburger, an engineer, who became a wartime captain of marines, and showed particular acumen in Beijing by selecting the second best quarters for his company and letting headquarters have the first.

Two university political scientists, Drs. Charles Rohlfing and Clyde King, were stimulating lecturers, and there were others.  Rohlfing had rowed on the Penn crew, had graduated from its law school, and acquired a Ph.D.  His knowledge of state and local government was impressive, as well as his clarity in conveying it.  He became my personal model.  King had been Secretary of Internal Revenue for the state, presented its first budget, and applied his deceptively homespun approach to teaching public finance and political theory.  Plato and Aristotle, aristocratic and democratic, for him in their varied dress represented the bulk of western political theory.  I am convinced both men assured my later graduate scholarships.  In Penn's graduate school, the provocative survey of economic development course was given by economist Simon Kuznets, later a Nobel Prize winner.  Illustratively he showed how intense competition to achieve a smooth cannon bore resulted in the steam piston. English Professor William Harbeson appealed to the idealistic instincts of his students and never seemed to repeat a lecture, always packing a large hall.  In a course on Shakespeare, his lecture on "Romeo and Juliet" was memorable.  After a quotation he softly concluded, "And that, gentlemen, is poetry in excelsis."  The hall had been progressively mesmerized.  He quietly gathered papers from his table on the low podium, and was halfway down the aisle before the students recovered and leaped into tremendous applause. *He gave full meaning to a liberal arts education.*

Occasionally we took long night-time walks from the dorms.  Spontaneously we would decide to walk out to 69th Street, the end of the elevated line, and then downtown to the Delaware river waterfront.  There, late at night on a wharf, we watched the magic reflections of lights from the Delaware Bridge and heard the haunting, waterborne ship sounds.  For some reason, we spoke in low tones.  It reminded me of my merchant ship night departures, the quiet commands from the bridge, the ship's whistle echoing between the empty wharves.  I wanted to be there again.

In another sphere, I can appreciate the effect of my New York grandmother.  As the  niece of the old theatre figure Joseph Jefferson, who named the Little Church Around the Corner, she had a lifelong love for the stage that she fostered in me. When I was ten she named me her escort, and together over a dozen years we saw copious vaudeville and the leading Broadway plays and musicals. Vaudeville was at its height, and all the stage personalities one heard of took their turns between legitimate theatre. Gentleman Jim Corbett, the oldtime heavyweight champion, had his act, as did young Bob Hope as a master of ceremonies before starring in "Roberta." The theatre of the early twenties into the thirties offered everyone, from John Barrymore and Will Rogers to Mrs. Fiske and Marilyn Miller. It was an unusual education. Later in college, on weekends I visited my grandmother in Manhattan, and she supplied a key to her apartment and theatre tickets that kept me fully occupied. As an understanding woman who knew young men, I kept her trust. She made possible my seeing a goodly share of Greenwich Village and Harlem entertainers and musicians so, when Benny Goodman's swing orchestra later played "Stomping At the Savoy", I knew that famous Harlem ballroom.

These were the Depression years, and they were traumatic, for at its depth one third of the single earner families endured unemployment, and salaries for those employed had been cut. There was a consequent sense of obligation among the students, knowing the financial strains on their families, so aware of this, I received a Phi Beta Kappa key and then won a scholarship (tuition and room) to the Fletcher School of Law and Diplomacy, administered by Tufts University with the cooperation of Harvard University. University undergraduate and graduate schools were good stations to observe the growth of Marxist ideology and the simplistic appeal of communism as an alternative to totalitarian fascism. Political extremes bred my suspicions for I sensed their similar face. Still this did not deter student demonstrations against fascism alone and urgings to accept the proclaimed idealism of communism. Prolonged hard times and wide public suffering encouraged the public growth of Marxist ideas and demagogic solutions. A foreign grown ideology was contending with traditional American radicalism. Those of my time faced all this. Academia for anyone alive was no shelter from pervasive realities and the disturbing events abroad.

At my Penn graduation a visiting new university president was justifying his position by declaiming upon world civilization. Sitting berobed among the mass, a classmate and I quietly celebrated by playing tick-tack-toe during his address. Unnoted by us, the speaker asserted that society had paid for our education. This aroused Dad, sitting in the balcony, to a low but clear commentary that produced a like reaction from adjacent parents.

Summer jobs were hard to find, and for two partial summers as a salesman I had been a convincing failure. In what were available as Depression jobs I had sold magazines and hosiery door-to-door, after daily morale-designed songfests of company words to familiar tunes. Despite the inspiration, in covering preselected precincts of Philadelphia I learned more about human nature than salesmanship. Successive door rebuffs rapidly ebbed my charge, and I was reduced to orders from family and friends. These the manager silently accepted, along with like orders from others in our legion of the inept. My folks were philosophical.

The summer after graduation and before starting the Fletcher School in quest of an M.A., then a one year program, I answered a newspaper ad and became garage manager and tour chauffeur of the Mayflower, a large Cape Cod summer hotel at Manomet. I was an incompetent mechanic, but I had an assistant, and since the title meant pumping gas and taking cars to and from the garage and the hotel, I coped. I boned up on adjacent attractions like the Pilgrim Monument in nearby Plymouth, where as a town guide I would inquire if, added to Myles Standish and John Alden, any of my tourists knew Priscilla's family name. My stumped group was impressed when I would point to Priscilla Mullen. In a variation, when touring the Cape, which I got to know well from Plymouth to Provincetown, and passing a tablet attached to a house, there was always the ultra curious passenger. For the inevitable query I would casually respond that the tablet recorded the home of one Captain Ebenezer Snow, a famous whaling captain. My best job so far!

In the autumn the Fletcher School began. The School had thirty three students from all parts of the country centered on the Tufts campus, and each of us could take four courses to assure the M.A. Of my professors, three were from Harvard, quartered in the Widener Library and the Law School. Among them, Phil Thayer, a broad scale man teaching international commercial law and with whom I had rapport, gave Foreign Service candidates a several evenings cram course on maritime law, and later in Washington developed a Fletcher offshoot, the well-known Nitze School of Advanced International Studies (SAIS) of Johns Hopkins University. Another course, American foreign policy, had a Clark University professor, Dr. George Blakeslee, a principled man and a leading authority. I liked him, for once after my overlong report he pointed this out, but paternally advised, "Keep your enthusiasm." There was also a bonus. The legendary emeritus dean of the Harvard Law School, Roscoe Pound, gave a lecture course I audited sporadically.

Our oldest student, Walt Horvath, had been a financial success in the fur business, but on an annual off-season cruise he fell in love with a young woman. Aware by contrast of his inadequate education, he graduated from Columbia, and, although his love affair ended, was pursuing a graduate degree. As a sophisticated older man, I always thought he was a good balance for the rest of us.

An echo of Penn proved profitable. As a senior I had seen our green but promising sophomore football team, eventually to be Ivy League champions, lose to Columbia's Rose Bowl winner in a very rough contest. The next year our team lost every game before the Columbia meeting. Undeterred, from my month's allowance, I offered Fletcher classmates even odds Penn would win. Our team did, with Columbia not making a first down.

Harvard Yard and its library became familiar to those of us commuting from a Tufts dorm. We liked the atmosphere of both campuses and merged into the student bodies. On free time we frequented Boston and the places, musical (the Boston Symphony), theatre (Ray Bolger's "On Your Toes"), and nightclubs (Fats Waller) known to our local students and my Penn friend, Bob Tucker's family. As the year progressed it seemed natural to eat baked beans and brown bread on Thursday, to prefer brown shell eggs, and to take scrod, clams, and lobster for granted. There were academic advantages. Four of us formed a dorm study group to review old written foreign service exams, and undeniably it helped.

Before the School's finals, the demanding two-and-a-half day Foreign Service written examinations took place in the Boston Customs House. Then with the school year over, I went to our new family home in Norfolk. A capstone was shaping with the notice of my qualifying in the writtens, along with Kingsley Hamilton and Harlan Clark of our study group. King, from Wooster College, had a pleasant low-key demeanor, and gave an unobtrusive air of character. Harlan, more extroverted and from Michigan State, was good to be around. Both are continued friends, and for we three the oral exam was next.

Because my family moved to Washington at the beginning of my college sophomore year, I visited the State Department Personnel Division on vacations and holidays to learn of new developments. The senior staff assistant, Mr. Shreve, a lanky, grey haired Virginian, and his aide, Mr. Marvin Will, both supporters of the Service, gave discreet encouragement and whatever new material they might have. From Mr. Shreve I gathered further details about the Service. Upon appointment, a new Foreign Service Officer (FSO) was given an unusual three commissions. The Service then had eight numbered grades and three lettered ones. The top was FSO, Class 1, and new appointees were Unclassified C. Unlike the Civil Service, there was an annual performance grading for eventual promotion or selection out, and seniority rank and assignments were set by class. The other two commissions were for a consular and diplomatic rank used in an assigned post function, such as consul or secretary of embassy. My current aspiration was to become an FSO, Unclassified C, a third secretary of embassy, and a vice consul. It was humbling.

Government work, I knew, would not give a sizable income, but the Foreign Service magnet as a career was its apparently guaranteed, venturesome stimulus, with the small Service encouraging participation from its seeming cohesion and morale.   After I became an Unclassified C, Mr. Shreve said that with no examination for three years there was a wave of applications.   Some 1,000 candidates took the writtens and approximately 150 passed.   Then in the oral examinations over 30 of us succeeded, so our odds were about 30-1.   Currently the odds are even longer and raise the query what competent people may be missed.

On finishing the Fletcher School and getting an M.A., I was set for a year at the University of Pennsylvania on a Harrison Fellowship in political science, which had me virtually self-supporting.   Here I met a challenging stipulation that the Fellow have a reading knowledge of French and German, both unknown since I had studied Spanish.   Another hurdle.   My family being in Norfolk, before I knew the Service written results, I arranged for tutoring with a student of the Norfolk branch of the College of William and Mary (now Old Dominion University), having a dual purpose in mind, since I needed a reading knowledge of both languages for a Ph.D.   Mother never would have thought of it, but Dad wondered how I could focus on study with my attractive tutor, until I confessed she was engaged.   My schedule was roughly comparable to the intensive language training which FSOs get today at the Foreign Service Institute.   Ten hours a day, six days a week, I worked mornings with my tutor and studied, until after 12 weeks I qualified by translating from Rousseau's "Social Contract" and from a German critic's appraisal (with dictionary) of Wordsworth's poetry.   Next, to obtain the bulk of academic course work for the Ph.D. in my Fellowship year, Dr. King, my chairman, took me to the Graduate School dean to say that I could handle the load.   The dean knew me from his course on classical civilization and agreed.   By a quirk of the Foreign Service, I later was pleased to have his son as a younger associate.

A corollary to the broad academic curriculum I pursued was the discovery that I had a liking for the law.   Business and international law as an undergraduate, and international law and international commercial law as a graduate student all made sense.   This culminated in the definite prospect of a three year Penn law school fellowship if I had not succeeded on my first try for the Foreign Service. I had Dr. Rohlfing's example of a Ph.D. and the law, and somehow it seemed logical not to have all my eggs in one basket as I sought both a varied and a professional satisfying life.   Either route meant I would be no financial burden for my steadfast family.   To be an international corporate lawyer in Philadelphia was a not unattractive alternative if I needed more time to enter the Foreign Service.

By the end of October of my graduate year, I was in Washington for the Foreign Service oral examination.   The procedure was simple and disconcerting, with the oral grade over a normal half hour counting as much as the lengthy written examination.   While 70 was passing for the writtens, few candidates scored higher than 75. Since an 80 average was required for a combined score, the oral panel decided success or failure. One brilliant Fletcherite got the unprecedented writtens mark of 86, but after an hour failed the oral. Clearly the panel was evaluating something other than knowledge.

Each of us had a story of his night before the test or of the oral itself, and afterwards a future classmate and friend, Milton Rewinkel, told me of his. On a solitary walk and while he stared at the White House, a distinguished older man began a conversation. The gentleman heard Milt's story of his hopes the following day, shored up his confidence, and identified himself as a Supreme Court Justice. Washington was then that kind of town. My Fletcher friend, Harlan Clark, his examination a day earlier than mine, enjoyed it, and made a favorable impression. Asked why Teddy Roosevelt protested when Woodrow Wilson paid millions to Colombia, Harlan said he thought it was Roosevelt's conscience for supporting an independent Panama. His examiners laughed, relaxed, and enjoyed the rest of his session. His advice: "Try to get them to laugh at least once."

A young woman from Fletcher I thought had the poise and personality to qualify. However, the hierarchy questioned her general Service utility, perhaps concluding that she would marry shortly and rationalized, for the small number selected, to exclude her. The later social revolution for women took me, like most young men of the era, by surprise. At social visits to Smith College I first became aware of women's professional limits when an attractive scholarship student claimed that after college she had no alternative but to attend secretarial school. The woman candidate's decision by the panel was apparent discrimination, but change was slowly coming.

My turn came to sit in the anteroom across a hall from where the oral examinations were being held. I had seen Mr. Shreve, who gave a brief pep talk. Then I was with a group of young men, all strangers and competitors. Time dragged, with sporadic forced remarks to break the tension. Finally I entered the sanctum to find a spacious, sparsely furnished room and six men seated in an arc. The escorting clerk introduced me to the chairman, who in turn presented me to the others. Wilbur Carr, assistant secretary for Administration and "Father of the Foreign Service," acted as chairman, while others included the director of Personnel, and representatives from agencies such as Commerce and Agriculture. I was sent to a straight, armless wooden chair at the hub, while my escort with his notebook headed behind me for another chair.

Mr. Carr began by mentioning my general background. A letter from the university president referred to my rowing experience, and this prompted a discussion of sports, which may have been a welcome change for the panel. One member asked if I had ever been interested in boxing. I replied I was, but "didn't box because I had a sensitive nose." This gave them the laugh that Harlan had advised. On being asked what I would do if not making the Foreign Service, I replied "I would try again." Another query, since I was going buoyantly at all subjects raised, was if there was anything in which I was not interested. I responded, "Gentlemen, at this point I cannot think of any subject in which I have no interest." Eventually when one of the panel members asked a repetitive question, Mr. Carr coldly replied, "That question has already been asked, Mr. Wilson" and speedily ended the session. In any event, as I told friends, I honestly enjoyed the interview.

My guide collected me, I shook hands with the panel members, and left for the anteroom. The guide returned to the panel room for the result, and escorted me to Messrs. Shreve and Will. We had been told, "If you pass, Mr. Shreve immediately arranges your oral language examination and sets an appointment for your physical." This he smilingly did for me. Next, I took the oral language test in a Spanish-speaking interview for which I had tried to prepare the previous evening by charting three alternative conversations.

The physical, the day after the orals, was held in a temporary Navy Building on Constitution Avenue under the auspices of Public Health Service officers, who gave us a thorough examination. A group of the successful candidates appeared at the medical facilities, stripped, and was given towels. I still recall Elim O'Shaughnessy, who was debonair even in a towel. Elim, who became legendary with us, was some years older than the average, and had taken the written and oral examinations once before. Because of his sophisticated manner he reportedly had been earlier told by the examiners to become more Americanized. His persistence paid off and he passed this oral.

Back at the University, Halloween, I celebrated with a group of my friends. Soon welcome notice came of my pending commission, but it meant waiting for the new fiscal year, the next July, when there would be money to fund further appointments. By then, I reflected, my life would have covered twenty four years; a prelude to build a career.

While awaiting an appointment, friends and I drove to the Texas Centennial's second year at Dallas at the end of the academic year the following June. By the close of this travel, Montana and North Dakota excepted, I had been in 46 of the contiguous 48 states. On our return we came through Georgia to Norfolk, where someplace I drank contaminated milk and was ill by the time I reached home. By July 10th I was hospitalized (before antibiotics) with an acute blood infection, fatefully coincident with the receipt of my assignment notice. Had blood transfusions been necessary, all of Dad's crew volunteered to be donors. I had

*✕ After massive liver injections,*

been riding high, but that illness taught me the great boons of surcease from pain and quiet exhaustion. July 30, released from the hospital†and facing a long recovery period, I tottered a few steps and began a daily, systematic effort to double my walking distance. When I could walk a quarter of a mile, despite parental trepidation, I meant to go to Washington and take my oath of office.

Traveling to Washington by the Norfolk nightboat, I arrived the morning of August 18, took my oath of office which Mr. Shreve administered with quiet sincerity, signed the necessary papers, got my diplomatic passport, and at 5:00 p.m. was on The Montrealer, bound for my first post as vice consul at the consulate general in Montreal. My world was opening.

Fletcher School
with Harlan Clark

On holiday with
Ira Lambert, Scotty,
and Bob Tucker

Ottawa Parliament
building

U.S. Chancery, Ottawa
with Bob Rinden

# CHAPTER 2

## NEOPHYTE IN MONTREAL

## August 1937 - July 1938

*Hitler's regime was in high gear, but the paralyzed European democracies inhibited any counteraction. The Sino-Japanese war began, adding to global instability. Americans, preoccupied with their economic depression, could not think global war was imminent. To save domestic jobs, migration into the U.S. was restricted and American consulates were sparing in their visa issuances. My assignment as vice consul at Montreal was devoted to probationary training, mainly visitor and immigration visas. Meanwhile I learned other aspects of the Service and its life.*

Imbued with a sense of adventure, I reached Montreal in the morning and was met by a consular officer, Lloyd Yates. As he stowed the baggage, including my violin case, into his little car and drove to the Mount Royal hotel, his friendly and natural manner made me comfortable. Next at the consulate general Lloyd introduced me to the people and the premises. It was my first working contact with the Foreign Service. This was reality; a lively consular office. Although nominal supervision came from our Ottawa embassy, Montreal in its consular district, Quebec province, dealt with area activities, its people, and local Americans. The brief excerpts read for the exams made it logical for our people to be interchangeably assigned. Now in Montreal, I was meeting secretarial and specialized cadres termed staff personnel. After introductions, Lloyd identified three as non-career vice consuls whom I came to know as comparable to military specialists.

The picture, reinforced by time, is of a bustling office of a dozen consuls and vice consuls, with a staff and numerous visitors. It was on the 10th floor of the Castle Building, off St. Catherine Street, serviced by elevators opening on an inner corridor opposite large glass doors into a reception room, where visitors saw one of two desk-seated officials. At one sat a veteran non-career vice consul, Henry (Pat) Kiley. Within the day I sat at the other. Prominent was a spreading tubbed plant, to which Pat regularly fed pills. Everything was stimulating, and I was too busy to be bewildered by its strangeness.

Since it was my first office, the blueprint is unforgettable.  The consulate general was roughly comparable to an elongated  "C", and Lloyd took me through it all.  The street side was a series of offices with a corridor along the windows.  These were in sequence:  the reception room; switchboard; notarials and consular invoices, its non-career vice consul the office accountant; the American passport and citizenship consul; the second-in-charge or the executive officer; two secretaries, and lastly, the consul general, who had a visual line of control to the reception desks.  At the top and around the  "C" were three visa examiners and commercial offices with two FSOs.  Correspondingly, the down side and curl held medical and visa processing rooms.  This arrangement I came to appreciate reflected consul general Byington's management approach.

Initial impressions merged with my year at the post.  It was standard for neophytes like Brewster Morris, an appointee six months before, to be my informal adviser.  Some years older, he was from my examination group, but appointed earlier.  He encouraged me to use his French language instructor, and I was expected to assume his role in advising two from the next assigned class. Brewster, in a rotation I was to follow, had been a receptionist and now was a visa examiner, while Pat Kiley, my goldfish bowl roommate, was a right arm. Lloyd Yates and Bob Cavanaugh, successive heads of the visa section, served as models, and Marie Chabot, their staff assistant, taught me visa routines.  An American some ten years in the office, Marie directed the work flow, and under a later departmental program became an FSO.  Of the group, we alone duplicated this assignment together in Tehran, and became good friends.

Learning my way around, meeting people, lunching with two, and starting to delve into the visa regulations were physically demanding.  That evening at my hotel I followed a ten-day pattern.  I was so exhausted on reaching my hotel room that I removed my coat and shoes, stretched out without dinner, and did not rise until the next morning.  As a receptionist I traveled over the corridors and between offices all day and until noon on Saturdays.  Pride prevented any mention of recovery from a serious illness, for I was enthusiastic about the work and wanted to do my best.  I sensibly followed my Norfolk physician's instructions to visit a local hospital for continued test monitoring of my recovery, where the physician proscribed exercise for six months.  It took eight months before I received full medical clearance, but I had to try skiing that winter.

I enjoyed the new life, but occasionally there was a reminder that this assignment was probationary.  Eventually I was told that the cautious State Department, unsure how our new contingent  would adjust to the work and environments, sent most of us to Mexican or Canadian border assignments.  This gave it discretion to end an appointment at minimal cost which, I was told, in one instance happened. I did not dwell on it, for having come this far I could not see dismissal as applying to me.

On being immersed in the world of visas, all its details fascinated me. Combined with this was the uniqueness of working in bilingual Montreal. Our clients were non-Canadian immigration visa applicants, for Canadian visitors simply passed through our immigration authorities at the border. The Canadian government had agreed that our office could pre-examine by mail visa documents of applicants in the U.S., legally or illegally resident, who as relatives of American citizens were entitled to preference, and when cases looked in order, that applicants could use our letters to enter Canada for interviews. If not qualified, they were allowed to reenter the U.S. and thus not be a Canadian problem; essential in view of the Depression.

The immigration cases and legal aspects were exceptional by normal consular standards because of the pre-examination procedure and the adjacency of Montreal to New York. We also handled public and theatre personalities. An English actress, the popular stage and musical comedy star ("The King and I" and "Lady in the Dark"), Gertrude Lawrence, got her immigration visa painlessly. To an early inquiry from her agent about possible Canadian problems in getting her visa, Byington by phone had commented, "The skiing is excellent." Miss Lawrence came to ski in the Laurentians.

Office visa traffic flowed efficiently: the reception room, a medical examination, a typed informal application, and an interview in one of the examiners cubicles. If approved, the applicant passed to the visa typing clerks, where the file was beribboned and stamped with the consular seal. Lastly the applicant saw the head of the visa section, who surveyed the file, took the person's oath, and issued the visa. The recipient then left for the Immigration Service office a block away. For our role in the procedure, we receptionists found spare time to do pre-examinations and interviewing of visa applicants. In fact, I handled every nuts and bolts feature of the visa issuing process. It was a busy, effective mill, and I found the process absorbing.

One incident unavoidably involved me with David Dubinsky's naturalization certificate. When an American sponsored an immigrant with an affidavit of support, a moral rather than legal obligation, he presented credible data on his citizenship and finances. Mr. Dubinsky, head of the International Ladies Garment Workers Union in the 1930's and a force in Roosevelt's New Deal, was a sponsor legally obliged to send either an original birth or naturalization certificate along with case relevant documents, which in this instance I received. My function was to review papers at my reception room desk, interview some applicants, and concurrently receive visitors and answer queries, but at the end of this busy day

Mr. Dubinsky's certificate had disappeared.  At dinner, Lloyd and Brew tried to cheer me up, since our work spotlighted visa mistakes, but the next day a conscientious applicant returned the certificate he had inadvertently taken with his papers.  Thereafter I gave him very special and speedy attention!

The man who organized our system, Chief Byington, formerly Chief of the Personnel Division, was a stocky, ruddy-faced, inveterate pipe smoker, scotch drinker, golfer, and poker player.  He was an old-line consular officer who could see no Service aspect on the diplomatic side which compared favorably with the familiar activities he did so well.  His was a strong presence.  The Consular Service was his world, and I came to agree with his advice, to use the Foreign Service regulations, of which we had copies that we were expected to update, to justify what your common sense tells you should be done.  Among his good stories, he had a favorite concerning a novice monk, a chain smoker, who asked the abbot if he could taper off, but was refused under a monastery interdiction. The suffering novice soon chanced upon an alcove with cigarette stubs and ashes and brought it to the abbot's attention.  The cleric smiled and said, "My son, those are for the brothers who do not ask."  The story had a later personal impact.  He gave a further caution; to stay away from diplomatic, political work, especially oil politics: "A nasty business.  Stay with clean consular work.  You meet a better class of people there."

An applicant I was pre-examining appeared subject to the alien contract labor exclusion proviso.  The visa section head and executive officer approved my draft letter, but only the Chief signed such correspondence.  He asked my views since he wanted his officers to examine their decisions, but in this instance believed it would be difficult to make the legal provision hold.  He would not sign the letter, and suggested another turn.  Then the Chief added, "Remember that visa letters are written for three purposes: 1) to get my signature; 2) to gain the approval of visa letter reviewers in the State Department, and 3) and last, to reach the person for whom it is intended."  There spoke a bureaucrat who had learned his lesson well!

The Chief had his own schedule.  He arrived at 11:00 each morning, looked at incoming mail that Dick Ford, his executive officer, had earmarked, and discussed significant matters with Ford and the section chiefs.  At 1:00 we all lunched together at a balcony reserved table of Macy's drugstore and non-alcoholic lunchroom.  Byington sat at the head and during an animated lunch heard and saw consular events through the eyes of his officers.  Back in the office at 2:00, the Chief signed letters, made phone calls, and conducted other business. Invariably by 3:00, if weather permitted, he and an invited officer played golf, presumably exchanging one-on-one views.  In bad weather after work we met at the Mt. Stephan Club (we were all members) for some wild poker (5s and 10s and buried 3s).

The daily office lunches and poker sessions were valuable to me. It was revealing to hear the men at their ease talking about professional matters, for they had ideas from the most technical in the consular field to observations on politics. These were upon areas in which they had served, and Nazi Germany and Fascist Italy were topics. They saw energetic movement and strong public support in Germany and Italy, contrasted with flaccid seeming Anglo-French actions. I recall only one comment upon the problems democracy faced with the nazi-fascist challenge. Although war was but two years away, none of these alert and well informed men mentioned it as in the offing, and perhaps it was just inconceivable before the Munich crisis of September 1938. Another impression of my immersion in the Foreign Service was its acceptance as a masculine monopoly. This surely was true of other professions, but no women of our Montreal staff were designated as officers. From my visa horizons I began to have unorthodox thoughts that some were competent to be visa examiners, or even do more substantive work.

I keep returning to Lloyd Yates. He marched to his own drummer, and liked the outdoors and the simple life. Then too, his visa examining techniques were worthy of emulation. I remarked his logical, down-east type mind, helpful attitude, engaging smile, and exceptional talent for handcrafts and building practical wooden furniture, which we would today call Shaker or Scandinavian modern. He was separated domestically and lived alone in a small apartment near the office, a convenient place for Pat Kiley, Bob Rinden (who came later with a married Randy Kidder), and me to visit. He usually ate dinner at Macy's, and invariably ended his meal with bananas and cream - no substitutions, ever.

Pat Kiley warranted close observation for his techniques of meeting people and taking care of their problems, and how he examined each case with its distinctive features. Our reception room was home for long hours, where frequently we returned after dinner, got our pile of pending cases, and worked away, thereby keeping Marie's correspondence leftovers down to size. Pat impressed on me that it is best to review each case against the visa laws and regulations, and to avoid personal involvement. He was a pleasant-faced, curly haired bachelor in his middle thirties, and loved to handle prominent theatrical or well-known visitors. (He once mentioned his family was concerned about a young nephew, Richard, who was trying to break in on Broadway.) Unfortunately Pat had a drinking problem, which I discovered one day when he started drinking scotch at lunchtime, and within a few days mixed it with coca cola in a paper cup, sipping on the job. Next, it was disconcerting one morning to find Pat at his desk, but incapable of operating. I had him refer all callers to me, while he sat ostensibly reviewing papers. Brew told me he had been exposed to a like episode and had taken the same step. The following day, contrite and the cycle having run its course, Pat furiously waded into his work. This was my first experience with a Service alcoholic, and through him I came to understand why it can be such a serious problem. The Service was a trap for alcoholic susceptibles, who, given the frequency of, and the need for, socializing and the availability of liquor, drifted into the habit. Tragically, another excellent Montreal officer and his wife died as alcoholics years later. It was endemic, I discovered, with an alcoholic casualty in some other assignments.

In a constant stream of visitors, each dominated by his own concerns, one gets to essentials fast without appearing to press. You appraise visitors as to type and character, and take appropriate action. When the reception room combines with later visa examiner experience, as in my case, this is a grounding for wider work. Certainly one gains by treating varied personalities, in not being surprised by unexpectedly revealed traits, and in acquiring an evaluative faculty every veteran officer needs. Over time I could spot an entrant who gave off an air of difference or even oddity, and in a city of Montreal's size and the affairs of our busy office, we drew our share of eccentrics. There was the man who tried to touch the ceiling, calmly replying to Pat's query by saying, "You would interrupt, wouldn't you." No unpleasantness or criticism came our way, for happily whenever a visitor commented to a ranking officer it was in appreciation.

As visa work became familiar, I gradually acquired more specific knowledge on other sectors. The executive officer, Dick Ford, was alert to office activities, an unneeded double check on Byington's practices. He also wrote excellent reports on provincial and city politics, as well as specials, such as the role of the provincial church. I did not get to know him, but years later an FSO who was an associate in Tehran told the story of how Ford, temporarily in charge and impatient to leave, was awaiting a new ambassador. He drafted a message: "I would like to know if my title is chargé d'affaires ad interim or ad infinitum." His subordinate, Jack Jernegan, persuaded him not to send it, but he was not dissuaded from sending a second: "I would like to know Ambassador X's plans. I realize in matters of this kind silence is golden, but I'm off the gold standard. Ford." An unusual, independent man.

Another officer kept a register of resident Americans, attested to marriages by a qualified authority, issued birth and death certificates as requested, and handled citizen problems and welfare cases of stranded Americans, such as seamen overstaying shore leave and temporarily on the beach. Montreal before the Seaway opened was Canada's leading port, having grain elevators brimming with cargos of western wheat. This meant hungover seamen showing up in our offices needing housing until shipped out on another freighter. I had more sympathy than most.

It was routine for the administrative or accounts officer to look after office expenses, to keep them within allotments, and to handle a good income source, consular invoices for products shipped to the U.S. The Public Health Service used two doctors and a nurse to examine immigration applicants under the health portions of the laws. It was on their recommendation I denied a visa to a Chinese acrobat because he was afflicted with trachoma.

Joe Touchette, the commercial officer, was a jovial energetic man, who by one of the spins of the Service later took me on a first visit to the Egyptian Pyramids. Denise, his French wife, was the only official Montreal spouse I came to know. She was perceptive, who after a first meeting told her husband that I was a convalescent. Perhaps this spurred her efforts to have me meet a French Canadian girl, my slight social chink into French Canadian life, then so isolated from the English. Joe and his deputy encouraged American trade with the province, found local agents for U.S. firms seeking them, were watchful for any discrimination against American business, and followed provincial economic life in reports to Washington, notably for the Department of Commerce. Their lively associations and correspondence with various firms were fully comparable to those of us working on visas. It was enjoyable in a vacation lull, with Joe's acceptance, to hold down the section, aided by its trusted secretary, for several weeks.

Impressions of a first post are most memorable. With Lloyd Yates in his Fiat we cross the frozen expanse of the St. Lawrence river by following a brush trail, accurate and direct. To me it is an unprecedented example of cold, with big, heavily laden trucks routinely taking the same road. In a foursome, I am at the Auditorium with Brew, watching from the balcony the antics of the dancing jitterbugs below. We have a comparable experience with a memorable Benny Goodman concert filled with jazz luminaries. Baseball season I am at the International League stadium with Marie Chabot and Louise O'Grady, the Chief's secretary, both fans. Although no golfer, I carry Marie's clubs one pleasant day, liking the greenery and prospects of the course. Happily Montreal is a port, I think, as I wander some off days along its downstream waterfront with basic features I know so well. After the bustle of activity ends, early clear evening adds its special blue atmosphere to the wharves and flowing water. It gives me a good feeling.

There were other incidents. New Year's Eve I was on my own. My bachelor friends were away; Pat Kiley in New York, Lloyd Yates seeing his family, and Brewster Morris transferred to Washington. That evening I was in a St. Catherine Street nightclub watching the show and enjoying it less. At 11:30

p.m. I left and hailed a cab for the Westmount Lookout with its panoramic view of the city. The night was clear and cold, the site deserted. While the puzzled driver kept the motor running, I walked to the parapet, and heard the growing urban sound, watched the start of fireworks, and listened to pealing church bells as midnight arrived. My spirits rose and spontaneously I found myself extending greetings successively to various friends and my family, culminating in good wishes to everyone. Then I bounced back to the taxi and its even more curious driver, who took me down to my apartment house, where I sang in the shower and went to bed. A later episode showed me that, whenever events brought depressed mood swings, I would instinctively react toward normalcy.

The Chief, a man of his time, may have looked quizzically at a young fellow for not playing golf and only infrequently poker. He could not have known I was more familiar with an oar than a driver or with a compass than a full house. Yet I seemed to get along well enough with everyone, from our somewhat-a-loner citizenship officer to Honest Joe Touchette. Even one with social pretensions and a pipeline to the Number Two in the State Department was civil enough.

My social life outside the office picked up slowly as my health improved. I moved into a furnished apartment with maid service covered by a $75 a month rent allowance, and lived on my handsome $2,500 a year salary. There were invitations to officers' homes, visits to the theatre, and dinners with Lloyd, Pat, Brew or Bob Rinden. The active sports life in winter centered on skiing and badminton. On Sundays, special trains took skiers north in the Laurentians to chosen waystops, where my initial efforts were awkward and unnoticed, as on a first gentle slope I broke a ski and was through for the day. Nevertheless it was good being outdoors in the cold sunshine. It was pleasant also to have an evening with a legendary skier, Mr. Johansen, who talked of cross country trails and was an area institution for years. During the week, badminton clubs were the vogue, and I belonged to one near the office where I played doubles, for I was not yet physically fit.

We had some fine American young women in the office: Betty Beddoe, a Smith graduate, was pleasant and good company; Muriel Baker was a poised and attractive McGill grad; Kay Wedge had an engaging open freshness, and I saw her into my next assignment. Then in November Pat made up a foursome for a military ball, to be my first date in Montreal. He knew an American lady, a Virginian married to a Canadian, whose beautiful nineteen-year-old niece also had an American mother. After Pat and I met her for tea at her aunt's, presumably social practice, I concluded this by extending the expected invitation to the ball. I was enroute by cab to the niece's home, when I suddenly could not remember the street. I thought it was a cigarette name, and the helpful driver supplied the word, Chesterfield. By that margin, perhaps, my life was changed. Virginia's father, a gregarious man, warned his daughter to beware of the man who doesn't drink or smoke. He must have hidden vices. Virginia and I had come from an evening movie when he returned from his club, and as an introductory gesture offered a cigarette which I declined. I fancied a slight tension when he suggested a drink which eased upon my acceptance. I had qualified. We occasionally dated while I was in Montreal, and some years later Virginia Wells and I married.

A feature of Quebec Province permeating the environment, of which I was dimly aware, was the two solitudes, as a novelist later called the French and English cultures. The two language groups were self-contained, but it is unconscionable that we new FSOs had no durable contacts with French-Canadians. Undeniably the Canadien culture and love of life were a vigorous contrast to the low key English style. Typifying this was a large sedate restaurant near the office, buried in quiet, and a contrasting restaurant in then French East. There the atmosphere was convivial, with good food and many hand gestures. Too, the Canadiens ice hockey team, the favorite of French Canada, was a leading symbol of Canadien identity.

It is hard to believe the half century change in Quebec. Then the provincial cardinal was a major political figure and the village priest a force to be reckoned with. Family planning was unknown and large families common, with the Canadien birthrate the highest in the western world. The English-Scots were bankers, stockbrokers, and storeowners, while the French concentrated on traditional professions; the church, the law, and medicine. Today politics is essentially secular, Quebec has the lowest birthrate in Canada, and the French are the economic leaders. The so-called quiet revolution has happened, and the dual relationship offers small prospects for English speakers.

The realities of the Foreign Service grew. Lloyd had been in the Service ten years, serving in countries including Germany and Argentina. He had picked up an ailment in his previous assignment and, aside from family separation, was recovering in Montreal. Pat had begun drinking in Germany and Bulgaria, and became an alcoholic. Bob Cavanaugh developed a bad case of dysentery while on assignment in Central America, and still had to be careful. The assistant commercial officer had been overworked at Warsaw and was recovering in Montreal. Of the others, at least one more had health problems. Montreal because of its healthy, cold climate was used as a recuperative post. Foreign Service rules allowed 60 days leave yearly, with an accumulation up to 180 days, in addition to the annual 15 days accumulated sick leave. These generous provisions, rarely used, were realistic in view of the health hazards and strains officers then were expected to confront. I came to know two leading officers who contracted tuberculosis abroad and had lengthy recoveries that used all their accumulated leave. Health conditions improved immeasurably, thanks to medical advances, but the growth of ever-present terrorism became as great a threat.

The Service had a discipline controlled by rank and office seniority, but what had not been fully apparent to me from the outside was its quasi-military nature. There were demanding assignments accepted without question, illnesses, and work breakdowns, but the officers followed their duty. I began to sense a common morale in my associates, strengthened by shared experiences. To my new eyes it still would take longer for the consular-diplomatic union to become fully manifest. There had been thirteen years of the consolidated Foreign Service, but in Montreal I saw its officers predominately had served in consular posts. The Chief himself, from the old separate Consular Service, had gained his reputation over years at Naples. Yet there was no talk of separate consular and diplomatic identities. I found it also was very unlikely that people would have similar views of their fellow professionals, such is the uniqueness of humanity and differing enviornments to which they were exposed. This became clear in hearing varying assessments of colleagues, particularly seniors, who had been more closely observed. An early conclusion I drew was to take my chances with seniors, on whom an officer's career and his annual efficiency reports could depend. If relations did not work out, I'd have to face the problem.

It was my personal fortune to have only the best recollections of the Montreal experience. The group of officers, stimulating and varied, reinforced my newfound belief in the importance of observing the profession through those qualified. This was not to say in the officer group at Montreal there were not likes and dislikes, other preferences of interest outside the office, and human frailties. I learned from each, even the weakest. As officers left the post I also realized that turnover was continuous and good friends may separate, not to meet again for years.

Each departing officer in most posts I later served was given a memento. When my transfer came it was a little cigarette lighter, customary there, with the initials of my Montreal officer colleagues thereon. All knew I didn't smoke, but though rarely if ever fired, it became one of my small treasures.

Top row, left to right: Herb Olds, Paul Paddock, Dave Thomasson, Jule Goetzmann, Gordon Mattison, Charley Thayer, Ray Thurston. Middle row: Harlan Clark, Roy Melbourne, Stratton Anderson, Fred Reinhardt, Bill Cole, Milt Rewinkel. Bottom: Ed Gullion, Aaron Brown, G. Howland Shaw,(Chief of Personnel), Francis Sayre (Asst. Secretary), G. Klahr Huddle (Director of Junior Officers School), Elim O'Shaughnessy, John Melby

Junior Officers Course — Spring 1939
Effort V — Spring 1999

# CHAPTER 3

## APPRENTICE IN WASHINGTON

### August 1938 - July 1939

*Approaching war became manifest after the Munich crisis, followed by Nazi territorial depredations. The American public observed the triple moves of the Axis Powers, but our government took no significant action. Capitalizing on Munich, the Japanese in their China war were strip searching democratic nationals in Tianjin to signal their increasing disregard of international opinion. In Washington's Visa Division, I learned of desperate refugees from Austria and Germany; met my classmates in the Foreign Service School, and saw how the Passport Division operated for businessmen and tourists, with war prospects still generally ignored. My assignment to Tianjin, China, as vice consul was changed "for Service reasons" to vice consul at Kobe, Japan.*

In Washington Avra Warren, the Foreign Service head of the State Department Visa Division, told me what to expect. He would use my Montreal training as a special assistant, to sit in an adjoining office with a secretary, and relieve him of the volume of phone calls from such places as Capitol Hill, while the plight of European refugees worsened. I started just before the Munich crisis. With the earlier annexation of Austria to Germany and the downfall of Czechoslovakia at Munich, the two events compounded the strenuous activity by private citizens and Jewish organizations seeking to get friends and relatives out of Nazi control. I was also to give helpful interviews to lawyers and others concerned with applicants. Immigration lawyers proved to be our most frequent visitors on behalf of clients, and I found them generally professional in pursuing their cases.

Frequent phone calls came from the offices of New York City congressmen, who were responding to their constituents. On a scale, the most pleasant to deal with was Representative Sol Bloom's office, but the most contentious was Representative Samuel Dickstein's. He was chairman of the House Immigration Committee, and, given that pressure, his staff made life difficult for our division. One day Mr. Dickstein called on the phone, and began a long colorful tirade about the ineffectiveness of the Visa Division and its lack of help in a particular case. It was obvious from the tenor that he was performing for an interested listener. I became progressively more irritated. When Mr. Dickstein paused, awaiting an expected feeble response, I hurriedly interjected, "Hello, hello, hello," to which he responded impatiently. I then added, "Oh, Mr. Dickstein? There has been something wrong with our phone connection, and I am sorry, but I haven't heard a word you've said." There was a long pause, and he began talking in a businesslike manner.

One of the problems about visa work was that only mistakes drew attention from the top. A single error counted more than long periods of effective operations. Once a serious looking Avra Warren came and said, "I have a complaint here about you." Seeing my concerned expression, he laughed and said that in reality it was a letter of commendation for some aid I had given. I reminded him to keep the letter in my file to counterbalance an inevitable letter of complaint.

A quiet, elderly visitor identified himself as Dr. Schick. He was concerned about his two nephews, also physicians, who were trying to get out of Vienna, and produced proper papers to further their cases. As we talked a thought struck me, and I asked if he was the Dr. Schick of the widespread Schick tests for diphtheria and tuberculosis. Yes he was. With his contributions to medicine in mind, I did all I could to help his nephews.

Another episode, not as happy, occurred when a well-known newspaper columnist came to ask for telegraphic transmittal of documentary evidence needed in our embassy at Vienna for his father-in-law, detained by the Nazis. The information was sent, and I had a reply with commendable speed from Vienna saying that the evidence was satisfactory and the visa would be available on the applicant's appearance. I phoned the columnist the good news and noted a strange pause. In flat tones he expressed appreciation for what had been done, but added that his wife had just received word of her father's death in a detention camp. Such instances brought home to us in the Visa Division the tragedy being enacted.

I came to know the congenial Visa group well in the detail period. The officers were an even mixture of Foreign Service and Civil Service, with the assistant chief being from the latter. Julian Harrington, later an ambassador, and Harry Troutman were agreeable FSOs. I also met the anonymous visa letter reviewers, who saw that the worldwide official mail was consistent with the complex visa laws and regulations, and who kept records on each letter drafter. They were reassuring and friendly.

State no longer has proprietary rights in the State, War and Navy Building, as it was called, though at the time the only military trace was the office of the Battle Monuments Commission, with its apparently unused chambers reserved for the General of the Armies (Pershing), as the placard proclaimed. Every FSO who served in the building has an affection for its unique atmosphere and architecture. The thick walls, the high ceilings with their fans, the heavy doors and their outer, latticed barroom doors, the wide corridors--all combined to make it well ventilated and comfortable in summer or winter. Senior officials could put their working fireplaces, strewn throughout, to use. The heavy closed doors and the short, swinging ones, through which people purposefully entered and exited, made me curious. The large identifying signs, with some office functions met for the first time, added to this, but their dimensions shrank to reasonable size as they became a part of the landscape. My Visa Division room was on a first floor corner, and in the basement was a little coffee-candy stand where people would steal for a brief mid-morning or afternoon coffee break. The office phones were used only for official calls. Each outgoing call went through the Department's switchboard, and you told the operator it was official. This implied suspicion always annoyed my secretary. Such practices, I came to realize, emphasized that the State Department's Washington personnel was small, so small at that time I saw a group photograph which included all. The entire Foreign Service Officer component was about eight hundred, but the portion in Washington headquarters was bolstered by a competent Civil Service. In the field, the FSOs were strengthened by Foreign Service staff and local national personnel, as in Montreal.

By good fortune I discovered the Gralyn Hotel on N Street, Northwest, off Connecticut Avenue, and its proprietors, Polly Morrison and Ralph Erskine, which over the years became my home leave oasis. Polly was a self-made woman, starting as a secretary, qualifying as a lawyer, and by astute real estate operations and because of her extensive holdings there, known as the unofficial mayor of N Street and the moving force in retaining its atmosphere. Ralph was the manager and created the climate that made the place so enjoyable for young professionals. The building was impressively combined from two town mansions, the furnishings were old fashioned, and the fabulous breakfasts were served in good weather in the rear garden. My sister, working for a Washington lawyer, was taken with the place, and moved in herself.

Washington was changing rapidly, although it still had aspects of a southern town. There was no talk of street violence or muggings, and people walked its streets with confidence. Construction of Mall museums, aside from the old Smithsonian and the Mellon (now the National) Art Gallery, had barely begun; the Lincoln Memorial was a decade old; the sprawling Navy Annexes still graced Constitution and Independence Avenues despite Roosevelt's efforts to remove them, and the most recent architecture was the Hoover-built, Roman-style government buildings on their side of Constitution Avenue. Street traffic was light, for government workers used trolleys and buses, and the Gralyn was within easy walking distance of the State Department. The city's atmosphere was friendly, and there was a sense of unity derived from familiar local personalities.

Radio and TV star Arthur Godfrey first gained attention in Washington with his radio jokes about the bedraggled bear fronting Zlotnick's fur shop; Arch McDonald, the Senators baseball and sports announcer, had a popular radio program, and Carter Barron was the theatre impresario and public spirited man for whom the Rock Creek park amphitheater was named.

For socializing, there were big hotels with their dance bands and visiting entertainers. Downtown were the Mayflower and Willard, while far out, off Connecticut Avenue, were the Shoreham and Wardman Park hotels. The last was Harry Wardman's, who cannily gave the British embassy its building site, knowing this would benefit his other properties. Then in the spring of 1939, the British king and queen toured America. It was the social sensation of the day, though one diehard congressman read the Declaration of Independence to his children at the outset of their Washington visit. For the moment, the press reported, Americans were royalists.

Since I had no radio, I missed a network program describing a Martian invasion, produced by Orson Welles. The next morning I gathered its impact, aside from press publicity, by hearing my colleagues talk of little else. Quite a sensation. So popular history is made.

Whenever there was the chance, I attended the theatre in both Montreal and Washington, but the programs were very thin. His Majesty's, an old playhouse, was the only English source in Montreal. On one occasion "Our Town" was presented and familiar Frank Craven played the Stage Manager. In Washington, there was only the National Theatre and the DAR's Constitution Hall for concerts, where I heard an old, weary Sergei Rachmaninoff perform - magnificently.

Aside from the Service health hardships mentioned in Montreal, in Washington I found a few more. One day in Montreal we had news of the assassination of the consul general in Beirut by a local Lebanese. Several of the men knew Ted Marriner, and emphasized the problem of doing your duty and running risks. Marriner never knew that the man who shot him had been refused a visa. In the rush of our Visa Division work, we began hearing of a trickle of officers in Vienna breaking down as hospital cases and requiring recuperation. These men would work demanding hours (there was no official overtime), and do their best to handle applicants trying to get out before the full Nazi impact made this impossible. Our men knew they were working against time in trying to save people from serious privations or death, all of which affected us new to the Service. The four month period ended, but not before I knew our visa people and learned some of the problems they faced.

It was unusual one day that the Chief of Foreign Service Personnel, an austere bachelor, requested I come by. I discovered he was intent upon probing for possible adverse elements affecting the recovering, earlier overworked, Montreal assistant commercial officer. He was not pleased with my good estimate, snapping that I presumably found the whole staff excellent. I agreed. Later in a training school talk, this Chief mentioned with satisfaction that he was seeking an added fourth day for the Service written exams. I am unsure if he welcomed my comment upon the added fatigue factor.

By January, a new cycle began in the basement of the State Building when I attended the Foreign Service School, then the only organized training done within the Department. The School's staff was one senior FSO-1, and one assistant-typist, which today can be contrasted with the multi-course and well-staffed Foreign Service Institute. Klahr Huddle, our chief, had held responsible assignments in the Department and in Europe, particularly Germany, while his assistant, Cornelia Bassel, was an institution herself in being known to many officers. Her job, as we later saw it, was to look after us, give advice where she could, and act as a buffer to Huddle, whose most lasting impression on us was the initial one.

Our group assembled in the classroom at designated desks in alphabetical order. There was no fanfare of welcome, no words of wisdom from ranking Department officers. They were busy doing their jobs. Mr. Huddle, announcing we would be under his charge for the period, devoted the rest of the session to reading from marked sections of the US Code. These centered upon penalties for absconding with the office cash and other felonies of which he presumably thought some of us might be capable and the consequences of which he gave due warning. By this time we averaged about one and a half years in the Foreign Service, and we thought his readings from the good book unnecessary. Further indicative of protocol and the compactness of our government, we were next instructed to leave our official calling cards at the Roosevelt White House, right corner turned down to show they were personally presented. That day, feeling slightly foolish, I left my card with the gate guard, who stoically accepted it.

For the first and last time, seventeen of our class were together in that basement room. Five were married, four became ambassadors, while all would have unique careers. My Fletcher friend, Harlan Clark, was there, as well as new friends like Gordon Mattison and Fred Reinhardt, with whom I would have later assignments, and Elim O'Shaughnessy, as polished as ever. Ray Thurston after our retirement arranged for John Melby and me, as full-fledged academics, regularly to serve as lecturers on Lifelong Learning cruises. Zeke Paddock I privately deemed the typical Princetonian, given his exuberance and joy of life. Then there was Milt Rewinkel, a Minnesotan and a regular fellow, a lifelong friend with whom I had related assignments. We look so young in the class picture.

Franklin Roosevelt was the dominant public figure of those years, and I met him twice. One summer day I was with my father as a vacationing student in Washington while he was assistant to the captain of the Navy Yard. The presidential yacht Sequoia came in with President Roosevelt and some of his friends from a fishing trip. I knew the yacht was stocked with sufficient potables and no tackle. My father, as usual, was at dockside to meet him, for Roosevelt preferred only one person ashore to meet his yacht, another contrast with current times. The president used a special gangway with railings at the right height to move himself along and at the end of the gangway, once again greeting my father, he saw me at a discreet distance and asked my identity. On being told, he said, "I'd like to meet the young man," so my father waved me over. We were introduced, I answered his several queries, and was so taken by his personality that in my first presidential election I voted for Roosevelt. Now while I was working in the State Department, there was an annual white tie and tails, with decorations, diplomatic reception at the White House, including all State officials. The president and Mrs. Roosevelt had a long receiving line, and at my turn I was tempted to mention the earlier meeting. Intimidated by the surroundings, I settled for a handshake. From what we know of Roosevelt, he would have welcomed that slight break from formality.

The Foreign Service School operated on a regular workday schedule, with the course segmented to cover specialized aspects of State's work. Virtually all our speakers were from State, with one each from the War Department, Commerce, and Agriculture, since foreign assigned personnel from the two last were being merged in our Service. Importantly, I had an initial opportunity to see the gamut of Foreign Service operations and to synthesize field and headquarters action. Aside from our one War Department, G-2, speaker, we had a half day at Fort Myer, where in the large training hall we had an exhibition of mobile warfare supervised by then Army Colonel George Patton. The pack mules and the borne light artillery pieces even then seemed anachronistic. Country desk and specialist officers talked to our class. We used the basic code books and cipher tables, became acquainted with the Commercial Division, the tie between State and Commerce, and had short intervals in Visas and Passports. With two weeks training in office accounts, we absorbed some of the Department's system of bookkeeping, the only phase of the course on which we had an examination by preparing office accounts for a hypothetical office. This training I later applied for one month in Istanbul, when I handled its accounts. Because of our initial field experience, we found the material meaningful, and it stayed with us.

During the few days devoted to shipping and seamen, we had a speaker who recounted his most difficult days as consul in Hamburg. "An American student school ship, loaded with some 150 young men", he said, "was attached for non-payment of expenses while docked in Hamburg." Mr. Hosmer went on to relate how he was the center of a volume of telegrams from anxious parents and concerned congressmen, causing headaches for the entire staff. After his talk, I introduced myself as one of the "Albatross" group, and thanked him for his inspiring performance in Germany which led to my being here in the Foreign Service. He beamed.

Before the School ended, Secretary of State Cordell Hull invited us to his offices for a little socializing. He circulated among our group and closed the session by making some private comments. After telling us his good opinion of the Foreign Service, he turned to the leading question of the Axis Powers. To paraphrase, he thought Germany, Italy and Japan as international brigands were engaged in a concerted campaign against the democracies, passing the crisis ball between them. Given our domestic situation, the best we could do was to keep them guessing as to our actions in the event of international conflict. This inhibiting role events might change. He concluded from his broad experience to give a bit of advice. He had found in public life there were times when the future looked murky and uncertain, but if he followed the principles he believed, when the fog lifted he was not far off course. We appreciated his confidence and thoughtfulness in giving us his personal philosophy.

By May we finished the course, coincident with our promotion to Unclassified B, a $250 salary increase, and the end of probation. During the final session, as new assignments were read, there was some tension as everyone waited, but we were veterans of one foreign post and confident in our ability to function in another. Tianjin, then Tientsin, China, was mine. Certainly it was exciting, for the Sino-Japanese war had been ongoing since 1937, and Tianjin, in the war zone, was subject to strains for foreigners. The Japanese military were strip searching all westerners, including officials. Much was happening as the Far East violence grew.

My assignment was typical, though, as a response to an officer's post preference. Each year by April 1 (it became known as the April Fool report), we listed our three choices and sent them to the Department. This report was supposed to help make assignments fit the abilities of the FSOs with their preferences, but it became a joke that you never were sent to any of these areas, which in my case proved true. I had indicated that I would like a Spanish-speaking post in Latin America or Spain to perfect the language before assuming another. So up came China! I never had a Spanish-speaking post, although admittedly when World War II came I gave up on preference. French became the language I found most useful, and in early mornings at the Foreign Service Institute I qualified with an acceptable knowledge.

Because June-July was a busy period for tourist passport applicants despite the international clouds, Mrs. Ruth Shipley, chief of that Division, had me and John Melby detailed to its front office to handle the public, taking passport applications in reception room fashion. During the six weeks in the Division I got to know Mrs. Shipley better, for I had met her in my Visa Division job on occasional business. Every day at 11:00, long before the coffee break became an accepted institution, she served coffee in her office. There were five to ten minutes of group conversation and then all would go back to work. Because of her responsible position and influence with Congress, and because ranking women in government were rare, she stood out even more. One reason we got along well was because she saw my kindred interest in the Department of State's traditions and historical atmosphere. Her office held furnishings from some of the leading Department men of the past, confirming that women are the great conservators of tradition. Our friendly acquaintance continued, and until her retirement, whenever I was in the Department on consultation, I dropped in for coffee.

Before going to Tianjin I said goodbyes to the Department's people I had worked with, starting with Messrs. Shreve and Will, and took a few weeks leave, visiting Montreal, and having a brief holiday. Then it was by train to San Francisco, changing as usual in Chicago. A ferry ride from Oakland to San Francisco brought me to the American President Lines office, where a letter from the Department was waiting. This gave me a jolt, familiar to many colleagues, as a change of orders. I wasn't going to Tianjin after all, but was to be posted as vice consul at Kobe, Japan. Originally I was to take a vessel there to Taku Bar for Tianjin, but I could not remember having heard anything more of Kobe. Before World War II it was customary, based upon a standing provision of the State Department appropriations bill, to close every new assignment with a set phrase: "This transfer is not made at your request nor for your convenience." An officer mentally saluted and accepted the assignment, in this case, Kobe.

Earlier I had been in the Far East Division of the Department for a week and had seized the opportunity to research the files on Tianjin. Since I was also looking for a Ph.D. dissertation topic that would be appropriately related, I found a potential use for the long-stored consulate general's records at Tianjin, and the embassy's at Beijing. The protection of American interests in North China from an historical perspective would be my subject. I had a momentary twinge when I thought how Jim Penfield on the China desk had tried to have me become a language student at Beijing. He had regaled me as learning Chinese in the embassy compound with an instructor, while seated poolside between dips.

Since I had two days before the ship sailed, I visited the San Francisco World's Fair, further reinforcing a conviction that San Francisco is my favorite American town. On boarding the President Lines ship I found three congenial North Carolinians, one my cabin mate, going to Shanghai and working for the British-American Tobacco Company, who also were escorting a young woman to marry an associate there. We all became friendly, saw Waikiki together, and ate and drank mai-tais on the beach of the Royal Hawaiian Hotel, little realizing how the essentially sleepy vacation atmosphere was to be transformed by war. Between times I read Steinbeck's new book, "The Grapes of Wrath." At last we docked in Yokohama where I was to check in with the Tokyo embassy. By now it was familiar to be met by an officer, escorted, and briefed, but here was a fresh assignment.

Kobe Consulate

Kobe Club

Kobe Regetta and
Athletic Club

My house and street, Fall 1939

# CHAPTER 4

# JAPAN FREE STYLE: KOBE

# September 1939 - December 1941

*Europe's war came, Japan's in China continued, and the Axis Powers worked with a concerted purpose toward global objectives. America's leadership was alarmed, and sought to aid the Allies within neutrality limits. In Japan an English colonial lifestyle of social activity and sports shifted to a discreet existence. International Shanghai lived a final frenetic hour, while occupied Beijing retained its indefinable air of permanence. In Kobe I shared the flow of foreign living, and emphasized consular work of visas and Japanese shipping, an extrovert life, and sports typical of young bachelors. This gave a taste of the prewar Foreign Service.*

The embassy arranged a room in the Imperial Hotel in Tokyo, designed by Frank Lloyd Wright and the sole structure to survive the great 1924 earthquake. Tokyo was strange and exotic, but after leave and the trip I was impatient to reach Kobe. There two days later I was met at the train by a dapper non-career vice consul, Otis (Dusty) Rhoades, who took me to the Oriental Hotel, near the consulate and in the port area. The consulate, my first full assignment home, was a drab, two story, red brick corner building, where I rapidly grasped its office plan and the roles of our staff. An American telephone receptionist graced the entrance. Dusty shared an office with a clerk, handled the office accounts, transient shipping and seamen, and signed the consular invoices, prepared by two Japanese clerks under our *banto*, the senior Japanese. My office, down a corridor, had a Japanese secretary, where I attended to visa matters and Japanese merchant shipping reporting. When other officers were away and as I gathered experience, I would do American passports and other economic and commercial reporting. From the entrance, a stairway opened to the consul's office and another with an officer and American secretary for citizenship matters. A third room held two translators and a typist, while the Treasury attaché, his assistant, and Japanese staff were to the rear. The janitor lived with his family in the basement. It was tidy and homey.

The principal officer or consul in charge made various political and economic reports, and the position changed three times during my assignment. The first, a shy bachelor, kept to his office and did not have the respect of his staff because, among other traits, the officers never knew what he thought and was reporting on them. Technically he was within his rights, since annual efficiency reports were then completely confidential. His number two or executive officer was Bill Affeld, who did some economic reporting and citizenship work and who, with Myrtis, his truly nice wife, was most supportive. He was succeeded by Gerald Warner, destined to be a lifelong friend.

After the first principal officer was reassigned, his replacement was an Old China hand, Samuel Sokobin. Sam was Jewish, his wife was Irish, and they made a good team. I particularly appreciated his understanding in my Jewish visa cases, for he enjoined me to be fair but strict, and he would support me fully in any of my decisions. He lived up to his word. In the fall of 1941, Sokobin went on home leave and in the interval, since we closed our post in Nagasaki, Arthur Tower, our consul there, was temporarily in charge before his scheduled home leave. Sam was captured in Manila and was held with other official Americans for two years of the war.

Sokobin as a Chinese language officer had a good consular career and was a thoughtful reporter. From a post in Manchuria he reported that the Japanese, despite war with China, were building a coal and steel backstopping empire for their armaments industry. This was not a popular conclusion with Sinophiles in the Department, so Sam became controversial, and ironically was transferred to Kobe. It was my first instance of an officer suffering professionally because of his informed insights. To his credit, one never would have known this of Sokobin, for his optimistic, yet realistic way of looking at life never deserted him. In Washington after his exchange from Manila, he was anticipating Birmingham, England, to be his last post. He remarked to me that as an FSO, Class 2, he had a good career, had done his best, and had no complaints. He was the Chinese language officer on my mind when those in the '50s went through the Senator McCarthy wringer, with John Service a star victim. It was fitting years later, when the Foreign Service honored a rehabilitated John Service at a luncheon, that he detailed Sokobin's unjustified reverse and the way he had faced it. Service's final post also had been Birmingham. We kept in touch, and I last saw Sam when he was 93, then a recognized Chinese specialist and a Judaic scholar, still brimming with ideas. A very worthy man.

The consular Japanese became familiar figures. Our *banto*, Mr. Suzuki, was a very conscientious, dignified older man who had been in the Russo-Japanese war. Then there were Mr. Muto and Mr. Noda, dependable and decent fellows. Tomori, the office messenger, was a happy youngster who sauntered around singing an American song popular in Japan, "My Blue Heaven." The translator doing relevant excerpts for me unfortunately proved a weak reed when things became harder, but a better example was the general typist, Miss Handa, a friend of my secretary, Miss Kawamoto. The latter was a Japanese Christian, missionary educated, who always dressed in traditional costume, requiring her to rearrange the long sleeves of her kimono when she began to type. She proved excellent for dictation and typing, and was of immeasurable aid. In fact, I came to appreciate the value of these national employees and to note how loyalty to the consulate, their organization, was brought into conflict with the super-patriotic zealots running the country.

Early I discovered my Kobe assignment stemmed from my predecessor's drinking problem, when he resigned from the Foreign Service by request, and it was plain, since I was en route to the Far East, that I was diverted to succeed him. He was a Japanese language officer and capable, aside from his drinking episodes. We struck a good bargain. I took over his house and furniture and his *obasan* (honorable old lady) or cook-housekeeper, and his dog. The house was Japanese with a few Western conveniences, and the Airedale was a house guardian. The *obasan,* Hino Yoshino, a motherly woman, came from a country village many years before, evolving into a tolerable cook and adequate housekeeper for a bachelor, and stayed with me throughout. My most memorable impression of that house was when it initiated me into Japanese earthquakes. At a New Year's party until 4:00 a.m., I was in bed at 9:00 o'clock, when I felt an earthquake severe enough to shake the house and to drop roof tiles, while I hopped down the stairs for the welcome outdoors before things got more serious. It is not an experience I would recommend to anyone with a partial hangover.

The atmosphere of my little alley or *kuche* was different from anything in my experience. Children played and people in native dress conversed or took the air in the evening, the men having changed into traditional kimonos. In the morning I usually awakened to the sounds of the night-soil carts going by on early morning rounds, since there was no sewage system. Clearly the Japan I came to know was not the West. Kimono-clad men and women, many in *geta*, the Japanese shoes; cart pulling porters with their headbands and toe-dividing sneakers; the Japanese calligraphy on shops and signs - all these gave an exotic flavor.

Kobe itself I became acquainted with as part of the Kansai or southern half of Honshu island. The heart of our community, however, aside from the port area in which I included the consulate, was the shopping streets of Tor road and Motomachi. Little restaurants, as an innovation, would have on outside display the most natural appearing, but artificial, food platters, so a customer would truly know what he was getting. We all avoided ordering the globefish, lethal unless carefully prepared, for we did not carry trust that far.

Because Kobe was the largest port in Japan, having more trade and business with the U.S. than Yokohama, we were kept busy with visas for Japanese businessmen, as well as foreigners. Many resident foreigners in Japan were applying for immigration visas and were on quota waiting lists for the countries of their birth. In my earlier days we had refugees from Norway, after the Nazis had occupied that country. A dumpy, sixtyish woman one day unobtrusively sat down opposite my desk, and in her I saw the most unforgettable deep blue eyes. She was Sigrid Undset, the Norwegian novelist, who had earned a Nobel prize for her novels, including "Kristin Lavransdatter." She had escaped from Norway, came across Russia, and was bound for America to join the free Norwegians. However, the influx of European refugees following the campaign against Poland was of greater dimension. Eventually there were over 2,000 Polish Jewish refugees, including entire rabbinical schools, staying in the Kobe area and seeking immigration visas after having come via the Trans-Siberian railroad. Similar larger groups were in Yokohama and Shanghai, but here I handled them alone. It was a busy reminiscence of Washington as congressmen and relatives cabled and wrote on behalf of various people.

It was customary to receive visa applicants in the morning, when they waited on benches in the corridor, and after lunch to do the voluminous correspondence or outside work. Effective refugee handling alone would have been impossible had it not been for a local resident German Jewess, the representative of the Hebrew Immigrant Aid Society. She was educated and efficient, and between us we worked out a realistic schedule of appointments and interviews, as well as the evidence of suitability which each prospective immigrant should have. There was still one problem. The strong atmosphere of the crowded office lingered after the morning's stay until the janitor opened windows and cleaned the office at night, only to have the cycle recur. Something had to be done, so I told the HIAS representative that I was going to ask two things of each applicant. Before each was interviewed he or she would bathe the night before and not have eaten garlic for a day. She effusively thanked me for this, and thereafter we had no atmospherics. One ingenious applicant hired a room in a European-style hotel and charged his mates for the use of the room and the hotel's hot water, soap, and towels. The hotel management shut him down.

A monthly report on merchant shipping in the Japanese empire was my added responsibility, and was done in Kobe as the leading port and as having the best contacts with shipping company executives and brokers, whom I visited in the afternoon. For the same economic reasons, instead of being in Tokyo, we housed the Treasury attaché, who concentrated on trade issues between our countries. My translator would cull shipping publications for items of interest, while I would clip stories and articles in the English language press, on which I based my interviews. The reports covered such features as merchant ship launchings, charter rates, shipping agreements, and related matters, so I collated my material and wrote my reports, always after hours because of the volume of visa work.

Although visas and shipping reports were a full occupation, I made a second try on a doctoral thesis, choosing the Japanese Cabinets. It would trace the transition of Cabinets from civilian to military dominance and follow the interlocking of these influences. The backgrounds and ties of the cabinet ministers could give sufficient clues, and my university thought it a good subject. I began collecting material and had a fair amount when we entered the war. My research perforce ended.

There were aspects of consular work which have been dropped or drastically changed. Consular invoices (and U.S. fee stamps) were required for all items shipped to America. This was a large amount of the office's business, which created a goodly income for the United States because of the trade from Kobe. World Trade Directory reports (WTD's) were required on all firms doing business with the U.S. It was an immense chore to keep these current, because it meant an interview by one of our consular personnel with a potentially unresponsive businessman, who was expected to supply fulfilling answers to what he deemed prying questions about the business. Frequently I went with local personnel to interview exporters, which because of the accustomed pace of affairs, could take some time over cups of tea. It was all part of the game to learn about commercial activities and important products such as pyrethrum, which came from flowers and was a staple of insecticides. In this assignment with its variety, I came to be assured in all phases of consular work.

American ship captains would come to the office and make their conventional marine protests, and there was usually a seaman on the beach who had missed his ship and who we sped by the next vessel. American shipping companies were obliging, especially the American President Lines, the main passenger and freight hauler under our flag. We would visit these ships charged with our duties to check papers, to deliver and receive diplomatic pouches, and while aboard might hoist a friendly glass. If a ship did not stop at Yokohama first, we would get pouches from the Department that a consulate courier would take by train to Tokyo. In turn we might have pouches from Tokyo locked in our supply room awaiting an American vessel bound for home or for Taku Bar (Tianjin or Beijing), Shanghai, Hong Kong or Manila. Some pouches for embassy Beijing were once locked in our storeroom for two weeks before being discovered, since Dusty was on leave. There was an irritated letter from Beijing, but this was the good old days.

We did have one shipwreck. The vessel, the President Quezon, piled on a reef, and the American crew delivering the ship to the Philippine government was brought into Kobe virtually destitute. There were a few days of flurry, which we devoted to caring for the men at the local seamen's hostel and seeing they had anything they needed. The ship's union stewards, directly to us, and the union headquarters in San Francisco were appreciative.

Citizenship activity was varied, in view of the complexity of our laws and the large number of nisei (second generation Japanese born in the U.S.) who had come to Japan to study or work. The Japanese Government considered all overseas born Japanese to be its subjects unless they had taken positive steps to the contrary, so there were problems of students being called for military service in Japan who considered themselves as Americans, but were pressured by their Japanese relatives. Sometimes the pressure was quite zealous, ending with a bewildered student finding himself in the army and not knowing how it happened. If he was in the army, unfortunately he had taken an oath of allegiance to the emperor and had divested himself of American citizenship.

As I pursued my assignment I became aware of a Foreign Service identity, aided by common entry trials. An added bond was its lore. When promotions seemed to have gone to an officer's head, it was said that he had acquired consulitis. Personalities were part of the lore, some classmates contributing to this. Charley Thayer, a Russian language officer, was the exuberant narrator of lively books, such as "Bears in the Caviar." And of course there was Elim O'Shaughnessy. Visas, my initial preoccupation, were a source of anecdotes. Chief Byington had told me of Naples days, when fraud and forgery always were in prospect. To foil this, he placed an extra dot over his signature for authenticity. I liked the yarn of the vice consul, who gained the commendation of his boss by reporting successively higher visa bribes. Finally he requested a transfer, explaining that the bribers were getting near his price!

The Japanese, I find, are a remarkable people, with discipline the hallmark of a culture that is essentially unchanged despite war and occupation. Students still are driven to do well or face deep embarrassment for their families, and it is a formidable sanction. Employees are usually guaranteed lifetime jobs, and loyalty to an organization generally persists as the height of virtue. Every large organization is in uniform: trainmen, train porters and station officials; the sales girls; certain municipal employees; the police, naturally; the ubiquitous military, and the students. Concerted company morning calisthenics seem to typify this. A substantial element in fostering such disciplined uniformity is the ethnic unity that makes foreigners stand out. As the Japanese observe, it is the popular bulk contrasted with the foreign few; we and they. The ethnic emphasis has drawbacks in the acts of discrimination against the many resident Koreans, but it is the Eta though, that make this unusual. The Eta are an outcast minority, ethnically indistinguishable from the average Japanese, who operate in caste professions as meat slaughterers and leather workers, similar to the Hindu untouchables. No average Japanese, knowing the official vital records, can countenance marriage with an Eta. Yet I could not find a locally printed word of the strange anomaly.

There were complex domestic peculiarities. The reluctance of people to have twins was the bias against multiple births, my secretary explained, for its aura of animal litters. Families also had unusual continuity over centuries that was only understood by the widespread practice of adoption, which to a foreigner explained the nationalist legend of the unbroken succession of the emperors. Many years after, when I was a tourist, the Japanese press carried stories of newly discovered tumuli in Kyushu, over a thousand years old and of Korean origin. The Imperial Household Ministry, the guardian of the imperial legend, apparently blocked further investigation. Every culture had its legends, but this was active conservation.

The roles of men and women were so different from ours. Even though American women at the time had fewer rights than they later possessed, the Japanese males were completely dominant. From the first day of marriage the wife walked a step behind the husband. Careers for women were unheard of and even later it was rare that a woman attained a middle level executive place. With all this, because of the cheerfulness, sense of measure, and courage that the women possessed, it was the unanimous judgment of foreigners that they were the better half of the Japanese race.

In another aspect, I witnessed a unique example of Japanese emotional reaction when a Shioya country club steward's little son drowned in the pool. The man, in the face of condolences, was laughing. It was my first encounter with a reverse emotion as an accepted feature of a national culture. Crying was simply not done in the face of tragedy.

It is understandable how foreigners can be taken with the artistic side of Japan, so different from the western. Flower arrangement study, new to us with its three elements of heaven, man, and earth, is best known. But there is the elaborate tea ceremony, sand sculptures, and the indigenous theatre, such as Noh plays (the oldest) and kabuki, the roles taken by men. Prints and paintings to me had the charm of the unfamiliar, as did the brief haiku poems with their single images. An example of the melding of Japan with the West came when I saw my first Takarazuka revue with its elaborate costuming and dancing, hybrid music and singing, the parts all taken by women. The revue was featured in Michener's novel, "Sayonara," which, as an ever practical Japanese goodbye, simply means "since it must be so."

As a kind of shorthand I think of diplomatic styles at cultural variance to be represented by different sports. Contrasted with American baseball as a way of thinking I place Japanese ju jitsu, in which I took many lessons. It is a samurai's method of wrestling, using only the necessary effort to attack an opponent's vulnerabilities. Strength and weight of the opponent are used against him as a means of leverage. Japan made me realize how important it is to understand the ways people think, for in the Foreign Service that could be crucial; judging probable reactions to moves that a country or the United States might make locally or internationally. Only after World War II, however, was the discipline of cultural anthropology recognized by foreign affairs practitioners for the good tool it can be.

A change in my living came when an English family left their house to move to the Shioya suburb, and I took it over for the rest of my tour. It was European-type with a gas heater in the single bathroom for the wooden tub. Being on a narrow kuche, or alley, with no sequenced numbers, it was hard to find, but here I had a phone with the only number over years I still remember: 7440. The Japanese deemed 4 to be an unlucky number, meaning death, and so assigned these numbers to foreigners instead. I had a spare bedroom, so occasional official visitors and friends would stay overnight. Also, it was good for entertaining, being in the city, and my *obasan* was able to handle guests at lunches and dinners. I had acquired a full quota of household effects, and there was never a problem in terms of food for, say, six people, if I gave my *obasan* a good hour's notice by phone. She would go into action, seeking neighbors who had food stored or readily available, recruiting helpers. Usually we were served lobster or steak and what else was needful, so by my bachelor standards it was a satisfactory meal. This spoiled me for later assignments.

For most young British, Dutch, Swiss and Americans there were three clubs, the first being the European males-only Kobe Club. Diagonally across the open square from the consulate it was an rambling old brick building that served as the focal point for the foreign community, dominated by the British, who were the principal foreign commercial representatives. Because of the war I did not meet Germans or Italians there, and they had their own clubs. It was convenient for men to lunch and have after-work drinks at the Kobe club, so I could judge time from my window by the growing number of groups descending upon it. The Club also had a good library that I used regularly. North, on the other side of the street, was an elongated, block size athletic field, with stands at the far end and its Kobe Regatta and Athletic Club building nearby. The KRAC, the headquarters for the younger male/female crowd, was devoted to baseball, soccer, and rugby, and I alternately lunched there. Again symptomatic of the illogical race relations, Eurasians could be members of the KRAC, but not of the Kobe Club. I enjoyed the KRAC, and needed little urging from some Canadians and British to start playing rugby. It was a strenuous game, but one I became attached to (no timeouts, no substitutions), which meant for a good portion of the year I practiced Tuesday and Thursday and played an occasional game on Saturday. Our competition was various colleges and universities, and once a year the Yokohama Athletic Club, our counterpart, was played in an Interport match.

Through young Britishers in the KRAC, there was a further change in my lifestyle. In my first autumn, I was invited to a beach house at Shioya, a suburb of Kobe some 20 minutes by the electric line, where a large foreign community was built around the Shioya country club, the property of an Englishman, Ernest James. These contained various new European type homes, while along the Inland Sea beach my friends had rented two wooden Victorian houses. Connected with the country club, of which I became a member, was an excellent gym adjacent to a swimming pool and, naturally, a bowling green. The friendly Italian gym instructor was on Mr. James' payroll, and he held classes Monday, Wednesday and Friday. I enjoyed his strenuous half hour sessions, and happily arranged to move part-time to Shioya, spending the other half of the week in town. To fill the week's calendar, after a game on Saturday and a dinner or a little mild celebrating that evening, I might go to Shioya. Sunday in our yard overlooking the Inland Sea we exercised with medicine balls and weights, ran in the surrounding hills, and after lunch would have a lazy day. Weekday mornings we would work out and swim in the Sea.

Jackie Tarr was our Shioya leader. A Cambridge grad and an excellent quarter miler, he worked for a shipping company and was captain of the KRAC rugby team. Then there were fellows like McWattie, a fervent reader of O. Henry, and Shaw Hutton, who liked chamber music, and four others including Colin Stanbury, living in the adjoining house, and nearby, a colorful Dutchman, Fritz Tuininga. An attractive young couple, the Howard Harkers, were familiars, as was George Kyd. In the unknown future, Jackie, Colin, Fritz, and Howard were longtime friends. Colin and Fritz had vigorous, joyful personalities, and as healthy bachelors were attracted by and attractive to women. While not hesitant in the liking, my friends genially dubbed me abstemious. With the war, Fritz joined the Free Dutch and graduated from Sandhurst, the British military college. In Indonesia he freed a Dutch woman from a prison camp whom he later married in Holland, before going on to a comfortable fortune in industry. Colin, fluent in languages, after the war became a partner in a leading Brazilian accounting firm, happily married a Frenchwoman, and finally retired to the south of France.

Our Shioya cook and housemaid were nicknamed by Colin Stanbury as Nitwit and Yotch. The smiling little cook, all metal teeth, had learned English cooking and was not very good, so it was years before my memories of brown brussels sprouts died. Each morning Yoshiko-san, a hefty woman who routinely carried our heavy garden weights, would wake us with trays of tea and milk - again

English style.  Our manner of living was simple English public school, and the salty conversation and ballads to hymn tunes also fitted.  Parenthetically, those earthy ballads served as passwords with later British colleagues.

Our sportive lifestyle was known, so Robertson, a sturdy, short Scotsman and rugged soccer player, one Sunday offered to take Colin and me on a hike to a locally known rural temple.  After we had gone some miles and reached a ridge, he pointed to the blue line of the next,  and said, "That's half way."  We made it, with Robbie, impatient with these "athletes," pulling away for home.  The final stretch we walked stiff-legged down from the Shioya hills.  Colin detoured for some club restorative beer, while I reached our home, spent.

An indispensable adjunct to our English colonial lifestyle was amateur theatricals.  While Americans had put on one play before my arrival, "The Front Page," it was known more for its exuberance than drawing room or mystery style.  This was marked by the mayor of Chicago, type cast by our assistant Treasury attaché, who feeling unconfined, broke up the audience by exclaiming in a tumultuous scene, "What's all the *yakamashi* (disturbance) about?"  My first winter I was drawn into a play, "I Killed the Count," which had the twist of different suspects each with a plausible motive, so all went free.  As one suspect, I struggled with the Count, an amiable Italian, so energetically that we broke the table.  A sturdier one was found.  That winter too, a big Anglo-French unity affair was held at the KRAC, where three very husky friends did a burlesque ballet dance of the flowers, but only after two double scotches apiece!

As an American among the British, I offered them occasional reminders.  Colin and I were running in the Shioya hills when, as ever enthusiastic, he made a sweeping gesture, exclaiming "What a delightful prospect!"  I responded, "Yeah, nice view," to which he rejoined, "You American!"  Early on July 4th morning I stole downstairs and, at full volume on the record player, started a band rendition of "The Stars and Stripes Forever" to a sleepy chorus of protest.

The life was healthy, typical of young foreign bachelors of our time, although there were few Americans.  The young British consular people did not engage in our sports, except for tennis, but one British vice consul invited me to his place for drinks which he selected from the straight sequence of his cocktail book.  As I recall, the man acquired stomach ulcers.  I thought of my three immediate predecessors and their brief careers.  All left the Service after a year or so: one for liking women too much (he became a successful historical novelist), another for liking men too much, and the last for liking liquor too much.  Meanwhile, I went in heavily for sports!

As always in the profession, there were storied personalities. Of the people in our Tokyo embassy by far the most eccentric I encountered was Dave, a Japanese language student FSO. He had a remarkable gift for languages, but was lost in the mundane world of consular affairs. On his arrival, Dusty Rhoades met his ship and escorted him to the Tokyo train. As Dusty wonderingly described it, Dave disembarked carrying all his baggage; a suitcase, a guitar case (his thumbnail so long he needed no pick), a dressing gown over one arm, and a set of maps, which immediately unrolled down the station platform. Safe in Tokyo, we heard he had immersed himself in the culture. His Service supervisor, eventually taken aback at his appearance, had him place a clothing order with Sears Roebuck. In doing this, Dave by chance revealed crumpled, uncashed salary checks, which on request he produced in quantity. After two years he passed the best Japanese language examination in memory, and on being queried, said he had gone to the roots of the language, which he defined as also learning Korean and Cantonese! His Foreign Service career was not lengthy.

Service people I came to know were not merely those in Kobe. There was another consulate at nearby Osaka, comparable to the relation between Yokohama and Tokyo. Officers there lived in a foreigners' compound between our two cities, and we tended to merge some social life. Of these, Walter and Dorothy McConaughy were most agreeable. I knew a few from the embassy, although I never met our ambassador, and when they travelled to Kobe they could stay with me. In further adapting to my Kobe base, I had some friends among the older men such as Fred James, brother of Ernest, so when a daughter married Shaw Hutton of our beach house, Colin Stanbury and I, with Fred in attendance, arranged a final bachelor party. Colin, who had an exceptional command of language, was my closest friend among the young fellows, a chartered accountant from England by way of Canada. We gave the affair in my town place, and it was a great success to the point of locking the garden gates at 2:00 a.m. to stop the local police from interrupting the party. Thereafter it took us two days of cooperative effort to rehabilitate the prospective groom to meet his wedding deadline. While Shaw appeared fit in his wedding togs, he privately admitted to be at 85 percent. Wisely the bride had decreed the bachelor party should be a full two days before the wedding.

Social affairs, aside from home invitations, occurred most often at the KRAC or the Shioya Club, both well equipped for these, and where our male society had the leavening mixture of English and Eurasian women at the KRAC, and at Shioya, of Englishwomen like Gwen James, Rosemary Winter, and Mary Bain. Gwen and Rosemary after the war, married George Kyd and my Shioya-KRAC rugby friend, Cyril Owen (who knew the novelist, P.G. Wodehouse). At club parties our male singing chorus on New Year's Eve and holidays would habitually hold forth on "Auld Lang Syne," so whenever I hear this, the picture brings understandable nostalgia.

Kobe today has changed. The city looks more scrubbed, if less picturesque. It has a large, man-created port island and more modern buildings. The Kobe Club is now a family club located at the Tor Hotel site, while on its old locale is the retrenchment idled American consulate. The former KRAC grounds are a public park. The Oriental Hotel, as a result of the widespread bombing of World War II, is a block removed. The people are well dressed in western style, and the traffic is suitably heavy to equate with current civilization. Our old Shioya beach house spot is predictably a gas station. You can't go home again.

Travel in Japan and the mainland had local restrictions, but I went to the Japanese Alps for journeyman skiing, Nagoya to see its castle and the cormorant fishing, where the ring-necked birds disgorged for the fishermen, and to Nagasaki and Tokyo. It was always by train, for there was no defined road between Tokyo and Nagasaki. Sold at every stop were net bags of tangerines or "mikans", needed since passengers were uncertain of the water. Outside Japan, twice through the circuit of Korea-Beijing-Shanghai, I determined within these limits to see as much as possible. After the ferry from Japan to Korea, vines and yellow gourds festooned the farm roofs. Then, at the border of Manchuria, set up by the Japanese as the independent state of Manchukuo, there would be frontier formalities before the run to China proper. At Shanhaikuan, where the Great Wall dipped to the sea, there was a delay of a couple of hours, and with the visible adjacency of the Wall it was irresistible with permission to climb and to walk along. Given the size and expanse of the project, it is believable that astronauts in space identify this single man-made feature. Tianjin was the next big city, and from there to Beijing orders were strict that the window shades be drawn. Careful peeks showed regularly spaced intervals of Japanese soldiers guarding the rail line from Chinese guerrilla action as the Sino-Japanese war continued.

As a foreign traveler, once as a diplomatic courier with an associate, I obtained a small train compartment. The trains were crowded in Manchuria with Chinese laborers, and the task of moving through the cars to the diner was distinctly unpalatable. The Chinese were close packed, unwashed, and as Teddy Roosevelt would have said, produced pungent bodily advertising. It did not take long to decide to await train stops, hurry to the diner while at the stations, and repeat this on returns.

Most intriguing was Beijing, for virtually no modernization had been attempted. The extensive old quarters, where craftsmen of a hundred kinds produced an amazing collection; the old walls and the massive tower gates of the city; the virtually deserted Forbidden City, the home of the emperors, with its remarkable architecture; the people, poorly dressed; the numerous rickshaws and their runners; the Japanese military, and the signs of war: all these elements made an indelible impression. In my war travels only two cities gave a similar effect. Beijing had the antiquity, the extensive craftsmen quarters, and the other intriguing aspects that rivaled Damascus and Istanbul.

For completely different reasons, Shanghai was unique. One could feel the subconscious weight of controls, a feature of Japan, fall away when crossing the Garden Bridge into the International Settlement. This regional effect was the secret of its success, for the area, with the French Concession added, was not under Japanese supervision, but was patrolled by locally recruited volunteers. Life went on freely, as if Shanghai were living in its own protective capsule. Our Shioya Italian gym instructor warned a young man of Shanghai's distractions when he was transferred to the city. Later the instructor and his wife took a brief trip there, and in a nightclub noted a woman singer focusing on an unclear man which a spotlight revealed as "My Donald," said the instructor.

Our consulate general in Shanghai had extensive business, from visas for the large refugee community to reporting on the turbulence that was China. There, liking the unconventional, I found the most unusual officer to be Monroe (Rhody) Hall, a Chinese language officer who proclaimed he wanted to study Japanese. He felt being a student was simply agreeable, but for Japanese was firmly rejected. Perhaps news of his colorful personality preceded him. His spirits were undampened, and he enjoyed Shanghai. In build he was a present pro football tight end, and his capacity for liquor was exceptional. Just before I made one Shanghai foray he had given a party that lasted three days and was much talked about, especially that part where he had camels for guests to ride around his garden. Rhody had another side on which I remarked when at the American Club bar, the longest in Shanghai, for while being seated he would clap and a barman would bring him a serious book, non-fiction from the title. With table friends he held an animated conversation while reading. When we left, he again clapped, and the barman took the book. I occasionally wonder if Rhody ever finished it.

There was a depressing aspect to international Shanghai that did not fully register with unfamiliar visitors. The squalor, the starvation, the deaths among the thousands of street homeless, had an unreal quality that contrasted with the lively patina. Early mornings the authorities would mark the street dead with straw mats, after which crews on special trucks would carry off the bodies for communal burial. Meanwhile, pedestrians would be uninterrupted, as traffic flowed around the mats. Begging children, seeing foreigners, would approach crying, "No papa, no mama, no whiskey, no soda, no *tansan* (tip)." These were spectacles hard to take, even for regularly commuting consular people. Today, at considerable cost, there are no street sleeping homeless or beggars visible in

Shanghai, but the old international portion is drab, deceptively spiritless, but teeming with no buildings save from the old days. The swank Park Hotel has no vestige of its earlier incarnation, and the race course, perhaps for the best, is a quiet public park. The packed crowds still move on Bubbling Well Road. For sights of sleeping swarms of homeless one must go to India's great congested cities, where it arouses speculation how long such conditions can be endured.

In Shanghai just before the U.S.-Japan war, the Bund and Bubbling Well Road with its great department stores were crowded and noisy. Given the black market foreign exchange rates, there were store choices from stateside profusion and stays in excellent hotels like the Park. A custom suit could be bought after two hotel fittings in twenty four hours. Across from the hotel was the race course. There was jai alai and the latest American movies. Nightclubs, from the so-called Blood Alley to the elaborate Arizona, and good restaurants were booming, along with, if wished, White Russian young women as pleasant table companions. The latest books and records were available in pirated editions. In brief, all of life's distractions were on display. The Settlement never slept, and its visitors did their best to keep up. With others, I estimated in my final stay that I averaged a few hours sleep over three nights  The good times became faded memories when the realities of war took over.

Kruger Park with Bob Rutherford
and Ned Brookhart

Right: Beijing: Temple of Heaven

Kruger Park with relaxing lion

Right: Beijing: Temple of the Sun
and Center of the Universe

# CHAPTER 5

# JAPAN AT WAR: KOBE AND THE EXCHANGE

## September 1939 - August 1942

*Japan, on the 1940 fall of France, acted aggressively in southeast Asia. It synchronized with Germany and Italy, drumming patriotism and austerities for a great national effort. Restrictions on foreigners created serious strains. Aware of the danger of sudden war, Americans prepared. Businesses cut back on staff and Japanese preparations recognized. From the Kobe consulate I reported on Japanese military rail movements and Japanese Empire merchant shipping. After Pearl Harbor, we followed Japan's triumphs from house arrest and an official exchange ship to Portuguese East Africa. There I was assigned, over objections wanting military service, as vice consul at Istanbul in neutral Turkey.*

Right after my Kobe arrival, Dusty Rhoades invited me to dinner with my departing predecessor. In its midst we heard the sound of tinkling bells, which the two promptly recognized as newsboys, bells around their waists, hawking fly sheet extras (*go-gais*). They bought one, and our language officer read aloud that war in Europe had come. We were briefly silent. This overwhelming event was to spread throughout the world and over the next six years to become our overwhelming preoccupation. Meanwhile Asia was not yet directly linked to it, and until the fall of France the pattern of foreign living in Japan remained reasonably intact. In the consulate I had a job to do. America was neutral. We in Japan were most sympathetic to the democracies, but our consular duties had to go on.

Americans, of course, knew some Germans and Italians, as well as the British, French, Dutch, and Swiss, but the Americans naturally gravitated to those called free. Increased strains of the war's progress found isolated, opposing nation friendships that survived, but one did not, and I was at the breakup. An athletic and convivial German married to a Canadian had a social confrontation of the couple with a former Dutch friend, Fritz Tuininga, during the Nazi invasion of Holland. It was affecting.

In the early period I was not as aware of the domestic Japanese responses to the war, but these gained in intensity. Suspicion of foreigners was officially encouraged, sources of information dried up, and food and materials became more scarce and shoddy. Train timetables were no longer published, and foreigners needed travel permits for the most routine distances.     Japan's war came to be revealed in two repeated domestic scenes. It was rare at a rail station not to meet a vociferous group assembled to give a loud send-off to a military recruit or to one returning to China. The nadir was the sight of boxes of cremated soldiers being returned to their families.

The press and radio covered Japanese military actions in China as perpetual victories, no defeats or retreats, although disparate dates and places of actions were never explained. Public information and official contradictions could be fully controlled, since radios were strictly censored and short wave broadcasts very difficult to receive. The campaigns thus seemed on a seesaw until the fall of France, when the focus changed from China to the south; Indo-China (Vietnam) the Netherlands Indies (Indonesia), and the Philippines, with indications of their extensive resource potential for the Japanese war machine. The Japanese military, after France's defeat, began aggressive moves against French Indo-China. The war became real, and the British, fighting alone, tightened themselves for the ordeal ahead. Their families began an exodus and the young men headed for training in India. There was a small Free French organization, but most of the French officials in Japan stayed with the Vichy regime, only outwardly accommodating Nazi Germany.

Overseas Americans closely followed developing American reactions. One that gave me a glow was an act by President Roosevelt. After France's fall he called for a national emergency mobilization. One cannot forget at the time there were slightly over 100,000 men in the American army. The president named two men, temporarily among the most important in the United States, to direct labor-industrial mobilization.     The labor "czar" was Sidney Hillman, who had immigrated as a 20 year old Jewish boy from Lithuania and was an important labor leader. As industrial "czar" Roosevelt named William Knudsen, who came as a 20 year old Lutheran youngster from Denmark and headed General Motors. On scrutinizing the stateside news, I found nothing but praise for the nominations and no questioning of their complete Americanism.

Americans had been startled and aroused to the stark dangers facing our country. To a tyro FSO, America's democratic fate  rested on the ultimate victory of Britain and France over the Axis. Yet reports from home, by mail and the press, showed a growing division on action: either help the United Kingdom and France as in American interest or follow strict neutrality to avoid involvement. Families of Allied nationals were only too well aware of Japan's direction and accelerated their departures through 1940 and into 1941. Pacific shipping was curtailed, and schedules became infrequent if not uncertain, stimulating the hesitant to move. Americans responded to the official warning with a large evacuation in November 1940. Through 1941 and aside from diehards and missionaries, the only nationals from the United States and western democracies left in Japan were single men on business deemed "essential". Colin Stanbury and I became the sole tenants of a beach house when earlier there had been eight in two adjoining homes. Colin was still with his national accounting firm, the only one left in the Kansai needed to look after British business interests. He was restive but cooperated with his consulate; I found myself spending five days a week in Shioya with two days in town. Showing changed attitudes, my dog was poisoned by unknown neighbors to my *obasan's* anguish. It began to be a bit lonely for Americans.

Over time I met Japanese, but by 1939 it was too late to make Japanese friends. For the Japanese, merely having foreign acquaintances was enough to cause the military to suspect them of traitorous intent. Through our American secretary, Mary Ogawa, I became friendly with a history professor, Dr. Takeuchi, and his American wife. I admired the dignified way they both met the situation as it changed to overt hostility. We in the consulate could see the war strain on the nisei who were being bulldozed by their relatives into declaring themselves Japanese subjects. Some tried to leave but there was erratic transport to America as shipping gradually stopped. A young Japanese in a silk store I frequented quietly described his situation as a nisei, saying he had not dared to come to the consulate to make inquiry. Since he had served in the Japanese army, I could offer no hope for his American citizenship. He thanked me.

In July 1941, the U.S. imposed an oil and scrap metal embargo on Japan, and things became gritty. Our Japanese employees were uneasy. One hesitated to ask them for translations of the most routine items, since they might be accused of spying. Press propaganda became strident, but one read between the lines. Their planes were never shot down, but always "disappeared in the clouds." Samurai-style movies became more frequent. Pictures of warriors were on all the billboards, swords drawn, with traditional tight lipped grimaces. Here were old traits of feudal loyalties, retribution, and unfeared death. The culture, which proved durable, would accept a suicide complex sponsored by military propaganda and exemplified by kamikaze aircraft in World War II. Years later there was an American public TV program in which an informed participant drew close comparisons between the earlier Japanese kamikaze training and that which promising business executives currently received. A cultural trans-location, not transformation.

It is my observation that what one nation loudly accuses another of in times of strain can generally reflect its own bias and by reiteration can draw a reaction.

Obviously Japan at the time of the war was stridently and ethnically nationalist, while blaming its problems with the United States on American racial prejudice. Foreign affairs have an excessive quota of the emotional and irrational, with the logical and rational too often lacking. In the heavy atmosphere there was one instance which struck me when I went to the port to see off the American retiring president of Kansai Gakuin University. The outpouring of sincere regard and singing by his students thronged on the dock in farewell was too genuine to be covered by military decrees. I still see them whenever I hear the hymn, "God Be With You 'Til We Meet Again."

My reporting on Japanese merchant shipping continued. For a time, as information became more difficult to get, this was partially compensated by my increased awareness of the subject and new sources. However, by the autumn of 1941 there was very little that could be obtained from other than vague press and magazine articles. I had received several commendations for my shipping reporting, and as the situation became more tense was spurred to do more, with the result that I received three department commendations in one month. Increasingly it was necessary to draw on past experience when analyzing a shrinking pool of sketchy indicators.

In October, through a long-time resident whom I had got to know in my shipping reporting, I was given a small handbook on India paper. It was a listing of every Japanese merchant ship over 500 tons as of January 1, 1941, at a time when we had no authoritative information on the extent of Japanese building of its merchant fleet since January 1937. The handbook gave the salient data on each ship, such as date and place of building, tonnage, fuel capacity, and engine type and horsepower. The invaluable handbook went by pouch in early November 1941, so we knew what the Japanese had in their merchant shipping, the major shipyards, and their rate of launchings.

Because the main railroad line between Tokyo and Moji-Shimonoseki, the strait between Honshu and Kyushu, passed across the road from the Shioya beach house, we could see the heavy traffic it carried. We could sense that things were building militarily, but it was not an original idea to stay home for a period in the fall under the pretext that I was ill. In the facing bedroom I marked the time and number of cars and every train going up and down the main line, together with my estimate of carriage; whether it was a hospital train, one carrying types of heavy military equipment or troops. Civilian passenger service had virtually ceased. Over two days I did this for a 24-hour period, and after an interval when I had a relapse, repeated it for another 24 hours to see what trains ran daily. My boss liked the effort and it was sent along in reporting channels.

After the July 1941 embargo by the U.S., we in the consulate began to wonder how and when the Japanese might strike. We worked until noon on Saturday, so it became a ritual to speculate aloud on quitting whether we wouldbe there on Monday morning. If we opened on Monday, we knew we the office would survive another week. We all believed that the Japanese would strike on a weekend, for we saw an ingrained psychological pattern to hit, as in ju jitsu, where they considered the potential enemy was weakest. In modern history Japan always attacked and then declared war, for international law practice was an alien concept in East Asia. Economic information was quite inadequate, but our Treasury attaché calculated that the economy had enough stored raw materials for the production machine to roll unimpeded for six months. On that basis, it was in the fifth month that the Japanese struck. Meanwhile our government was closing offices and curtailing staffs as the war signs intensified. There was one chuckle about an officer with the reputation of a curmudgeon. The consul general at Keijo (Seoul), Korea, grew impatient to close and leave. He thereupon did the deed, brusquely announcing to Washington, "I see no further reason for my remaining here."

As far as I knew, we had no military attaché visits during my stay, but an assistant army attaché was to come at the end of November and stay in my house. I left word with my *obasan*, since I would be away. With no leave all year, I was combining a trip with official duty by taking a small courier pouch to Shanghai to meet the American President Lines ship scheduled to evacuate the 4th Marines there. The year before, with a clerk from our Tokyo embassy, we were couriers to Beijing, taking numerous pouches, two being classified. The Japanese military would unhesitatingly open any pouch not under our eyes, so the pouches were crowded into our train compartment. We barely had room to sleep and, of course, only one of us at a time went to the diner. Now, berths were virtually impossible to obtain and one chanced them after getting a train ticket. As a courier I did get one for Nagasaki after talking to the Japanese representative of Thomas Cook Travel in Moji. He hinted broadly that he had been educated in a mission school, followed American life closely, and very much wanted a copy of the famous novel, "Gone With the Wind." I guaranteed one if I could get a berth on the return, and we later made the swap for a pirated Shanghai edition.

In Nagasaki, as our office was closed, my official courier material by arrangement was stored with the British consul before the ship departure for Shanghai. That evening, after dinner with him and his American wife, he and I went to the Nagasaki Club, one structure with a past comparable to the Kobe Club. It must have been the first organized foreigners' club in Japan, but was reduced to two members, the consul and the German manager of an American oil installation, who did not use the club at the same time. When we entered, the houseman in his white jacket was there to meet us in a small lighted room, but the rest was in darkness, and all the furnishings covered. The consul and I played on a billiard table surrounded by darkness and draped furniture with beers served by the jacketed attendant, then walked out on the long, bare veranda with its lighted, magnificent view of Nagasaki harbor, marred by the large canvas drapes concealing the local shipyard. Feeling a little pensive, I returned to the hotel. When war did come, the consul and German national briefly met and declared the club terminated.

On the ship to Shanghai was the Eurasian daughter of a Frenchman I knew in Kobe, who was going to Indo-China to work as an interpreter for the Japanese. Apparently there was no way for her to engage in more meaningful work in Japan, and, accomplished Paris-educated pianist and all, she was leaving for this job. Life for Eurasian men and women was not easy, as I had seen from the KRAC. Despite, in many cases, being striking in appearance and intelligent and educated, their lives could be frustrating.

Again I crossed the Garden Bridge, entered the International Settlement, and left Japanese military control. The Shanghai flame still burned, and if I had remained to be caught there by the war, I could have stayed in one of its large hotels from 6:00 p.m. to 8:00 a.m., with the rest of the day free in the Settlement. Two days later I attended a memorable farewell party given by the American community for their erstwhile guardians, the 4th Marines, who shortly were fighting on Bataan in the Philippines. Further, the thin crust of impending war on which we existed was manifest when the captain's orders for the evacuating President Lines ship (I was in his group) were stolen in the American Club to the studied ignorance of the staff. After two more comparatively carefree days, there was a published speech by the Japanese premier, General Tojo, which sounded a tocsin for war, whereupon our acting consul-in-charge, Ed Stanton, encouraged me to return to Japan, to be there when war came. I arrived in Kobe after a spartan trip on December 2.

The morning of December 8 (December 7 in the U.S.) was a Monday, and Colin Stanbury and I walked to the Shioya station on a warmish day. Colin in his customary style hailed the children with his *"ohayo buchan"* (Good morning, youngster), while the youngsters greeted him as *"ohayo-san"* (Mr. goodmorning). I swung, as customary, into the consulate's rear entrance and found the Japanese employees huddled in the semi-gloom of drawn shades. Mr. Suzuki, in halting terms, said that war had started between Japan and America. Mary Ogawa, our receptionist and phone operator, confirmed this, and I raced upstairs to the consul's office to find Arthur Tower and Jerry Warner in a quick huddle. Tower was staying in Jerry's house, both had heard radio news that morning of American installations in the Philippines being bombed, and had come prepared for the worst. Jerry had simply grabbed a tooth brush. We quickly organized. Arthur and Jerry took care of the fee stamps and passports to be destroyed or mutilated, as well as office seals. I handled certain office seals and confidential visa files. By 9:00 a.m. we started the destruction, burning papers in several fireplaces and even in coal scuttles. The Treasury attaché was similarly busy. Mary was on the alert to warn us when the police or military came. Some time later I learned that she had used ingenuity to forestall what would have been a premature descent by the gendarmerie. She had one phone call, from a commercial firm next door complaining that the burned ashes of paper from the chimneys were coming in their windows!

In Kobe I had affiliated with a Masonic lodge, and after monthly trips to Yokohama I received the thirty second degree. As lodge secretary one of my current actions was to place the large wooden box of lodge records in a filing cabinet among my personal papers. After the war the reopened lodge was the only one whose records were intact.

I finished my portion of the destruction and had gone through my personal papers before I was told that the gendarmerie or *kempi* authorities had arrived. I locked the file cabinets in my area, and joined the others upstairs. This was about 11:00 a.m., two precious hours for needful steps, despite our earlier efforts to strip files and equipment to the minimum. It always takes longer than one might think. While I had been busy burning, Colin had come and left some traveler's checks, which he hoped I could pass to his mother in England. We shook hands and he left, shortly to be imprisoned, then interned with other foreigners, and finally freed.

The *kempi* were clearly chagrined when they saw the burned paper in the fireplaces and the preparations made for their arrival. As they traversed the offices there was a lock cabinet ajar, which Jerry noticed and in which Arthur had just put the office accounts. Jerry moved over and found a pretext in answering how the cabinets worked to respond, "In this way," and twirled the lock closed. We had lunch brought in from the Kobe Club, while the *kempi* waited for orders and took photos of the charred fireplaces. We took stock of our numbers. Dusty was on a courier trip to Tokyo and was under house arrest there. In addition to Arthur, Jerry, Martin Scott (the Treasury attaché), and myself, there were nisei staff members: Mary, Martin's secretary, Jerry's secretary, and a male clerk Arthur had brought from Nagasaki.

Late in the afternoon we were bundled into cars and taken to the Tor Hotel, the second of Kobe's two European-style hotels and up the hill from the commercial area. Here we were in separate rooms off a first floor corridor, each with black-out curtains. The next several days I was confined to my little hotel room with its bath; three times daily a guard would bring food, and that would be it. My room was bare except for a bed and a small table with a box of matches, so I spent hours making wooden fences and designs and counting wall patterns while huddled under a blanket, for it had turned cold. After several days, we were allowed to gather in Arthur Tower's room to find, other than Mary, the nisei had left. She alone resisted the official and intimidating interrogation to which each of them had been subjected at *kempi* headquarters. She said she was an American, her folks had raised her as one, and she intended to remain so. Arthur had been taken to the consulate and threatened if he did not open the various safes and locks. He refused. He was a stubborn and courageous man, and I am sure he would have suffered bodily harm before giving in. In any event, the five of us had a chance to be together briefly, to gain moral support, and to respond to the *kempi's* question whether we wished to be interned in the hotel or in Jerry's house. We said the former and the next day were shifted to the latter.

Before leaving the hotel my *obasan* came with a suitcase of clothes from my town place, which in the guard's presence she stiffly presented. He left us alone for a minute, at which the old girl broke down. She showed her true feelings by crying over the terrible war, while I sought to comfort her with a few words and personal good wishes. Those clothes were supplemented by others she brought from the house before leaving for her home village.

Jerry's house was sizeable, with four bedrooms, one a sleeping porch. I had the latter, while next to me was Jerry, and down the hall on the same side were Arthur and Scotty. Across from them was Mary. There were also two bathrooms, one opposite mine and Jerry's. Downstairs was a large general reception entrance with a fireplace and four guards, two on each twelve hour shift duty around the clock. This was house arrest. Jerry and Arthur converted a small, first floor storage room into a food and liquor storage area for shipments that only the week before had come through Japanese customs, a cache that proved a lifesaver in supplementing some meager fare. Our major base though, was the large living and dining rooms with a door into the big entry area. Scotty's cook was permitted to work for us, while Jerry's housemaid continued. Mary was in charge of them, and in one meal each day she prepared an American dish for five. The expenses were split four ways among the men, and for a period I was on credit, on the cuff as we joked, until the Swiss were able to allocate funds.

Details remain sharp. A small space along the side of the house, about 20-25 feet wide, had a path down the center 26 steps long and wide enough for two. Since Jerry was tall, it took him 24 steps. We had the numbers exactly. In the adjacent rear was a tennis court as part of the grounds of the British consul general. Later with routine established, we had the chance to talk with them briefly through the fence when their guards and ours were not around. Finally, we got permission to watch Jerry play tennis with them. We had no visitors or radio, but simply the Japanese press and three English language newspapers, the Japan Advertiser, the Osaka Mainichi (English edition), and Kobe Chronicle, wherein nothing cheered us as the tide of war swept the U.S. back throughout the Pacific. We could recognize that Singapore and Java had fallen, and in the Philippines, Corregidor too. Obviously staged, there was a photo of the tunnel at Corregidor lined on both sides with typewriters, but there was enough truth in this impression of bureaucracy to irritate.

The Foreign Service generally brings tolerance for religions and races. Many Protestant and Catholic missionaries claimed my regard for their faith and staunchness in adversity, since men of each Christian branch had suffered prior to our exchange. We also learned of the variation in treatment afforded American officials by the Japanese military. I cannot forget FSO Oliver Clubb, later hounded by a malicious senator, who endured six months harsh solitary confinement in Hanoi, where he had been consul, and who had come courageously through the ordeal. There were, of course, Japanese I liked and respected, and the many Japanese-Americans who stood by their country. I can understand, knowing these, the motivation of the legendary Hawaiian infantry battalion of Japanese-Americans that became the most decorated unit in the American army. *The exceptional senator, Daniel Inouye, lost an arm at Cassino.*

Our house routine quickly made a pattern. We would breakfast at 8:30 a.m., after which we could walk in the garden, read, study Japanese, or take a turn at "schnellbach" in the living room. It belonged to Jerry and was a Dutch game played on an elongated, raised sides ironing board on trestles, with four slotted compartments at one end into which we slid 20 wooden disks. Five disks in each slot gave a perfect 100 score By the end of internment we all regularly scored in the 80s. At 10:30 a.m., Arthur and I would take a strenuous half-hour of calisthenics on the side terrace. Like Scotty, Mary took no exercise. Once when we teased her she silenced us by effortlessly doing a high, feet-to-hands back arch. She exercised privately.

I had gone to the Shioya gym classes regularly, and as the foreign community diminished, found myself in the last several months running the class, mostly with a few British, Dutch, and Swiss. Among the latter I remarked a bachelor Swiss named Bossert, a quiet, nice fellow with whom I was friendly. Here the exercise was an excellent way for Arthur and me to let off our nervous energy, and sometimes we did 45 minutes, but it was a strenuous daily session in which we consistently tried to exhaust ourselves. A shower followed. After lunch we again read or studied Japanese. We were fortunate that Jerry and Arthur had a wide collection of books, so in an atmosphere where you could place yourself in the era, I read Plutarch's "Lives", Dante's "Divine Comedy", Lawrence of Arabia's "Seven Pillars of Wisdom," and Shakespeare. We had two favorites,

Mark Twain's "Innocents Abroad," the finest American travel book, and Roark Bradford's "Old Man Adam and his Chillun," source of the Pulitzer play "The Green Pastures". Excerpts from these two certainly lightened our feelings.

   An official ship exchange was on our minds, and we created a pool of dates when we might be exchanged for Japanese officials in the U.S. The latest date was early May. This came and went, and the pool stopped. I do not mean to exaggerate the conditions under which we lived. We had food and drink, which the Stateside stores of Jerry and Arthur supplemented, with what our cook purchased on the open market at inflated prices. Each Saturday night we made a special occasion, with one of the five seeing that my little portable record player kept going, as the other four played bridge, and we had extra drinks. There were breaks too, when we visited the tennis court and watched Jerry play with the English. On a few memorable occasions some of the British and an exuberant Australian sneaked into our living room through the side window, for we early established the practice that the guards would not come upstairs and into the living-dining room area. Thus, while we would see them in passing through the front entry hall, we could for a period be on our own.

   What proved to be our only dissension was brought on by developing strains. Isolated as we were, Jerry and Scotty pressed Arthur to demand that we see the Swiss, our protecting power. Arthur resisted, not wanting to ask the Japanese military, asserting the Swiss were taking every practical way to reach us. In a climactic evening Mary sensibly retired and I, disturbed the difference could disrupt our unity, did my best to follow a lighter perspective, apparently bridging the two views, as Jerry later confided. Nevertheless, the frustrations of our internment remained significant. When the Swiss did get to us, we had various difficulties to overcome with the Japanese for ordinary living arrangements, such as finances and the disposal of home effects. Three times all was supposedly set for an exchange and three times it was indefinitely postponed. While it finally took on the fourth attempt, to our knowledge, we were not optimistic that we would leave Japan. We certainly believed the United States would win the war, but we also knew enough elementary Japanese psychology to expect that after heavy bombing of the fragile cities and impending military defeat there would be small chance for any diplomatic exchange. A scorched earth, military dominant mentality gave little ground for comfort. Considering the hundreds of thousands of Allied prisoners in East and Southeast Asia, and heavy American and Japanese future casualties in an invasion, there was no reason to decry the future use of the atomic bomb for a quick end to the war, seen, as in China, that Japan had lost the mandate of heaven. It was a subject we never talked about. Added to all this were various tensions with our guards, one of whom was obnoxious. Once I heard an argument between Arthur and the obnoxious guard, and plunged down the stairs in time to grab the poker he was aiming at Arthur's head. We were not sure of the consequences, but fortunately there were none, for the guard had lost face.

Among the five of us we worked out an unspoken live and let live philosophy, realizing that we were in the same boat and had to get along. Each of us was entitled to his share of bad days and, again unspoken, two people could not have the same bad day. In this way we accommodated and found the qualities in each other. After all, we were together virtually every waking hour, so by June 1942, when we left Kobe, we had the equivalent of several years in a normal family. Arthur and Scotty I came to think of as uncles, Jerry as an older brother, and Mary as the lady of the family. The test came when on the exchange ship all four men ate together, and Mary couldn't because women had a separate seating.

Arthur Tower tended to be reticent, a leader of our little group. In some ways he showed the strain more than the rest of us, but he had a quiet sense of proportion, his tensions were greatly relieved by the exercise, and he was a man I respected. Jerry Warner was a good companion, who did his reading, took his diversions in schnellbach and tennis, and studied his Japanese some six hours a day. He was a Japanese language officer, but he was striving to become more proficient to use it after we were exchanged. I liked his temperament. Martin Scott was a Kentuckian with a keen mind and a grand sense of humor. He was a gentleman, and one who knew his bridge and juleps. As a Kentuckian, he had mint from his home planted on the side of our house and we had that home pride. I had earlier known him as a leading Kobe Club personality, highlighted by his semi-annual bar standing speech of that earthy American classic, "Change the name of Arkansas?" Being one of a foreigners' local champion bridge team, he also taught us the game, but after internment and a game with an obsessive devotee, the contrast was too strong and I no longer play. Mary Ogawa was a graduate of the University of Idaho, who had to be the best humored of us all, with remarkable psychological strength. I think on occasion we men might have spoken out, perhaps to our regret, if she hadn't been there.

Two memorable forays came about because of our combined campaign. First, we insisted on church at Easter and second, that each of us have a physical examination before leaving Kobe. The *kempi* finally agreed, and we went to a nearby Catholic church for the service. The guards stayed in the back of the church, while we split up and sat among the congregation. A young Eurasian woman I knew sat beside me, and we had an animated conversation without the guards knowing, during which I learned what was happening in the foreign community and gave her news of us. Then came individual visits to the doctor, a Czech. He gave me full marks and when I told him of the strenuous physical routine, he shook his head.

There was a third sortie, this time to Shioya, where I made final disposal plans. The house was silent as somberly I surveyed it with a guard. On the stairway, by an impulse, I removed the only two articles I retained. They were Interport championship pennants that I could not leave, but hoped someday to deliver to Jackie Tarr, who had put them there. I succeeded. Here I must recount Jackie's saga. After training in India, he joined a Gurkha regiment that was captured at Singapore. He escaped and tramped the length of Sumatra to be picked up by a British destroyer that took him to Ceylon (Sri Lanka). He joined a second Gurkha outfit, fought through southeast Asia as a major, and was with the British during the Allied Occupation of Japan as a colonel. After resuming his shipping career, his last assignment was the Hong Kong office before retiring with his wife to a country cottage in his home county, Somerset. A married brother, also a retired colonel, lives nearby.

About noon on April 18, Patriot's Day, two of us were watching Jerry play tennis when a plane came over the Rokko hills very low. It had markings we did not quickly note, but it headed to the port area, we heard the sound of bombs, and saw smoke rising. Our obnoxious guard, now jittery, herded us into the house. We were greatly excited, since we knew one of ours had been at work. A Doolittle raider had hit Kobe, although I was told later by a pilot on the raid that the plane and crew never made it. However, it was a harbinger, and culminated in a postwar Kobe unrecognizable from bombings.

I arranged to sell our effects in Shioya and to leave the returns with the Swiss to help Colin if it should be possible to get him the money. As well, my effects in the equipped town house were left and I was never to see them again, but our government later settled my wartime claims for a fraction of what they were worth, which thereafter made me wary when assembling new households. Insurance does not cover war or riot.

As an avocation while interned I followed the three English language newspapers and got Jerry in his reading of Japanese ones to pick items that would have a bearing on Japanese merchant shipping. In time I collected quite a bit, and about May began to draft a report, to which I added as fresh information or impressions came. When a definite date for our departure from Kobe was set, I finished the report. Mary typed it on flimsy paper, single spaced and no margins, and I tried to memorize the result if searched. Until arriving in Lourenco Marques I kept the report folded in my buttoned shorts pocket if our effects were examined. At Lourenco Marques, when we were free, I gave the report to a non-State official, which apparently was a bureaucratic mistake. There was no reaction from Washington, and I could only conclude its origin had disappeared. Although I was temporarily taken aback, this was not deep, for regardless of author the information was useful.

After some time the Swiss succeeded in visiting us infrequently, but became more regular when an exchange seemed definite and we prepared to leave Kobe. The day arrived, and we entrained for Yokohama under guard, being joined in Osaka by its four consular Americans. They had an easier time than we, and had even been allowed to go on outside forays. We also found with us the Latin American consular people from Kobe, for the exchange comprised all countries in the Western Hemisphere. The Brazilian consul general in Kobe and his niece were along, and, after we arrived in Yokohama, to be held in the Grand Hotel, she entertained us every afternoon with a piano concert in one of the large reception rooms of the deserted hotel. We circulated freely in our segment of the hotel, and the stimulus of new faces and events helped. Noteworthy from the Peruvian consul, who had it from the Spanish ambassador as his protecting power, we got belated radio news of the battle of Midway. This really cheered us up!

The guards had us on a schedule. Each afternoon we went for a group walk, where once we happened to meet a group of consular personnel from Manchuria and Korea, interned with the Yokohama staff. We mingled, to the disgust of the guards, and were able to swap more information. Afterwards our walks were deliberately staggered, but that one time I did get some bad news. After Pearl Harbor, the Swiss legation at Tokyo increased personnel to look after Allied interests, and Bossert, my Shioya gym associate, was sent to check the American consular premises in Taihoku (Taipei), Formosa (Taiwan). The Japanese military were most reluctant to permit this. After an interval of no contact and when he should have returned, his legation received a cable from the authorities saying that Bossert's body had been picked up in Nagasaki harbor, a suicide. The brutality sickened me.

Finally the promised day came and in mid-June we were taken to the Asama Maru, the exchange ship. There we were joined by our embassy crowd and other official personnel from the Western Hemisphere, by numbers of missionaries and their families, as well as by some businessmen. American officials and businessmen had been without their families, who left in November 1940. The missionaries had steadfastly refused to part with theirs, and it grated on some to see them all coming aboard, for the missionary component, we were told, had been an obstacle in the exchange. There were a few hitches that kept us in the harbor about a week but on June 25 we started for Lourenco Marques in Portuguese East Africa, now Mozambique.

We learned of the harsh treatment that numerous Americans received as prisoners supplemented by accounts of those shipped on at other scheduled stops. Our Tokyo embassy people told tales of the sweeping actions by the Japanese authorities on our embassy grounds and the delaying tactics that were used on press messages, in effect, to invoke a complete censorship. The bulk of our non-official Americans told of prolonged prison and military interrogations. Psychologically many were conditioned not to hope for any release or exchange for Japanese in the Western Hemisphere. There were, of course, treatment inequities on both sides in the course of the war, such as our mass relocation of Japanese- Americans, but their own experiences were vivid to our internees. Many years later, a Dutch national on a world cruise recoiled when he saw the seated line of uniformed Japanese immigration officials at our cruise port. The memories of his Java prison were too strong, he said, and he remained aboard.

At that time members of the Service were accused of being out of touch with America, whereas this idea was not broached for respected Americans who had long professional residence abroad. Early on the ship I had a conversation with a missionary who was quite concerned about the ability of Americans to meet with equal vigor the fighting qualities instilled in the Japanese. Hiding my resentment at his thinking and feeling he was brainwashed by years of Japanese propaganda, I told him forthrightly that we could bank on our Americans to do the job.

The ship was very crowded and, aside from ambassadors and most senior officers, we were housed in compressed steerage compartments of eight bunks each. Adjacent steerage sections held people like Charles (Chip) Bohlen, the Second Secretary in Tokyo, who became an outstanding career ambassador. When we picked up those in Hong Kong, Joe Alsop, the later well-known columnist, shared my transformer for our electric razors. The food was deliberately terrible, causing digestive problems, and one acquaintance, a Maryknoll priest, used to close his eyes and stab with his fork. There was no empty space, even on deck, but the weather was good. On the way we were joined by an Italian ship from Shanghai, the Conte Verde, caught there by the war and now carrying the people from China;which paralleled our course, say a half mile or more, as we rolled along. While the two ships traveled with full lights and huge electric light crosses amidships on both sides, we were happily unaware that an American submarine stopped seconds short of delivering a torpedo attack on the Conte Verde. A fifth immunity message, the earlier four not received, was decoded just in time, according to Clay Blair, Jr. in his book "Silent Victory," Volume 1.

From a distance, Hong Kong was a shattered hulk as the result of the fighting, and our men there, including Bob Rinden of Montreal, had some hard stories. At one point the consular staff had been lined up in the belief they were to be shot.✗In the Saigon River we took on more passengers, including my Fletcher friends, Harlan Clark from Bangkok and Kingsley Hamilton from Saigon. We were told that the Asama Maru, after adding our repatriates from Hong Kong and Saigon, had about 900 passengers and our companion ship, the Conte Verde, carried about 600, so both ships were crowded. Yet we were all United Nations

Insert ✗ at a later stage the consul general collapsed and the ✗✗✗ took over.

nationals, so despite the known presence of police agents among the crew, we were comfortable to be with our compatriots. Voyaging on, by the first week in July we were, they said, at Singapore. Although out sight of land, Japanese military aircraft flew over us for two days until we departed across the Indian Ocean for Lourenco Marques, beyond Japan's military control.

A fellow inmate of my steerage quarters was an Osaka vice consul who met a Navy nurse being repatriated after her capture on Guam. They fell in love and were determined to marry. Fred Mann received his orders for Brazzaville, French Equatorial Africa (now Congo), and Jo Fogarty was under naval regulations. Despite residence requirements, different religions, and professional disciplines, within the exchange ships stay, they were married and proceeded to Brazzaville. Afterwards I saw them in Washington.

Every life has exceptional days, but a personal best was July 23rd, when we entered the harbor at Lourenco Marques. The first sight was an American flag freighter (later sunk, we heard) near the entrance. It blasted its whistle and we all cheered, because we felt near the end of a trying period. The Japanese and Italian ships docked bow to end, and ahead of us waiting was the Swedish ship, Gripsholm, with its Japanese cargo from America. The time was not long, but it seemed so the next day as we collected our gear. Single lines went down the gangplanks, the Allied contingent walking on one side of a long warehouse, while the Japanese took the other. Our people were only able to take what they could carry, but we were told the Japanese had been given generous limits, including refrigerators. In the midst of this there was a small scene. Japanese youngsters from the stern of the Gripsholm and American children from the bow of the Asama Maru, began talking to each other to compare notes on the food aboard. This is what interested them as they talked to their peers.

When we reached the decks of the Gripsholm there was tremendous confusion. Suitcases were strewn all over, and everyone was carrying on animated conversations. There was some official order in the turbulence, since I got my next assignment. It was telegraphed, and assigned me to Istanbul; a crusher. I wanted to get into the war, so as soon as possible I wired the Department requesting leave of absence to join the armed forces. I thought with my experience on Japanese shipping that I could be useful to Naval Intelligence, and I wanted to see some action. I got a brief reply denying my request and ordering me to proceed as directed. I knew by then that no one could travel without official orders and, not satisfied, sent a dispatch making my request at length and by protocol addressing it to the Secretary of State. Later in Istanbul I received a reply which, although longer than the earlier telegram, said the same.

There were a few rosy days as we all celebrated freedom and friendship, and one of the most vigorous was Rhody of Shanghai. When I asked why the notable extra enthusiasm, he gave his reasons. Notification of a promotion had been awaiting him. Next, an aunt he had not seen for years had died and left him a mink farm. And lastly, his ex-wife had remarried, and this meant no more alimony! With my friends, we younger ones did our celebrating ashore.

The time came for the Gripsholm to leave, and in the prior evening I searched the ship, finding each of my surrogate family. On reaching home I later learned of our group's various assignments. Arthur performed war-related work in the Department. Scotty, in San Francisco, had a like Treasury mission. Jerry followed Japanese activities from a post in Buenos Aires, Argentina. Mary, on Jerry's strong recommendation, worked for G-2 of the Army upon Pacific order of battle intelligence. For the present, from the cliff beside our hotel and with a new Foreign Service group, I silently watched the ship's morning departure. My mood reflected a vagrant ▓▓▓▓▓ aphorism: Courage is the one virtue that makes all of the others possible.

In Istanbul

New York with Virginia

On Capri

# CHAPTER 6

## JOURNEYMAN IN WARTIME: ISTANBUL AND WASHINGTON

### September 1942-October 1944

*The United Nations gathered offensive forces in Europe and the Pacific. Attention shifted from Allied North Africa and Red Army advances to a possible Allied invasion of Western Europe, eventually D-Day. The State Department had Axis peripheral reporting posts, with coverage of the Balkans and Eastern Europe concentrated in Istanbul. In Washington it coordinated inter-agency intelligence of political value. After the official ship exchange, my Service assigned group pioneered an air route through Africa to the mideast, where in Istanbul I became executive officer of the consulate general responsible for the Rumania reporting. There, from an informed source, I prepared five major economic reports on Japan, deemed by the Board of Economic Warfare as the most complete since the start of the war with Japan. After transfer to Washington, I served in State's intelligence coordination office and in Balkan Affairs prior to assignment to wartime Rumania and our political mission under the Armistice. Before my departure, Virginia Wells and I married.*

Walter Birge from the Istanbul office checked me into the Tokatlian Hotel on the Pera, and from there took me to our consul general, Samuel Honaker. He greeted me saying, "Melbourne, I'm glad to see you, but I don't know why the Department sent you because, for the amount of work here, you're not needed." Privately devastated, I remember telling him how hard I had tried not to come, but I have no recollection of the rest of the meeting. Alone in an assigned office, I dispiritedly mulled over the long interval since Lourenco Marques.

Waiting in Lourenco Marques was difficult for our Service contingent, bound for the Mideast, India, and China. A plane from Johannesburg one uncertain day would take us through Africa. First, to get acquainted with home and war developments, isolated in my hotel room, I read seven months accumulation of "Time" magazines, wherein I learned what the term "G.I." meant. Still waiting, a small group of us visited Kruger National Park by car and stayed in guest kraals, when it was unusual to have parks with wild animals roaming free, lions undisturbed by the roadside, and elephants in early morning mist at a watering place.

Finally the DC-3 plane arrived. On takeoff each of us had 80 pounds of baggage and we were at a plateau altitude not reckoned in the crew's sea level calculations. Compounding this, the copilot forgot to release the brakes fully until halfway down the runway. We saw little of Johannesburg since we were too close, but it did give us respect for the DC-3, the workhorse plane of the war.

The Pan Am crew had another assignment, to map a wartime transport route from South Africa to Cairo, for the airline was under government charter since the military air transport service (MATS) was not yet operating. Victoria Falls, an extraordinary sight, we saw at close range, a gift from the crew. Since it needed time to complete route mapping, we stopped over at Elizabethville in the Congo, Nairobi, and Khartoum. There and neighboring Omdurman, where the Blue and White Niles merged, were comparable to a Beau Geste movie, with its people in Arab dress and with black aquiline features. At Cairo the end of August, Rommel was threatening an attack, so after a hasty meal we left for Palestine. Five of us for Turkey arranged to go by train from Beirut to Ankara, where my four companions were assigned, and the next morning from our flea bitten Beirut hotel we saw General de Gaulle there on a brief Free French visit.

The Taurus Express passed through the Cilician Gates into Anatolia and its midpoint, Ankara, where at the station under the ancient hill fortress I was surprisingly greeted by an old Visa Division associate, Harry Troutman, serving in the embassy. This made me appreciate that the Service spanned the world. An overnight run bridged Ankara with the Sea of Marmora on an early September day, and on the European side of the Bosphorus I could see the minarets of Istanbul. The Gripsholm, I was later told, entered New York harbor a good week before.

It had been prolonged, but we were at war, I was here, and it was up to me in an unclear assignment to do my best. The consul general was competent and well intentioned, but to my great relief he had not known of the special plans that the Department had for the office. He left in December, overlapping with a new chief, and an unexpected operation began.

Burton Berry, the fresh consul general, was a Middle East specialist, a bachelor with a private income, a discriminating collector, and, for us, an excellent chief. His assignment was to organize peripheral reporting on Eastern and Southeast Europe occupied by the Nazis. When the operation got into high gear we had an officer assigned to each Eastern European country, with two each for Greece and Yugoslavia, and we had close liaison with all allied representatives in Istanbul. The post did no work on Turkey, aside from local consular services, a relief to our embassy having a problem coping with numerous unstructured American activities. The Istanbul press summary, for example, was done by a unit strangely reporting to the embassy commercial attache, who had offices in the consulate general, and the results were sent to Ankara. The embassy's army and naval attaches also were stationed in Istanbul. It was wartime improvisation. Local frictions were avoided, and we concentrated on those eastern parts of Axis Europe we could reach, subscribing to every publication coming from those countries which appeared in Istanbul. The material, current magazines and newspapers, as an instance, reached us from Bucharest a few days after their dates. One essential of our operation was a group of translators in German and the Balkan languages supervised by an American clerk, Dan Brewster, who later became an FSO. Further, we talked with various people who came out of the Balkans through the Istanbul funnel or who entered Europe from there.

As the senior (just promoted to FSO-8) among three junior FSOs under the consul general, I was designated the executive officer. This meant administrative responsibilities set by him in addition to the country I was expected to report upon, which was Rumania. It was purely random when the countries were being parceled out for reporting assignments that I selected Rumania and started on a Balkan background which lasted actively nearly eight years. I had good Rumanian and German translators, also an excellent Greek secretary educated at the American girls' school. Using our extensive coverage and talking to those who knew something of current Rumanian conditions, I supplemented these by reading until I had a respectable knowledge of the country. It was a busy time, work continued until we were done, and I turned out some eight dispatches weekly. Truly we knew why we were there.

In our consular group there were others designated as Foreign Service Staff or Auxiliary officers, the last a wartime rating, while Berry, Bill Fraleigh, Walter Birge, and myself were the FSOs. Bill was quiet, and for a time not well physically, but pleasant and conscientious. Walter was gregarious, with an energetic personality and quite a ladies man. Then there was Lee Metcalf, who when I arrived was secretary to the consul general, next a non-career vice consul, and after the war an FSO. He proved to be my best friend among the group, and we have remained very close. We added academic people to our staff, such as Dr. Davis, the former president of the American College in Athens, heading the Greek section. Dr. Black, who followed Bulgaria for us, had headed the American College at Sofia, and I respected him as a gentleman of the Wilsonian generation, who later became president of Robert College (now Bosphorus University) in Istanbul. His son Cyril, a well-known Princeton historian, and I later worked in Balkan affairs, both in Washington and the field. Then too, with time we began to get added specialized, auxiliary people, like Herb Cummings, an economist, but none with Balkan experience.

As part of the number two job, I was supposed to follow and track the clearly erratic activities of several wartime agencies blossoming in Istanbul, as well as to handle interagency liaison. That large Istanbul branch of the Office of War Information (OWI) required attention, and the initial director, in a job too big for him, was a free-wheeler who made a poor impression on the embassy, being deemed careless with his accounts. Liaison tasks with the Naval and Army attaches and the various covert activities of the government, included the Office of Strategic Services (OSS), the forerunner of the CIA. Then there were some Americans who gave us no clear indications for whom and what they were working, undoubtedly OSS in some form, which gave rise to anecdotes. One American overcome by his secret mission used to have the then deserted Turkish castle Rumeli (European) Hissar, on the Bosphorus, as his rendezvous point. It was the same man who semi-furtively approached Birge in his office. Walter, who handled our routine consular business, as well as doing Hungarian reports, expected something significant, but the operative, revealing a paper bag, whispered, "Have some nuts." George Earle, former Democratic governor of Pennsylvania, had a naval commission with an intelligence tie to the president. Earle was so direct and open that he drove Axis intelligence crazy trying to keep up with him, but the operation was of dubious value.

Meeting foreign officials was part of my rounds. There was an English colonel I saw regularly, together with the Free French. One of theirs was M. Man'ach, later the French government's expert on China. We also knew the Poles and enjoyed their company, and found, from the partition of their country, they were deadly serious in their assignments. In the city it gave you a strange feeling, because Turkey was neutral, to find Germans, Italians or Japanese at the next restaurant table. Then there were plentiful agents and double agents. American exuberance would not be downed, and in restaurants during my first winter, Americans would burst into chants of Timoshenko (the winter offensive Soviet general) to the rhythm of "The Volga Boatmen." However, social-political lines were well drawn, so among foreigners we gravitated to other Allied people and to pro-Ally Levantines and Turks. Among those of European background with Turkish passports was one jovial and sharp businessman, who, with humor and an eye for opportunities, came into our lives. He I chiefly remember in later noting the romantic record of the Gabor sisters and recalling the one piece of advice of his Hungarian mother: "Koca, never marry an Hungarian."

My first Service post inspection was done by Inspector Cochran, the sole such official State had operating during the war. He and Berry, I detected, had a personal animosity, and this would have subsequent career consequences for me. Still, I seemed to have no problems with him, and as customary he was my dinner guest, this time at the Taksim Casino, where we spent a pleasant evening. There or later he told me an inspection story. Malaga, Spain, was then a post, and Cochran inspected it, including a lunch at the consul's home. There the guileless wife, apparently not reckoning on a misunderstanding of Spanish social life marked by late hours, said, "Mr. Cochran, I am so pleased you are here, for my husband now is rising and getting to the office in the morning." To this the husband interjected, "Shut up, dear." Cochran, some said, was a prickly character, and Burton Berry was not the only officer to fall afoul of him.

This was world war, and there were any number of espionage activities which fitted the environment and could be recounted, and were in several books. Our people knew, as did other allies, but a part of these. I will mention one. A pretty cafe singer was trapped into having her Polish boyfriend unknowingly betray another Pole among those infiltrating back and forth from Axis territory. A Polish official with whom I was friendly, grimly said that the enamored Pole was encased in cement in the Bosphorus, and the woman blacklisted by the Allies. Other unusual happenings arose with my work on Rumania. One of these was, through the Free French, to meet with two Rumanians who had just flown out of their country in a little biplane. They had avoided pursuit or anti-aircraft action by literally hedge-hopping all the way to Turkey. These two, as well, had instructions from opposition groups forming in the country. I later met one of the men in Bucharest and we exchanged hearty greetings.

There was an acute housing shortage in Istanbul, so for an initial period I stayed at the Tokatlian Hotel, which gave my first bill, addressed to Roy Bey, a cultural experience. Then I discovered the hotel was the rendezvous for successive circumcision parties with the youthful honoree, nightgowned in a bed in the ballroom, surrounded by food, music, and dancing couples, presumably making him welcome to a man's estate. Next I roomed with an old White Russian couple named Pilkin, who ran a dairy shop. They were very nice to me, and one fine Sunday we spent picking mushrooms on the Marmora island, Byukada, a Russian hobby on which they were expert. Fortunately the AP correspondent in Istanbul, Frank O'Brien, was being transferred to Ankara, so I sublet his furnished hillside apartment, where from the balcony I could gaze over the wide, bush covered ravine down to the Dolmabahche mosque on the Bosphorus. The ravine top is now the Istanbul Hilton. On the floor below, Mr. Yalman, who became the leading Turkish journalist, commented with a smile that my bathroom baritone in the shower carried through the air shaft and made him think I played a loud radio.

The atmosphere of Istanbul grew as its impressive past penetrated my life and as neutral Turkey gave it another gloss. In location it was unmatched, and to me its nearest rival was San Francisco. Istanbul had the swift flowing Bosphorus from the Black Sea, opening into the Sea of Marmora with its islands and beaches. One could imagine Jason and his Argonauts heading against the current, bound for gold bearing mountain streams of Black Sea Anatolia, where sheep skins in streams collected gold in their fleece; ergo, the golden fleece. It too, was unique in its convergence of Europe and Asia, and by its mixture of cultures. Here Islam and several branches of Christianity (deliberately inconspicuous) were represented. The Greek heritage was maintained by a large indigenous Greek population. There were Levantines and Jews diffused among varied European and Mideast passports, and colonies of English, Russians (White and Red), French, Germans, and Italians added their variety. Turkish Islam was dominant in architecture, culture, and population, and the imposing mosques and palaces of the sultans gave the city its distinctive appearance.

War does not encourage public works, and the city was definitely shabby. It was the most cosmopolitan place in republican Turkey, but its appearance, more noticeable in the three-month wet and cold winter, was drab, and many buildings ramshackle. The narrow cobbled streets, up and down hill to the Bosphorus or the Golden Horn shores, were muddy and grimy. The people also looked shabby, and clothing generally was simple and worn. Museums, in which category the Turks placed Haggia Sophia Mosque and other structures like the Galata Tower built by the Venetians, were sparsely attended, for there were no tourists. The round Tower itself was an empty, dirt floored edifice crowded among uninspiring tenements. The famous Galata bridge over the Golden Horn was filled with ragged hamals (porters) bearing their back packs. The contrasts with the upscale present are startling.

The Golden Horn stream divided Old Istanbul, with its minarets and old bazaar that gave the city its flavor, from newer Istanbul. Across the bridge, in the Galata, Pera, and Beyoglu areas and beyond, was the bulk of the town. Even as today, rapid ferries crossed to and from Europe and Asia, and coursed the Bosphorus with stops at villages along its length. The mined Black Sea entrance was off-limits. The Pera area, with which we were most familiar, was at the top of a hill and had a main artery, Independence Avenue, known as the Pera, filled with shops, cafes, and movie houses up to Taksim Square, where avenues branched to other sectors. Sundays brought throngs to the Pera, when street traffic (including trolleys) moved slowly, and the movies drew heavy patronage. While Turkey was a neutral nation, it operated under a national emergency regime, so soldiers were everywhere a part of the civilian crowds. Regularly of an evening from a Turkish nightclub at the Square would come loud bursts of Mideast singing, painful until listening to hard rock music.

An early spring was a rebirth. In cutting through city byways one could see flowering vines and greenery that meant the nine good months were arriving. Rain ceased and sunny days were the norm. The delightful Istanbul, its beaches and night strolling took over, together with some magnificent sunsets over the Golden Horn that we could see from our Pera office windows. These aspects of nature were combined with the city's literary flavor. There was a large open air cafe hung with festive lights looking on the Golden Horn that I passed daily, which Graham Greene described in his novel "Orient Express." Then there was the Regence, an indoor and outdoor restaurant run by White Russians, given a brief mention in Ernest Hemingway's "The Snows of Kilimanjaro." Other sites added to the charm of the place.

Istanbul was Burton Berry's favorite city and he helped me see it through his eyes: the extensive bazaar with its treasures of fine craftsmanship, and the bazaar merchants he knew so well; the small shops selling Turkish delight candy; Pandelli's, the best bazaar luncheon restaurant, with its unvarying menu, and Abdullah's, the city's finest restaurant, on the Pera. As a lifetime collector, Berry bought only the best, his specialties being ancient Greek gold coins and Mideast carpets. He told me when serving in Tehran he bought many good Persian carpets, but when leaving took them all to a trusted bazaar merchant and exchanged them for one magnificent product. His collecting abilities allowed him in time to make bequests to the Chicago Art Museum, the University of Indiana (his school), and the American Numismatic Society.

So much the city had to offer in architecture and edifices, mosques, picturesque fountains, ancient walls, and city walks that we were fortunate to know an elderly American, Professor Tom Whittemore. He was in charge of uncovering the Byzantine mosaics in Haggia Sophia, hidden by Moslem decree for five hundred years, so with his wide knowledge he guided us on Wednesday afternoons to various sites. Three of us, Whittemore, Birge, and myself, went with Bill Fraleigh in his little open Fiat, to Tom's designated spots. Among other places, the professor showed us the extensive underground, many pillared reservoir in old Istanbul, which had been the city's guarantor against siege, closed to the public because it was unrepaired and dangerous.

Several Turkish customs or religious aspects appeared unusual to us. In modern restaurants like the Taksim Casino, it was proper for a young man to escort his date to the ladies restroom, attend outside, and return her to the table. Another was a positive gesture for the negative. If to a query one made a short affirmative nod, accompanied by a soft tick of the tongue, this would be a definite negative, confusing to the unfamiliar. If with two fingers you shook your coat lapel, this gesture meant you would have nothing to do with a situation. The Turkish bayrams or religious celebrations were noteworthy. On one occasion two of us visited the Suleiman Mosque on the Night of Power, escorted furtively by a guide through a side door up to a latticed balcony overlooking the carpet of male worshippers below. This was the anniversary of the descent of the words of the Koran to the Prophet, where the living texture of the prone assembly indelibly displayed the conviction and vitality of Islam. It struck me that Islam, over six hundred years younger than Christianity, might be contemporary with the height of Christian religious zeal.

Ataturk, founder of modern Turkey, died less than four years before I arrived, so memories and anecdotes were fresh. He has since been memorialized, statued, and converted into a national icon, but he was a remarkable man, and at the time as much of a presence as any major feature of the city or country. First, he shifted the capital to Ankara, in Anatolia's center, to make it less vulnerable to foreign influences or attack. In building the new town he was asked whether it should have a sewer system, and replied, "Put the money where it will show." He doffed the fezzes from the men, banished traditional garb for women in the towns, required everyone to have family names, abolished Arabic script, and obliged all to learn a new Latin alphabet, thus creating a modern literature. Perhaps from boredom with the success of his single party system, Ataturk proposed to a trusted aide that the country needed to develop a more pluralistic government. He thought the answer was to form an opposition party with the aide as leader. The reaction, I am told, was at best ambivalent, and the proposal quickly withered. Additionally, he was quite secular. Awakened with a hangover in the Park Hotel by a nearby muezzin call, he had the mosque torn down.

Men have their weaknesses, and Ataturk's were liquor and women. He was a great raki drinker, and the liquor, arrack, is native to Turkey, comes from a special bush, and has a licorice flavor. The Greeks call it ouzo. Told that unless he stopped he would die in a few months, he firmly declined, named Ismet Inonu his successor, and fulfilled the forecast. He was so drawn to women that stories blossomed of Turks keeping their wives and daughters away from receptions he attended, which a respected Turkish lady confirmed to me. The man liked Americans. When his yacht moored at its place on the Bosphorus opposite Robert College, the young American teachers would sometimes swim across, and if Ataturk was there, he would invite them aboard. A tangible sign I saw of the late leader was in the Tokatlian Hotel, where the bar had a huge mirror with one side partially smashed. It would not be changed, the manager told me, for Ataturk had broken it by hurling a glass.

Before the capital was moved to Ankara the large consulate general building had been the embassy, the ambassador's residence, as well as the chancery or business offices. In fact, there was a large apartment on the second floor, which Ambassador Steinhardt and his family used whenever in town or briefly during the summer. I met the ambassador when he was in Istanbul or I briefly in Ankara. There are strong differences of opinion about political appointees such as Laurence Steinhardt, but in Istanbul and Ankara, from personal excursions, we got to know his male secretary quite well. His private observations dovetailed with those of a later ambassador of mine. Steinhardt was energetic, skillfully implementing his instructions in Turkey and recommending steps to meet changing conditions. When he believed subordinates were trying to be helpful, he invited their suggestions, and credited these. From my worm's eye view, I would generally concur with this.

In the building floor space available for our operations, we wound up in varying size rooms not ready of access, nor intended as offices, where Lee Metcalf and I shared one during his work on Yugoslavia with Bill Fraleigh. We young men worked hard, but also had good times at either the Taksim Casino or at the Florya beach on the Marmora. One birthday did make a sobering impression, for it was my thirtieth, but despite this I gave a big party at my apartment in which Lee prominently figured.

We might occasionally be angry with the Turks who, while handling their neutrality masterfully, for reasons I still do not fully understand, imposed a virtual confiscatory "varlik" tax on the minorities living in the country, causing much suffering. Affected by this, tall Lee late one evening, put his hand on the shoulder of a short Turkish policeman, and cussed away with his broad smile, while the bewildered man, not knowing a word of English, kept nodding away. Afterwards Lee said he felt relieved, and as a spectator, life for me had a better perspective.

The atmosphere had its other strains, aside from omnipresent espionage, which I suppose affected all of us working there, so that what might be considered bizarre or unreal today seemed somehow natural to us. We took it in stride when the British military attache, a bluff, hearty type, committed suicide. We were bachelors, and in the Taksim Casino there was a small group of Hungarian girls in the show with whom we might on occasion have a drink or dance in the "snake pit," the late hours bar. To avoid a return to Budapest they reported to an Hungarian official once a week for a relay to the Nazis of what they picked up from talking to Allied people. We knew it was part of the game and concocted stories they passed on. The ambassador's secretary once joined us there and shared in the laughter of his mock surprise when one of the girls addressed him as "Phil, darling." "Never saw her before," said Phil in unctuous exaggeration. Americans like myself naturally dated English-speaking young women, and the impact of American schools and the teaching of English extended this to various nationalities, so that among these was a young Turkish woman, a former leading university fencer.

Health hazards, not unexpected in wartime, appeared. Bosphorus shellfish, we learned from friends' illnesses, were taboo. Then a serious outbreak of typhus brought an American medical team headed by Brigadier General Fox, that organized a mass inoculation which, from the strength of the inoculation and dull needles, gave painful and dizzying reactions. Lee and I took the shots together and we knew. The common mode of city transport was streetcar, and in one crowded trolley passengers drew away from a man as an accompanying bug appeared. Beggars and porters had been taken by trucks en masse for compulsory fumigation, but this fellow had been missed.

Because of wartime conditions, we traveled little, and given the environment of Istanbul, this was no hardship. One trip I did take, aside from three on business to Ankara, was with Burton Berry, Bill Fraleigh, and Dan Brewster to Bursa, the capital of the Ottomans before they captured Istanbul. It had a special atmosphere, that early center of the empire, with its simple mosques and great plane trees. From here we climbed the legendary mountain, Uludag, near the city, and later visited the ruins of the Hellenic city of Cyzikos. It was a relaxing several days interlude, my single leave.

After one year - I was only in Istanbul 17 months - in the autumn my work on Japan proved helpful in an unusual way. The Argentine chargé in Tokyo, strongly pro-Ally, traveled through Russia to Istanbul, where he awaited onward travel permission. We became acquainted, and I found his loyalties genuine, as well as being struck by the incredible amount of press and other printed English information on the Japanese economic situation in his baggage. I made a deal. In return for using his material I would give him a copy (suitably expurgated) of what I sent to Washington. Then I went to work with Burton Berry's hearty agreement. The result was five economic reports, one on Japanese shipping. Coincidentally, his material on this last picked up where mine ended, and continued until his Tokyo departure. I later received a commendation from Washington for the reports, and it was doubly satisfying to be shown by the Board of Economic Warfare man in Ankara a letter by Livingston Merchant, then a deputy in BEW and afterwards a prominent ambassador. He said the reports comprised the most comprehensive economic information our government had available on the Japanese Empire since the start of the war. So while I was initially disappointed at going to Istanbul, for the moment I was there at an appropriate time.

Professionally I learned much. I had, as the exec, to help arrange workloads, to have regular relations with other agencies, to be concerned with other countries on substantive matters, and on two occasions to be in charge. Burton made two trips to Cairo, each for two weeks, to check with Allied military headquarters there, in view of the growing importance of our work and relationship to Allied Balkan operations. We could cite many instances of our office reporting on matters of wartime value. Our organization had progressed so well that after the first American air raid on the Ploesti oil fields in Rumania, we had fairly reliable damage reports within three days.

As air raids over the Balkans continued, there were American aircraft crews interned in Turkey after being forced down on its territory. Their number grew, but the Turks adopted a more lenient policy as the war favored the United Nations by allowing them freedom within certain areas of the country. To check on their welfare, an air officer was assigned as assistant military attache to look after his fellows. The major and I met and, as natural with Americans, exchanged names of our hometowns. He admitted being from a small Pennsylvania village called Muddy Creek Forks, and was taken aback when I asked how Uncle Jess and Aunt Amanda were doing. The hamlet literally had a half-dozen houses, the two ran the general store/post office, and I had stayed with them for a weekend when in college. We became instant friends.

Tom Whittemore, our onetime guide, lived in Bebek, the site of the famous old guardian fort, Rumeli Hissar, and of Robert College, the American institution. Tom lived there with a Balkan old timer, Arch Walker, heading Standard Oil operations in Turkey and helping OSS where he could, and we would attend infrequent stag gatherings there when Arch would tell stories of his Balkan days, particularly Bulgaria. He was King Boris's friend, and was invited frequently to lunch, where he noted that despite delays in lunch scheduling, the souffles were always perfect. Curious, he sought out the chef. Said the chef, "it is no problem. I make a new one every five minutes." Bulgaria had plenty of eggs!

My first solid association with journalists came in Istanbul, where they were attracted by the same potential for Axis news as our government. Frank O'Brien I have already mentioned, but there were others such as Sam Brewer, who worked for the Chicago Tribune, later to go with the New York Times, and Reuben Markham of the Christian Science Monitor, with whom I was friendly. Sam seemed fated to have bad luck in marriage and was being divorced. His next wife, not with him in our assignments, after divorcing Sam married the subsequently uncovered Soviet agent, Kim Philby, earlier a leading figure in British Intelligence. The American correspondents were great story tellers. Once Archbishop Spellman of New York, appointed by President Roosevelt as Vicar to the Armed Forces, visited Turkey, and Frank attended his formal reception in Ankara. As he told it, in the receiving line each person was announced before meeting the Archbishop. After a procession of Turkish names, the churchman's eyes lit when Frank Joseph O'Brien was announced. He placed his hands on Frank's shoulders and said, "Bless you, my son." "He looked so happy," Frank said, "I didn't have the heart to tell him I wasn't a Catholic."

Through nebulous, bureaucratic channels, I was told that I would be granted home leave and transfer in a chain of these early in the year. Sure enough, in January orders came for the leave in a succession of seven transfers, but with no onward assignment. However, plans were afoot in the Department to send our reporters on Balkan countries to those states as soon as possible, and it was indicated that I would go to Bucharest. Nevertheless, I had my accustomed mixed feelings on leaving our energetic factory on a gloomy day at the end of January and crossing the Bosphorus with the same companion, Walter Birge, who had met me on arrival.

On my way home via Cairo I resolved to see a bit of the Middle East, so after retracing the route to Beirut I drove to Damascus. The place intrigued me as I rambled around its mosques and the bazaars with their finely worked products. Our bachelor consul in Damascus had a Service reputation as a linguist and lived in my hotel, but regrettably I never saw him, for vice consul Bill Porter, to be several times an ambassador, explained he was on a bender. Later that year, leaving from New York, I had unhappy news of the consul from the military airlines people. He had been flown home with a case of the DTs, and later left the Service. Drinking, as ever, was our problem.

It was a day's drive to Jerusalem as we passed along the Sea of Galilee and into the city. I learned something of the area, visited the religious and historic sites, and went down to Jericho, to the Jordan, and even waded in the Dead Sea. I found the books were right in that each holy place, regardless of religion, suffered the same malady, the commercialism surrounding it. Typically, in the small chamber of the Church of the Holy Sepulchre, supposedly the site of Christ's tomb, I found a black-robed priest of an Eastern sect with hand outstretched. I have not returned.

Cairo was crowded with military personnel, so since I had only civilian priority, I waited a week for passage and investigated Cairo and made a few false starts to the airfield. In one case I had an animated encounter with an Army doctor who wanted to send me home by ship on a stretcher. He misread some old lung scar tissue. In another, I was delighted to fall in with Joe Touchette, the former Montreal commercial officer, who took me to the Pyramids, arranged a guide as pilot to the top amidst the massive stones, and then accompanied me into the bowels of the Great Pyramid. This last was eerie.

Finally there was a seat adjacent to two Standard Oil men from Saudi Arabia, out in the early stages of its development, who gave my first indication of its remarkable oil deposits. After an overnight stay at Khartoum, we had two more such intervals across the bulge of Africa before reaching Accra. I was in the Service network, meeting there another old Montreal friend, Bob Cavanaugh, who in a day got me a seat on the trans-Atlantic plane traveling via Ascension Island to Recife, Brazil, up the East coast and through the West Indies to Miami. Strategic Ascension was a unique volcanic island with an unusual airstrip ending in a precipice overlooking the ocean. Refueled, we lumbered down the strip, dropped off the edge, and started climbing. The best attention gatherer was the West Indies, for as seen from the cockpit, one jewel of an island succeeded another as we flew up the chain.

At night in Miami, a WAVE (naval woman) officer arranged billets for official travelers. I had become friendly with my Standard Oil acquaintances, so the WAVE found us a large hotel room. After a good rest, we celebrated my first morning home in four and one-half years by ordering enormous breakfasts: six half-pints of fruit juice, 12 half-pints of milk, three orders each of bacon and eggs, pancakes and sausage, and toast with the fixings. We enjoyed it.

After a Norfolk reunion with my folks, I traveled to New York to see Virginia, who worked in the Convoy Control Office, to Philadelphia to visit my sister and brother-in-law, and reported in Washington. My home leave ended after a trip to Palm Beach, Florida, with Virginia and her mother.

Washington was overflowing with men and women in uniforms and war workers, and the tempo of life and variety of restaurants and night clubs had noticeably increased. The Department decided that I should have a Washington assignment until the opening of Bucharest, so I sought congenial quarters at the familiar Gralyn, also filled with military. Initially I was assigned to State's Liaison Division, a wartime innovation, where we followed Naval and Army Intelligence of interest to the Department and marked material State received of interest to the military. I simply accepted this as a worthwhile job, not knowing it marked the start of the broad interagency coordination now so accepted. Mornings I helped cull State's input of reports for their potential military intelligence value, and afternoons I went to the Pentagon with a stenotypist to review the military reports and to dictate from any relevant political portions. I was at this June 6, D-Day of the Allied invasion of Normandy, so I happily brought my senior Departmental people information regarding our progress. Incidentally, just before and for a week after D-Day, Army Intelligence was being reorganized in the Pentagon and disorganization was the condition.

Cavendish Cannon, acting as chief of Southern European Affairs when I reported there, was an excellent draftsman and knew the Balkans well. Among those working with him were two academicians who had moved full time into the Department, Cy Black, son of my Istanbul colleague, and Rumanian desk officer

John Campbell, intimately associated with the Department and the Council on Foreign Relations, who is now an old friend.  As I learned how headquarters viewed the field, Cavendish warned me I would meet a different kind of thinking when I got to the Balkans, of which Istanbul only gave an inkling.  In illustrating this, he told of meeting an unsavory political figure on a Sofia, Bulgaria, street. The man remarked that it looked as if it would be a fine day.  Walking on, Cavendish found himself thinking, "Why does that S.O.B. expect it to be a fine day?"  Then he realized he had been in the Balkans too long!

The Bucharest assignment came nearer and I had a personal decision to make. Virginia and I had expanded a relationship in New York and Washington previously restricted to years of letters, so by summer's end we both knew our lives had to be together.  The Department ruling stared at me:  FSOs could not marry foreigners, and Virginia's mother, first cousin to General Douglas MacArthur (their mothers sisters), had lost her American citizenship when she married a Canadian, and Virginia was a Canadian citizen.  The State Department had earlier refused exceptions to the regulation.   Then I remembered Chief Byington's story of the monastery novice, and I did not ask.  We made our decision, married in New York, and I left for my war assignment, Bucharest.  In my transient life I had a mooring.  The coup in Rumania on August 23 had spurred things, so by the end of September I was on my way.  On the close of the European phase of the war, but with the cold war critically affecting Europe's future having begun, Virginia came out on the first passenger ship to Europe, and with Washington's approval, we remarried in Rome.  When I had the opportunity during my Washington home assignment, I submitted the facts with my resignation to the chief of Foreign Service Personnel.  The Department, then prepared to accept the situation, gave its approval, and our lives went on together.

Flying from New York, I reached Allied Force Headquarters, Mediterranean Theatre, then located at Caserta outside of Naples, where I was assigned to the staff of the political adviser's office pending arrangements to open a political mission in Bucharest.  Since it was a military armistice situation, we could not have a legation, but for the unspecified interim Caserta was to be our supply backstop and message relay point.  The political adviser at Allied Headquarters was Alexander Kirk, an old career man and wealthy, unconventional bachelor. Kirk used a well-arranged bowl of frost light bulbs as a centerpiece during formal dinners.  Then, to bridge what he termed the inevitable table conversation pause, he would clearly make an unexpected remark, such as "When I stopped taking cocaine.."  Talk picked up.  Kirk generally stayed in Rome, while the office at Caserta was run by Carmel Offie and Fred Reinhardt, my Service School classmate.  An attached army major, George Morgan, and I shared a large tent. We all ate in the Palace orangery, listening to a string group play the perennial "Lili Marlene," and spent our evenings in the Officers' club, where one of our good companions was a personable colonel, Jock Whitney, later ambassador in London and a news media figure. We also had a small convivial session with Archbishop Spellman, continuing his travels as Roosevelt appointed Vicar to the Armed Forces.

The OSS in September had opened a station in Bucharest, and I was impatient to get there. Delays continued until signals were set on what political missions would be doing in the Balkans. Americans, British, and Russians finally agreed these were to be distinct from the military allied control commissions provided under the various armistices with Rumania, Bulgaria, and later, with Hungary. These states had been at war with the Allies, and the control commissions were to be under the chairmanship of the Russians in dealing with armistice matters. Each state would have a separate political mission with rights of communicating with its home government and having direct contact with the people and regime of each country. They were to be diplomatic missions, but because of the armistice they could not have the name, for our countries were technically still at war.

In after years I realized how the war forced a faster pace of Service career development. With associates as internees, we were acutely aware of the war's consequences. Then as executive officer of the consulate general in Istanbul, engaged there and in Washington upon intelligence on the war's progress, I learned something of analytic methods and of staff employment for effective results. In Bucharest I would eventually find a new political dimension on which to build.

Some resources began to accumulate, and Charley Hulick, knowing Rumanian, came on from Cairo to join me and begin a close friendship. While impatiently waiting, we were accompanied on a trip to Rome by FSO Carl Norden, whose father developed the Norden bombsight used in the war. Our first stop was Cassino, where we saw the war damage to the monastery, and then went on to Rome. While there, orders predictably came for a quick departure to Bucharest, so Charley and I hurried to Caserta and to Foggia, headquarters of the 15th Air Force. Journeyman days were ending.

King Michael, Queen Mother, General Schuyler and Burton Berry

Left: Mark Ethridge and
Cy Black arrive

Below: Left- Lee Metcalf
in Mission courtyard
Right:  with King Michael

# CHAPTER 7

# COLD WAR: BUCHAREST

## October 1944 - November 1947

*The Allies were heading for military victory in Europe. Under armistices, an American-directed military Allied Control Commission (ACC) was established in Italy, while Russian-directed ACCs controlled Rumania, Bulgaria, and Hungary; all former allies of Germany. The U. S. and U. K. with Soviet agreement established independent political missions in 1944, analogous to legations, but before V-E Day, the Russians began the cold war in Eastern Europe. Too late, Americans understood the USSR intended to expand its empire. For three years from the Bucharest political mission, serving as deputy and acting U.S. political representative, I witnessed the destruction of Rumanian and Balkan freedoms, despite efforts of the king and supporting politicians like Iuliu Maniu. Our actions were fruitless and the assignment ended in sweeping defeat.*

The two B-17s, ready for action and covering each other, flew over Yugoslavia as the Nazi armies retreated. We were on the lookout for fighter attacks, but the bad weather made it unlikely. The weather worked to our disadvantage, for when our B-17s were separated, our pilot had to rely on dead reckoning to find Bucharest. For a time I rode up front in the fuselage bubble with the navigator, and when the pilot phoned for a location, the navigator responded by raising a small crystal ball on a tiny stand. The pilot nodded vigorously, and that was his last request for location. When he thought we should be out of the mountains and over the Danube plain, we began to descend through the thick cloud cover, and at a few hundred feet found a clear pool, and followed the railroad tracks to Bucharest and Baneasa airport. The other B-17 had arrived, so on this October 29 we went into town using transport of the Office of Strategic Services (OSS) operating there since early September.

We chose the Athenee Palace hotel on the central square, for living quarters and met the personable and professional Lieutenant Commander Frank G. Wisner, USN, in charge of the OSS unit. After the disarray of OSS operations in Istanbul, I was told, he had reorganized the office and developed excellent relations with all government components there, particularly with Burton Berry. During his stay here he gave us unstinting cooperation with varied sources and was of immeasurable help in providing offices in the OSS building and full-time transport with drivers. In peacetime, he had been a lawyer and we found Frank unusual in his ability to maintain a balance amidst the highly charged atmosphere. I respected the man immensely, and over the years we were friends. I believe he fully merited his exceptional career with the CIA as director of its overseas operations under Allen Dulles.

The Red Army entered Rumania when galvanizing war events made this feasible through the weakening of dictator Antonescu's control. In a remarkable action, 22-year-old King Mihai (Michael) had turned the entire Rumanian army against the German troops there at enormous personal risk, arresting the dictator Antonescu, and making an inspiring radio speech to the nation on August 23. The quietly organizing political parties united in support for his action. These acts gave valuable military aid to the Allies, for Rumania, after Italy, had been the strongest element on the Nazi side fighting Russia. The Red Army under Marshal Malinovski, with help from the Rumanian army, now was pursuing the Nazis into Hungary through Transylvania.

When we arrived, there still were many Russian military in Bucharest, where for a brief period we enjoyed a friendly association with them. I remember General Vasiliev, whom we privately called "Old Billiard Ball," and General Vinogradov, deputy to the Russian general in charge of the Allied Control Mission. In meeting them socially we were cautious of their vodka, but taught them a favorite American toast, "To the Japanese Navy." They could not understand toasting an enemy until we explained "Bottoms up." The worm in the apple appeared when the political commissars began to take over. Our associations with the purely military rapidly faded, and we found ourselves surrounded by deepening suspicion. For unclear reasons other than the ingrained spirit of suspicion, efforts were made to get an American drunk in order to pump him. The most familiar tactic was to have a Russian group at a reception insist that the American drink separately with each, or at a table a Russian might be served water in a liquor glass while the American got vodka.

My Istanbul journalist friends popped up for long stays in Bucharest: Sam Brewer, Frank O'Brien, and Reuben Markham. Sam, thinking to foil Russian hospitality, adopted a legendary technique by swallowing olive oil before a Soviet reception. Things went well until something told him to leave. His last recollection was moving down a corridor toward his chauffeured car only to wake up in his hotel room the next morning. The technique has dangers.

In our first days there, Sam and I were driving to the hotel before curfew and passed Russian guards with tommy guns. It seemed to Sam that one guard shouted at us. He looked back and, sure enough, the guard was bringing his gun to bear. Sam yelled frantically to our driver, who stopped, and then we were allowed to proceed. Soviet military discipline was poor, and all of us had encounters with soldiers bearing tommy guns. While driving I was shot at by some passing Russians, bullets shattering my side view mirror. On another occasion, in the Carpathians as a passenger driving with a king's aide, Major Vergotti, we were stopped by two armed soldiers who clambered into the back. The aide drove as fast as he could to the center of the town of Brasov, where we let them out. He speeded up because a week before, under comparable circumstances, the driver had been shot. Even off-duty Russian soldiers carried guns, and I became an early convert to the dangers. A patrol in Bucharest, for instance, would fire down a street and duck behind a building, knowing that a fellow patrol would reciprocate. Such antics slowly subsided, but as urban troop discipline took over, the soldiers still were dangerous. When Mrs. Hulick, a later Bucharest arrival, was entering a theatre for a benefit, a Soviet guard jabbed a tommy gun into her fur coat. She froze until it was made clear to the unsmiling guard that she was a guest. An American secretary of the eventually established information officer's section lived with a Rumanian family at a time when Russian troops still would make unhindered forays through town. Late one evening two Soviet soldiers tried to break into her room and the owner of the house shot one in protecting her. The landlord was arrested and imprisoned.

The Bucharest's public atmosphere, reflecting the country, was fearful; fearful of the Russians and fearful of the war's consequences because of Rumania's role, despite the important military support given the Red Army by the king's successful coup d'etat and by the Rumanian Army's accompanying advance. The abrupt change in political fortunes caused the Russians resentfully to note the small evidence of war's tragedy in the country. Food was ample and signs of the good life apparent. It was not easy for some of the fashionable and bejeweled Rumanian women to adjust to the times. As Burton Berry, later my chief, remarked, "One tends to blink when they become emotioneé." Rumania also had been the breadbasket of the Nazi war machine, as well as its major oil source. Added to these human antagonisms was Soviet military awareness of the tremendous losses and suffering of the Russian people.

Emotional ambivalence was a human level of the Soviet attitude. Another, actually surpassing, was the realistic power politics of the leaders that characterized Soviet strategy. Although not clear at the outset when the aid of the Rumanian army was so welcome, the evidence became overwhelming of Soviet objectives toward Rumania and all Eastern Europe. In the tradition of realpolitik, the Soviets were intent on forging, through a range of punitive measures and economic domination, an area of controlled communist states. To later democratic protests that the Yalta Agreement for freedoms in Eastern Europe was flouted, the Soviets replied, in essence, "It depends on your definitions."

We had regained the former American legation, a two story mansion, from the Swiss as the protecting power, and set up the U.S. political mission and lived under that title since the Three Powers had formally agreed to allow a political mission to have direct access to the governments and the people. This practice held until the peace treaty was concluded and until an accredited minister presented his credentials to the Rumanian government.

Eleven days after my arrival, so compressed were time and events, I welcomed my old chief, Burton Berry, as U.S. political representative, who brought one secretary, Doris Magnusson, engaged to Lee Metcalf, and Jean Nelson, our early code clerk and files keeper. The skeleton political mission was operative. Indeed, there was plenty to do in the early months for our core of five, Burton, Charley, Doris, Jean, and myself. For Charley Hulick I came to have high regard, as the intensive working months showed his ability, exceptional character, and dedication. He was a balance wheel, and for a lifetime we have been close. Doris as the sole secretary and Jean were under unusual pressures, and I know we did not fully understand this as we drove to do our wartime duty. Sunnie Hulick arrived, and eventually Lee Metcalf to join his fiancée.

The mission came to have Berry as chief, a deputy (myself), and a political section with Charley Hulick, later joined by Vaughan Ferguson. Fergie had requested a post like wartime Iran, but with modern plumbing. He got it. Fortunately he proved an asset. He had a nearby house, and we saw much of each other. Every pouch brought him a packet of mystery stories, which kept us in escapist reading, and I remarked his low key personality and wry humor. Our economic section held two specialists, as did our information office, while Lee Metcalf was excellent in our important consular services. After Doris and Jean, we grew until there was a good support staff. The local Rumanian employees were a real bulwark, and some later suffered arrest and imprisonment because of their association with us, but a few later escaped to work in our Paris embassy.

Much has been written about the communization of Eastern Europe. Burton Berry contributed a two volume chronological manuscript, his memoir on Rumania, to the Indiana University library. In my view it is the best official style record of Rumania in those turbulent times. Accounts of active witnesses, like

Berry, still were said to lack perspectives that later opened archives gave. Next, the "revisionists" insisted that the West was wholly to blame for the area's satellite status and focused on America's atomic bomb monopoly as a threat. Neo-revisionists sought a synthesis, but it was hard to differ with realities exemplified by everyday terrors, disappearances, imprisonments, and executions of respected people, who were democratically inclined. Books by other early credible witnesses like our minister, Arthur Bliss Lane, on Poland and Christian Science Monitor correspondent, Reuben Markham, on Rumania added to these realities.

American interests, reflected in the work of the Bucharest political mission, involved three points: 1. three-power collaboration; 2. relations with local political elements as they built a framework within United Nations' concepts, and 3. traditional protection of American citizens and their interests. We recognized inter-power problems would arise, but did not expect that these would proceed to the point of total disruption. Muttering by ranking Americans seriously disturbed by Soviet actions could not affect a public conditioned by the Soviet partnership. It would have required too abrupt a stripping of political gears for Americans. The three pronged policy held.

To the Bucharest curfew, the omnipresence of Soviet troops, including Red Army women directing city traffic, and those off-duty carrying their weapons as they saw the town, the Rumanians offered a contrast. The quiet civilian movements, the few Rumanian soldiers, and the discreetly opened shops revealed public apprehensions for the future. Rumanians during the curfew for mutual reassurance would hold all-night sessions featuring the latest news and rumors. Fears became reality. Initially the Russians ordered all Rumanian residents who had been residents of Bessarabia before the onset of war to be transported to that province. Terror struck those who were, in truth, political refugees. This was supplemented by a later order, on two days notice, that all the male adult, German-speaking "Saxon" minority in Rumania report to designated points, each with a bag of clothing. Many had been actively pro-Nazi, but the punishment for all was harsh. More than 90,000 men were herded into several thousand freight cars and shipped to Russia to work in various mines. Their suffering was great, and those who trickled back about two years later carried reports of high casualties.

About this time the startling report spread of the Churchill-Stalin 1944 meeting and their agreement upon a 90% Soviet and 10% British influence in Rumania, with varying percentages for other Balkan states. The arrangement was frankly cynical and unrealistic, although Churchill seemed to be trying to protect

British interests in Greece, but it was a public opinion handicap that dogged us throughout.

Regardless of the past and the regime of Marshal Antonescu, the current reality was the overwhelming public support given young King Michael, coupled with an energetic Rumanian army working with the Red Army. General Sanatescu, the court official whose two cabinets supported the king, was succeeded by General Radescu, reluctantly accepted by the Soviets, but fully so by the Americans and British. The Soviet Deputy Foreign Minister, Andrei Vishinski, assured the king that there was no intention to communize Rumania, but we took the view that conflicting interests were for the future to face.

My initial job as deputy was to help organize our personal contacts. I had begun with key members of the Rumanian Armistice Commission, such as Savel Radulescu and Ion Christu, who were to implement its terms to provide assistance and indemnities to the Allies. One man we came to respect highly was then foreign minister Constantin Visoianu, a perceptive man, an adviser to the king from that position, and importantly, of clear integrity. Two people near the king with whom we became closely associated were Mircea (Johnny) Ionnitiu, his personal secretary, and Jacques (Jack) Vergotti, his military aide and later administrator of crown properties. Jack was about my age, Johnny about 23, and together we struggled for our beliefs on the road toward full Soviet control and communist re-making of the country. At points of acute strain, we young men gained resolution from chanting Admiral Farragut's old order, "Damn the torpedoes. Full speed ahead."

The political parties before the coup had made a covert coalition of National Peasants, Liberals, Social Democrats, and Communists. They pledged support promptly on the king's galvanizing action, and I came to know the leaders well. Iuliu Maniu, the overwhelming leader as head of the major National Peasant Party, was a bachelor whose life was politics. Dinu Bratianu, the tough old leader of the Liberals, the so-called landowner and business party, cooperated with Maniu before and after the coup. The Socialist leader, Titel Petrescu, was a theorist, decent and well-intentioned, who had his photo (profile, with hair flowing) prominently in his apartment. Communist leaders included Patrascanu and others, who over time either fled abroad or were "liquidated," to use the Stalinist phrase, with a select few who became leaders in the state. Chip Bohlen, in his memoir, gave Stalin's definition of democratic regimes. "If the government is not fascist, the government is democratic." He did not define fascist.

Since the Soviet transformation of the country was being done with little help from the bulk of the Rumanian people, the communists exploited party members who had lived in exile in Moscow and who were from the country's minorities. New names appeared as the country's leaders, such as Laszlo Luca, Hungarian; Ana Pauker, Jewish Rumanian; and Emil Bodnaras, Soviet Moldavian. At an opportune time, regardless of their official standing, these figures were swept away. While Iuliu Maniu was the epitome of integrity, Rumania had its politically compromised types. One of these was Tatarescu, completely unprincipled, who served any regime that offered advantage and who desperately sought to play with the communists. They used him for a time as foreign minister, as they did Ana Pauker, then imprisoned him.

Among western foreign diplomats there were a few cooperative Free French, but we were closest to the British and Burton's counterpart, Ian LeRougetel. He was lively and supportive, and we had frequent contact with him and his deputy, James Marjoribanks. Among the British units, I formed lasting friendships with the press officer, Ivor Porter, and Colonel Leslie Forster, the oil executive expert who had bomb targeted the Ploesti oil fields.

While I have dwelt upon the political aspects of activity, our military component of the Allied Control Commission was being fleshed out. Brigadier General C.v.R. Schuyler came to head it; an able man who later became the deputy chief of staff of the Army. He and Burton teamed well, so well, that for the area we had a unique and harmonious relationship between military and civilian components. General Schuyler, Burton, and I occasionally, used to discuss how we should react to and report the latest in the never-ending series of incidents which featured the turbulence of those first two years. These were caused by efforts of those wanting representative government to slow or halt the communist takeover and of the communists to press on with their plans. There was one incident over which the general and I chuckled. After a crisis discussion Berry dictated an action cable. The code clerk promptly returned and asked what priority he wanted on the crisis message. Berry thought a few seconds and in uncharacteristic language replied, "Oh hell, mark it routine." In that interval, he said, aware of the press and volume of messages in Washington, this put it in perspective. Nevertheless, by March 1945, when the Russians insisted on a *de facto* Soviet controlled government, we found ourselves in the midst of what became an overlapping cold war.

Both political and military mission staffs prepared, in addition to spot and analytical cables, dispatches and long reports giving body to country conditions and to communist plans. Some of the military reporters were not trained, but did the best they could. A colonel, with his Rumanian staff employee doing most of the work, prepared a report on the country's transport system, which he labeled "Secret." I remarked, since we were friendly, that this was unusual in view of the local employee's major contribution. "Not at all", said the colonel imperturbably. "He doesn't know it's classified."

With the shortage of personnel and the need for long hours and of relieving people, I sometimes found myself dictating a telegram, approving it, and then helping to code it for transmission. One early evening I coded a message describing the tense situation and ending that the city was quiet. On the last sentence firing broke out, some of it on our street. We cleared decks for the next telegram, which began, "At 5:00 p.m. shooting broke out in the city." Communications truly have been revolutionized. Our mission used slow working strip ciphers, and well into 1945 operated with one full time code clerk. When messages were pressing and in volume, the core staff dropped other work to handle them. Messages through Allied Force Headquarters in Italy were sent to the State Department, which decided the posts for further relay. Bucharest rarely saw cables about the Balkans on the Washington-Moscow-London circuit, such as embassy Moscow's estimates of Soviet intent. For the Balkans, the interchange was minimized, with the overload effect in mind. Happily our military mission was fully staffed and had healthy exchanges with its counterparts in Sofia, Budapest, and far military points. With our good local relationship, both Burton Berry and General Schuyler saw that we were on the same wavelength.

Early it was clear that the ACC designation of the Soviet chairman was to be taken literally, with the Soviets entirely responsible for ACC actions. Added to this was that inexpressible Anglo-Soviet 1944 area percentage accord. The seeming close analogy with Italy and the American ACC direction there, although deeply divergent by totalitarian practice, was not questioned for a time. Our separate political mission function, agreed by the three foreign ministers, was able to maintain full contact with Rumanians in and out of government, which we accomplished through extensive travel. We avoided visits to areas of Soviet troop activity and, even on a few early occasions, had junior Red Army officers along.

Travel expanded, whether by precedent or prior notification, until all sectors of Rumania had been visited. Burton and I, by car with an American soldier driver from our little team, travelled from the Prut river on the Soviet border to Turnu Severin and the Iron Gates on the Danube, throughout Transylvania, Moldavia and the Dobrudja, even down to Sofia in Bulgaria. I got to know the countryside and its people better than anywhere else on assignments. While traveling down the Olt river valley from Transylvania, we noticed a hilltop monastery which simply invited a visit. The inhabitants were two lonely monks and a white-bearded abbot, who warmly welcomed us. The abbot was even more affable when he learned we were Americans, for despite his almost forgotten English, he had warm memories of working in an American shipyard in 1903. One could anticipate as almost inevitable in every village to find those identifying themselves as old U.S. residents, some as citizens who had retired there, which made evident strong American Eastern European ties. Because of widespread travel, we three, Burton, Charley and myself, gained a first hand knowledge of Rumanian domestic and foreign attitudes that was valuable for our analyses and recommendations. This was buttressed by our talks with well placed Rumanians, who generally spoke French or English. Further we could point to our military mission and to established American journalists and other correspondents who remained for varying periods and gave continuity in factual stories that paralleled our mission's reports.

One valuable reporting technique that Berry developed has been in my kit ever since. We termed it the pyramid system. First would be a large number of factual messages from which we would exclude comment. At an appropriate point we would segment the reporting and liberally reference the factual messages in a series of sector analyses. A third stage, an appropriate event, drew upon the sectors for a general evaluation and recommendations. In this way Washington could follow our reporting with more confidence, since the means to our conclusions and recommendations could be followed. Just as important was avoiding emotion or subjective adjectives. In the devastating circumstances we witnessed, facts spoke for themselves, making a more powerful impression than emotionalism. This was as pertinent as the conclusions drawn from the facts. The technique is not as easy as it sounds.

Ultimately a crisis came over a Bucharest street incident on 14 February 1945, resulting in some deaths. Soviet communist pressure on the king called for Prime Minister Radescu's dismissal, and Vishinski, who had reluctantly accepted him in the first place, arrived again. Washington instructed the political mission and embassy Moscow to make clear the United States wanted the continuance of a broadly representative Rumanian government. After all, the Yalta Declaration was fresh in mind, and the king was aware of American and British views on this. The Soviets refused an ACC meeting for this purpose. Vishinski also was elusive to the American and British representatives. Berry, not to be denied, wrote to Vishinski asking that action not be taken before talking to him. The upshot was that Vishinski forced Petru Groza on the king as prime minister of a so-called coalition, the National Democratic Front. Unless his choice was accepted, Vishinski told the king, he could not be responsible for "the continuance of

Rumania as an independent state. " If Michael agreed, the king heard, there would be "a great improvement" in relations. Marshal Malinovski, heading Red Army forces in the Balkan sector, added his weight by a personal visit to the king, who decided to accede, not abdicate, but to stay and help the Rumanian people. Further jockeying between an adamant, coached Groza and a reluctant king, together with more Vishinski pressure, brought the communist dominated cabinet. On 6 March 1945, the new government was announced, a date Americans in Rumania marked as the start of our cold war.

In appraising the development, Burton Berry expressed the belief to the Department that the United States should be prepared to expect the imposition of communist dominated regimes with ever-greater assurance as the Red Army moved west.

Secretary of State Byrnes gave a quite similar account of the Rumanian crisis in "Speaking Frankly." American and British members of the Rumanian ACC were refused a request to meet and discuss their tripartite responsibility. Vishinsky arrived and demanded Radescu's dismissal, claiming he was unable to maintain order and fulfill the armistice. On instructions our Moscow embassy could not accept a single party provisional government and called for three party ACC consultations. Our ambassador was erroneously told that Vishinsky was holding them, so Burton Berry, unable to interview Vishinsky, wrote to him our view that no decisive action be taken before consultation. After Vishinsky's demand was resisted by the king to appoint Petru Groza, head of the National Democratic Front, as premier because of the unrepresentative nature of his cabinet, Vishinsky issued his ultimatum, and the king was forced to accede.

The Groza regime came to office outside the terms of the Yalta Declaration. When at the Potsdam conference the issue was discussed, Truman made it clear the United States would not establish diplomatic relations with Rumania. General Schuyler went to Washington in the spring where he saw the president, and gave a most helpful, factual rundown of our situation. Our government agreed the Yalta Declaration overrode Soviet political claims through the ACC, while locally we deemed the Groza regime a mere front for Soviet exploitation.

Vishinski, for us the spearhead of Soviet aims, was a strange man. He had gained great notoriety as the Soviet communist party's hatchet man, serving as prosecutor in the notorious purge trials of the '30s, and he maintained the role in the foreign ministry. In seeking an explanation of his career, the most likely reason stems from the unique culture of Stalin's communist party. Vishinski, it is credibly reported, early was a social democrat. With the ascendancy of the communists, Andrei Vishinski continually had to prove his loyalty by working hard as the party's trial prosecutor and ruthless figure.

The Rumanian assignment was my first lengthy duty in the vortex of a major international policy event. Operationally it was a hard, tension-filled period, physically unrelenting. The working days were long, the hours unbelievable. After a great effort Doris's health broke down, and she was obliged to go home under medical care. Most happily, she returned as Mrs. Lee Metcalf, when they were married on his home leave.

Many people mentioned in this Rumanian segment made me realize diverse American personalities loomed as large as ongoing events themselves. Their environments and glimpses of motivations could be threads in the varied issues. In Bucharest, the major diversion from the pressures was the people we came to know. It was integral while witnessing the totalitarian revolution around us, the acts of amoral ideologues, and the suffering of Rumanians. Aside from our Bucharest official circle, by personality and inadvertence three active Americans contributed.

The mission in Bulgaria was comparable to ours. I made two trips there, unfortunately after my friend, Milt Rewinkel had left, and met our remarkable representative, Maynard Barnes, and some leading Bulgarians, like the later martyr, Petkov. They were having a hard time. Barnes was a brilliant officer with several ideas each day, one of which might have real utility, who made me appreciate the rarity of a true idea man. He was flamboyant, and enjoyed a rivalry with the major general of the military mission. The general flew on his car the two star flag of his rank. Maynard, not to be outdone, flew his American flag and a 3-star flag stemming from his Service rank as minister, with the equivalent military rank of lieutenant general. He had the biggest he could find, so that in looking ahead as the car proceeded, with both banners acting as blinders, you were peering down a tunnel. Maynard, a courageous man who gave instant political asylum to the democratic leader, Dr. G.M. Dimitrov, later had his difficulties with Washington, including Secretary Acheson. Burton visited him shortly after he retired to a farm in southern Maryland, and when Barnes talked about cutting down trees, Burton asked if he didn't find it hard work. Maynard replied with his old spark, "Not if you give each tree a name!"

While we had regular liaison with Italy, we would get periodic visitors from there, and one of the most unusual was Carmel Offie. He was acting political adviser at Caserta, and came in an Air Force plane allocated to him for a trip through the Balkans, and which returned loaded with his purchases. As Offie recounted it, he asked us to send him cans of the fine Danube delta caviar, which we would do to keep relations agreeable with our base in Italy. Offie sent two kilos as a present to the Pope, for which he was duly thanked. Then an Air Force general wanted a private audience with the Pontiff, and using his caviar credit, Offie got it. Thereafter, Offie presented his bill to the general in a request for an aircraft for a trip. In those days two kilos of caviar went far! Years later, sadly, Offie's influence with an Italian ambassador resulted in an Alitalia flight being held for his arrival. The plane crashed on takeoff with no survivors.

Among our American circle, we had a Papal diplomatic representative. Bishop (later Archbishop) O'Hara of Savannah, was an extroverted and witty Irishman, who was in the Vatican's diplomatic service, and rarely saw his diocese. Both he and his American monsignor were a refreshing change from the local clergy, whom the monsignor scandalized by playing tennis in shorts rather than a clumsy cassock. Bishop O'Hara organized an interdenominational service our first Christmas, and in the hard environment we all appreciated it. Then he was caught by the regime's sudden substitution of new currency for the old, as we all were, and Lee Metcalf included his currency with ours for redemption. The grateful bishop, with conviction, told Lee that his place in heaven was assured.

Americans realistically know in the practice of our democracy we have significant deviations. Stories are frequent, but because we know ills can be remedied, they are tinged with an open humor that totalitarian bitterness cannot touch. A human comparative is incomprehensible to an ideologue. Rumanians were drawn to our complex giant and strove to understand our practical politics. One story they grasped. In a big American city, two political machines were contending for power. A day before the election, a local democratic committee-man entered a bar and saw Sam the Barfly. Heartily greeting him, the democrat hoped he would vote the right way, and the bartender saw him hand Sam $10. Later, a local republican official saw Sam, enthusiastically proposed he vote right, and the bartender saw him dispense $20. The next day, the polls closed, the curious bartender privately asked Sam which way he had voted. "For the democrat," said Sam. "How could you," said the bartender, "for the republican gave you $20 and the democrat only $10." Said Sam, pulling himself up, "I always vote for the party that's least corrupt."

We knew a change of scene from Bucharest tensions was essential, so after a sporadic search, we learned of Lake Snagov, about an hour from the office, where we leased a villa in the spring. The villa was a morale booster, so on a priority basis we scheduled overnight stays. We kept the place filled, but Berry stipulated that he would use it some weekdays and the rest of us could use it on long weekends. He might drive there several evenings a week, have a swim in the early morning, and come back to town. While in Bucharest, all serious business, he lived in the Athenee Palace Hotel. As a bachelor, Berry had his eccentricities, but we deemed him an exceptional chief for the time and place. He was a devoted collector, and this soon became known. As he visited numerous shops he met, always by chance, well-known politicians and other good contacts. Then we had mission visitors, who knew the risks they were taking when they saw him or us. One I especially liked was Liviu Nasta, a courageous Rumanian journalist, who later suffered for his convictions.

Old-style Balkan aristocracy, what remained, was inconspicuous. However, there was one outmoded duo, Prince Bibescu and his wife, a daughter of a former British prime minister. Berry lunched with them one day at the Athenee Palace, during which the lady asked who was our ambassador at the Court of St. James. When Burton replied, she sniffed, "I've never heard of him. He must be a parvenu." As a grande dame her time had passed.

This is no place to detail the many means - widespread arrests, relentless censorship, communizing the economy, and making democracy virtually impossible - by which Rumania became a Soviet satellite, reversing its war role as a Nazi one, and for this I would cite Berry's manuscript. Three major events and two subsidiary arise for me as markers. The first was 6 March, the advent of the pro-Communist Groza government. The second was the king's constitutional strike in the summer of 1945, which followed the clear American statement that it would not recognize the Groza regime, as installed in violation of the Yalta Declaration. Two subsidiaries were the Ethridge investigative mission and the Three Power mission to Bucharest to clothe a vague Moscow tripartite arrangement. Lastly, in the autumn of 1947 a joint U.S. Senate-House committee came to Bucharest and investigated the human rights violations and repressive nature of the Groza government.

In the flow of substantive issues that followed hard upon the installation of the Groza National Democratic Front aggregation, I am not alone in being unable to pinpoint V-E Day, that overwhelming event of the European war. For those of us in Eastern Europe, the war simply continued. The work was all-absorbing, for we strongly believed in the policy our government was pursuing, and I don't believe I had a day free for nearly a year. Once at Burton's request I took an afternoon off. It was strange and liberating to walk the sunny streets, strolling with nothing in view. We came to accept the onerous hours and the unremitting work, but it was here I saw Berry at his professional best. Unsteady from fatigue, he could dictate a lengthy cable without having to change a word. After an official dinner with the king, Johnny refused to believe that I was returning to my office until he dropped me there at 11:00 p.m. Steady nerves and strong constitutions were indispensable for us all, since the stark realities we dealt with were sobering. The strains inevitably brought their maladies. Mine came to be a painful spastic colon, which release from constant tensions would greatly modify, but most of our core staff came to nurse some physical weakness.

Showing that life went on despite politics, I am reminded of Claire, my competent secretary. She hadn't been with us long and wasn't happy She confided that she wanted to get married, but the prospects were dim, and unless a secretary stayed abroad a specific time she had to pay her own passage home. There is nothing like a feeling of kinship. I arranged for her transfer to Vienna where there were plenty of Americans, and when Virginia and I later passed through, Claire and her army major husband met us at the airport.

Meanwhile, the communist consolidation progressed. The National Peasants, the Liberals, and the Socialists were worried. We saw their growing harassment, arrests, the censorship and intimidation, the pyramiding communist power through control of key organs of state, and the trade union use for muscle and demonstrations. Now it is all classic. The king told Burton that the government kept trying to have him sign unconstitutional acts designed, he believed, to discredit him eventually. Still, the Soviets, for unclear reasons although merited, gave the king their highest military decoration, the Order of Victory. The award meant that Michael shared it with only three other foreigners; Eisenhower, Montgomery, and Tito, which our mission reckoned as a signal that the Russians still needed him. All this was part of an education in political realism integral to any systematic understanding of the Soviet Union. As the episodes mounted, I remembered a wartime State Department meeting with my Fletcher professor, Dr. Blakeslee. Ethics seemingly lack the same impact today, but when we discussed the wartime U.S.-Soviet alliance, with thoughtful insight he remarked, "The thing that troubles me for the future is the lack of any common ethical meeting ground between us." In ensuing years, in varying locales, that apt observation recurred. It was no accident that the officer I most admired in our Service, Loy Henderson, had posthumously published memoirs focused on this concern. That volume, dwelling on U.S.-Soviet relations, was called "A Question of Trust."

The large oil installations at Ploesti, were being reorganized under the new regime, but it was these oil installations that caused economic difficulties between the Americans and the British, with their large investments, and the Russians. The Russians confiscated, as war booty, oil equipment from the Standard Oil of New Jersey subsidiary and British companies, which the Nazis had confiscated in

1940 and used throughout the war. The Allied foreign ministers sought to delegate the problem through negotiations in Bucharest by a U.S.-Russian committee and a U.K.-Russian one. It became my temporary task to head the American group negotiating with the Soviets. We had a meeting at their military quarters, in which we did not get off the ground, and after our frustration were served an elaborate buffet by our Soviet colleagues. Each side had stated its views, and later we tried and failed to get agreed minutes. We wound up with two sets, each side maintaining its freedom. We had eight meetings in all, typified by the attendance of a special American economic emissary and our mission's petroleum attaché, while the claims issue dragged on in fruitless frustration until its dusty non-conclusion. This was one experience with Stalin's communism which impelled me to take a realistic view of accommodation.

By the summer of 1945, President Truman, to reaffirm the Yalta Declaration and aware of the millions of Eastern Europeans living in the United States, resolved to meet the issue forthrightly. He earlier had told Stalin at Potsdam that we would not establish diplomatic relations with Rumania. The American position was known and galvanizing, as exemplified by President Truman in his 9 August speech to the American people on the Potsdam Conference results. He asserted the three governments' common responsibility to help reestablish democratic governments in the liberated and former satellite nations, also recognizing jointly that Rumania, Bulgaria and Hungary not be spheres of influence of any one power. Until their international rehabilitation, these states were of combined Allied concern.

Two days after President Truman's speech, the Bucharest mission was instructed to make our position clear to the political groupings in Rumania and to the king in measured, yet clear terms. Burton was home on leave and I was in charge. Aware that to Washington I was unknown, I detailed in cables the successive steps I took. First, on receipt of the instructions, I informed the British representative, Ian LeRougetel. After careful consideration and noting the lack of instructions from his government, he made the excellent suggestion that, while it undoubtedly was well known, I might formally convey to the local Soviet embassy my government's non-recognition of the Groza regime. This I did, paying a call on my Soviet counterpart, and giving him the full import of my government's views by discussing the local situation, the Potsdam Declaration, and the clear plans and opinions of the United States. I do not think he realized their significance.

Of Rumanian elements, the king was the first entitled to an answer to his queries. This was done in a private interview. Then came the opposition. It was apparent to the king and political leaders that the mission had no instructions in the event the Groza regime or the Soviets used threats or strategic arrests, as in the past. The Rumanians were on their own, despite the position of America. Rumanians were not bereft of elementary geography. They realized the risk in following a policy antagonistic to the Soviet Union, having doubts and fears of Russia and that U.S.-Soviet differences might prove transitory. They were on the border of a victorious Soviet Union, with its troops in their country and the length of the Danube. The king and men like Maniu nevertheless thought that they could, through free elections, be in a position to reach a modus vivendi with the Soviet Union to retain essential elements of their national life. Hence, after this American pressure, hopes of free elections and of representative government they did not deem unreasonable.

On informing King Michael, I expressed to Washington my doubts that Groza would resign at the king's request unless the Soviets agreed. The British mission finally was instructed to tell the king that, if he requested Groza's resignation, the U.K. government could not protect him from the consequences. Still Michael did act in an appeal to the ACC, saying Groza's government did not have the confidence of the three allies and could not obtain a peace treaty. Groza refused to resign. The strong adverse Soviet reaction, the hands off British position, and the failure of U.S.-U.K. pressure on the Soviets, impelled the king to caution. Yet he and the political opposition wanted the Anglo-Americans to implement the Atlantic Charter and the Yalta Declaration. Until then he would approve no acts of the Groza regime; in essence, he would go on a constitutional strike. Soberly we assessed to Washington that to follow Groza a technician government alone had a chance. After the king's move I pointed out to affected opposition leaders the vital need to obtain Soviet cooperation in any United Nations' conference on Rumania and to avoid public signs of hostility against the regime or demonstrations for the king's action.

As the daily developments of our crisis unfolded, from the State Department cable of 11 August until the king's appeal of 21 August and beyond, I kept close contact with General Schuyler. His military mission's experience of frustration with the Soviet run ACC had been part of the common American record in Rumania which brought the United States to the position it had taken. Our mission sent daily reports to Washington on developments, and over what seemed a long stretch there was prolonged silence from State. I acted, reported, and acted again. Not for over two weeks did a Washington indicator arrive expressing concurrence with the train of mission activity. It was quite educational. While going on my best judgment, taking into account those in whom I had confidence, it was not wholly facetious when I would tell Charley (with mental apologies to that then quiet post), "Tegucigalpa, here I come!" Unknown to me, Charley alerted our American army drivers to be ready for possible trouble whenever I was a passenger.

Angered by the Americans, the Russians made an issue at a rare meeting they called of the ACC's three representatives on 23 August, at which time General Schuyler stated that our political mission had only furnished information to leading Rumanians on the official U.S. attitude toward the Rumanian situation. This attitude was fully public. Further, said our general, the acting political representative had so informed his counterpart on the Soviet political mission staff.

The Secretary of State commented on 22 August that we could not establish diplomatic relations, since the Groza regime was "not adequately representative of all important elements of democratic opinion." We were prepared to consult with our allies on measures to discharge our Yalta Declaration responsibilities. Meanwhile, he believed the three governments would take no action which would complicate a solution. We in Rumania rode with the guidelines, which shortly included avoidance of local political leaders. This was rescinded, since Soviet contacts with Groza's regime were encouraging communist supporters, while the ban dampened the democratic leadership. An accompanying injunction, unneeded except for the record, enjoined no opinions be given the king on whether he should sign any of the regime's decrees.

Burton returned from leave - consultation, spurred by events. After an interval when brought up to speed he heartened me with his approval, and I prepared to leave for Italy after a grueling first year comprising both the war and the cold war, capped by the summer constitutional crisis. The first ship bringing civilians came to Naples in September 1945, and I was on the dock to welcome Virginia, my bride. After a hectic period demonstrated the need to be remarried, we finally had a ten day honeymoon on Capri in a villa put at our disposal by the Air Force.

That fall further evidence accumulated for Washington. Secretary Byrnes sent Mark Ethridge, a prominent journalist, to double check on the situations in both Rumania and Bulgaria, and accompanying him as aide was my Balkan Office associate, Cy Black. Our mission got him appointments with all political elements, including the Groza cabinet, while he spent a long evening with our hard-bitten American journalists. His report, given to the Secretary of State on 26 November, confirmed the factual situation. If America wished to maintain the principle of getting representative governments and not conceding an unlimited Soviet sphere of influence, said Ethridge, it must "bring direct pressure" on the

Soviets and maintain its attitude on Rumania. Any Soviet attitudinal change, he thought, would be reflected in holding free elections.

A memorable outbreak of Rumanian nationalism and urge for freedom came on the king's Name Day, 8 November. We knew there was to be a demonstration in the palace square, so I went to Sam Brewer's room in the hotel, where he had a front balcony. The outpouring of the population of Bucharest waving banners and roaring cheers for the king as a symbol of their continued independence and freedom made an impressive spectacle the length of a main avenue, Calea Victoria. This was interrupted by the communists, who began using trucks to break up the crowds and shooting. We watched from the balcony, prone on leaden stomachs.

I have deferred comments upon the king, such an important factor that he warrants an appraisal only the full period can give. King Michael or Mihai, as the Rumanians called him, was a big, good looking young man, who liked Americans. We saw quite a bit of him and his fine mother, Helen, and in turn were taken by his good sense, his stubborn resistance to the communists, and earlier, by his courage in arousing the country through his August 23 coup against the pro-Hitler Antonescu regime. While the Russians awarded him the Soviet Order of Victory, the United States also gave him the Grand Commander rank of the Legion of Merit. We used to see Michael socially and for serious talks at his aunt's palace in Bucharest or Sinaia in the mountains, and we got along well. Years later I saw him in Bern, Switzerland, when he and his wife lunched with Virginia and myself. There he unburdened his hopes that his country would have the chance to see freedom again. As for himself, he had not taken anything from the country and had resolved to act as honestly as he knew. I believed him.

Maniu of the National Peasants was a recurring name in Rumania of the period. Amid the environmental pressures for survival that inevitably bred opportunists, he stood as a rock of integrity and a symbol of the better forces of Rumanian nationalism. He supported the monarchy, but in its period of independence, said a critic, he opposed the kings. Maniu could reply that there was something to criticize. The man, in his sixties, a lifelong bachelor, was of medium height and build, dressed always in an old fashioned high, stiff collar. Daily, as the clue to his unrivaled knowledge of public attitudes, he saw whomever visited him, and there were many. From these attitudes came policies. All circles respected him after he won his spurs as a Transylvanian nationalist in the Austro-Hungarian empire, opposing Rumanian second class status. United Rumania had been a lasting goal, and when the United Nations restored all of Transylvania to that country, he came to thank the United States, through Burton

Berry, for its position. During the war, Maniu and Bratianu, as their party leaders, often addressed memorials to Marshal Antonescu protesting the folly of the entire offensive against the Soviet Union. When the king, as the foremost symbol, called for a United Nations regime, Maniu was a main supporter. He resisted communist plans to change the state fabric, but was not rigid. In a remarkable meeting which Burton described to me, Maniu had declared that, if the United States was not prepared to follow through, to inform him promptly. He believed that he was in the best position to make the most constructive deal with the Soviets that could save the Rumanian way of life. Whether he could will never be known, but probably not, for the man died valiantly of studied neglect as a prisoner of the communists. In dealing with varied politicians, Iuliu Maniu was the man in my foreign assignments I most admired. His Rumanian antithesis, Tatarescu, was in my view the nadir. To retain personal integrity under the great domestic strains described was a remarkable achievement. Additionally, it served to evaluate the importance of character, aside from superficial brilliance, in the demanding profession of politics, which was life itself.

The diverse Rumanian public men I came to know were torn by the conflict of the time and had families to consider. I think of two decent, happy family men who were crushed by inexorable events. Those who succumbed I had no heart to criticize, even the beset politician at my home early one morning, pathetically thinking his dark glasses (a rarity) would disguise him from the communist police.

Given the unforseen turns of Rumanian politics, it still was surprising that figures like Tatarescu and minority group communists like Luca, Pauker, and Bodnaras, were trapped into believing their work for Soviet objectives would impede discharging or punishing them when there was no further need for their services. If from partly personal arrogance, it was also a kind of naivete. These people simply had not thought their futures through.

Amid the political tumult, Virginia began planning for the birth of our first child, bringing most of the essential equipment from our own home to the hospital since medical shortages were acute. With Virginia giving hospital birth to our daughter April, two friends helped me celebrate, joined by Lee Metcalf returning from home leave that day. After the event, I wired the news of April's arrival to my parents. With the message my mother jokingly asked a suddenly passive Dad, "Roy, don't you like being a grandfather?" Spontaneously and with a twinkle, he replied, "I just realized I am married to a grandmother." Our family life came to be my haven from tragic politics as I early began the practice of never bringing office business into our home. It also meant that Virginia did not have to worry about inadvertently disclosing classified information.

Among the communists, rifts widened until the strains of the conflict became apparent to us. The fault line we early detected was between the former Kremlin resident communists and the national ones, whose experience was confined to the country. Because of the ramified sources we maintained, democrats and communists as well, it became necessary to evolve ways of communicating to avoid endangering them or embarrassing us. This required care. There were at least four separate circles of prominent communists, each unbeknownst to the other, as well as diverse democrats, whom we had to safeguard and for whom we evolved procedures. Thus the transition from men coming to my house, then to meeting outside at night, and finally at various out-of-the-way places. My house was watched, with a new street light making it easier, and my phone tapped, so one had to be prudent. Illustratively, I found a listening wire beside my living room sofa. One couple solved the home communication dilemma to their own satisfaction by sitting next to each other and writing pad messages destined for the fireplace.

One communist provided steady and valuable advance information of communist plans and projects, not only for Rumania but for other parts of the Balkans. Importantly, he once gave the results of a general communist meeting in Belgrade, which he repeated when our embassy there could find no evidence. I supported him as a valued source, and had the satisfaction of getting essential confirmation from Budapest several weeks later. Prominent communists and leading democratic politicians held regular private meetings with Charley Hulick, who spoke fluent Rumanian and German. A National Peasant figure, who had saved many communists under the Antonescu regime, in turn was protected by appreciative communists against the Kremlin. So effective were they that, while the government actively searched for him to jail, he was concealed and moved from place to place for several months until he could be smuggled out to the West. Under very tight conditions I once saw him when he was in their hands. It was a complex, risky situation.

When I was in Washington after being reassigned, the head of the European bureau asked what I might say, not reported when in charge. I made one point. I considered the democratic parties essentially destroyed. Our only hope for change in Eastern Europe and Rumania was to exploit the widening schism between the home grown communists and the Kremlin variety. Focused as everyone then was on the idea of a united communist movement, despite the evidence from Rumania to the contrary, my views were politely heard and I was urged to take my long leave. I gently reminded Jack Hickerson, earlier in charge of European affairs, of the meeting when he was my ambassador in Helsinki. He took it well, for not until the Cominform denunciation of 28 June 1948, signaling the open quarrel between Tito of Yugoslavia and Stalin, did people begin to appreciate the differences and tensions within world communism.

A telling stage of the cold war drama for the Bucharest mission came in the December 1945 Moscow foreign ministers conference. Berry reflected our local view when he urged that we could come out of the stalemate "with colors flying if we match Russian firmness with firmness and, if we add to firmness, frankness and friendliness." A depressing compromise in Moscow simply added two cabinet ministers without portfolio to the Groza regime from the major Liberal and National Peasant parties. There were reassurances of free elections and universal suffrage and secret ballot, as well as press freedom. The tripartite commission of Vishinski and Ambassadors Harriman and Clark-Kerr reached Bucharest at year's end, with the task of activating an impossible compromise. The two powerless ministers were added to the Groza group over the voiced fears of the democratic leaders, but with assurances of sorts obtained from a government still clearly orchestrated by Vishinski. As subsequent events outlined a sorry prospect, as the crucial elections were delayed until communist control was a certainty, American officials were saddened. The compromise was revealed as a facade, and members of the mission began applying for transfers.

There was one heartening development amid the gloom. A long telegram from embassy Moscow in mid-February 1946, drafted by George Kennan, was promptly redirected by the Department to our circuit, among others. This catalyst of our containment policy we greeted with satisfaction, for it gave a guidepost to all of us concerned with Soviet relations. Our satisfaction was all the greater in recognizing that here was an influential element that we joined in understanding Soviet aims and devising a practical counter.

An addendum can conclude the depressing aspects. It was a persisting conviction of American area officials that we should adhere to the principles the United States had enunciated as its policy for Eastern Europe. Combined with this was a patriotic belief in American ability to take meaningful action, justified by military victory. The State Department, as late as June 1948, accordingly held a conference in Rome of representatives from its diplomatic missions in Eastern Europe essentially to put them aright on our domestic realities and the international scene. The factual situation was brought home: the United States was powerless to help the Eastern European peoples as to basic freedoms or civil government.

In the shifting details and patterns of developments, fragments of events or seeming jagged bits of the record can always give rise to distorted interpretation or to the path one fancies. It is the human environment of the time that is important, the aspirations of those affected by the atmosphere of the locale, which may, as in the case of Americans in Rumania, give the substance of how it was.

For Rumania by late 1946 it was all anti-climax. The communist victory was unmistakable, and Berry had recommended to Washington that he and I be transferred without delay, since our usefulness would rapidly diminish. The Department listened and he was transferred in mid-May 1947, but my turn did not come until November, almost a year after the recommendation. Charley and Sunnie Hulick also left in late spring. Lee and Doris Metcalf remained. The Department, I learned, wanted to hold me there as an officer familiar with the local situation until the peace treaty with Rumania was formally concluded and a minister to Bucharest appointed to resume diplomatic relations. It was difficult duty, but I was able to keep diverse contacts, helped by the staff, for the intervening period. At the same time during the four and a half months I was in charge it was an unusual organization of our political mission. By now I was an O-4, after changes made by the postwar Foreign Service Reform Act of 1946, but when I signed the payroll it was a distance down the list, for there were three senior O-3s and one O-2 as subordinates. Cavendish Cannon, our ambassador to Yugoslavia, first held his assignment as an O-3. The war sped responsibility. Dispositions were being made in Bucharest for the eventual shift of the political mission to a legation, but until minister Rudolf Schoenfeld arrived the Department did not want to change.

Schoenfeld finally came in October, but I remained at his request to aid the transition and to help greet the large, joint Senate-House delegation scheduled for several days in Bucharest. This was the third major political event Rumania provided us. The delegation, known as the Senator Smith and Representative Mundt group, was seriously bent on learning the realities of what had happened in the area since the war. Senator Smith had been a Princeton professor of my eventual number two successor, and he trusted his information from him. Among other members of the group, Senator Barkley, the former vice president, Senator Hatch, author of the Hatch Act, and Senator Hickenlooper were well known figures in whom we had confidence. The group saw every political faction, including journalists, and Groza and his cabinet. A roundup meeting with the delegation came after it had seen Groza. Senator Barkley recounted what he had been told, the antithesis of the facts. The senator, puzzled, wanted clarification. To the discomfort of our new minister and using the forthrightness that the assignment had given me, I replied, "It is very simple. The prime minister is lying." This cleared the air, and the meeting was very successful. Thinking on it, I believe our mission made a basic contribution, even in defeat, to help the legislators understand the conditions and tragedies of the harried region. Dispassionately, and perhaps too somberly, I judged that we delayed the Soviet program about six months, but since then I have been a hearty supporter of congressional visits no matter how personally taxing.

Some American officials not exposed to Soviet tactics understandably were slow in grasping their dimensions. Minister Schoenfeld felt he could somehow get along with the Rumanian communists by using the diplomatic skills he undoubtedly possessed. He did not accept my view that to negotiate with the Stalinist communists in any substantive way, the communists had to believe you held a countering weapon. For Schoenfeld the cold war was to begin.

So many friends Virginia and I had come to know and value went through painful times of persecution and imprisonment. Some were fortunate enough to get out, but others like our good friend, Lucia Cretu, for whom our subsequent second child, Lucy, is named, did not escape to the West for twenty years after enduring touching hardships.

For the first time I was a responsible officer over a prolonged period as an international crisis of magnitude evolved. Everything was compressed: reporting on developments; obtaining the best and widest contacts; spending physical stamina; confronting the new dimension of cold war; witnessing widespread suffering, and maintaining morale and mission effectiveness in the emerging political era. I became a veteran officer.

With our baby, April, we took a military mission plane 2 November 1947, bound for Vienna, indeed glad to leave three years and four days after my arrival, but unhappy that our Austrian nanny, Mrs. Strasser, stayed behind. As a slap at me, the communist authorities refused her an exit visa. Again, as in a recurring film, there was a feeling of unreality, that one actually was not leaving, and that the tangibles and people on the ground would always be there if you returned.

Left:  Inscribed:
"Staunch friend
Excellent colleague"

Signed: Burton Y. Berry

Right: Inscribed
"To my dear friend
Roy Melbourne with
deep appreciation of
his cooperation over
the years."

Signed: Loy W. Henderson

# CHAPTER 8

# COLD WAR PRACTICE & THEORY: ROME AND WASHINGTON

## November 1947 - August 1951

*The cold war dominated our lives. Under the Truman Doctrine, the U.S.
aided Greece in its civil war and Turkey in independence from Soviet
pressures. Italy held its first free elections in some 25 years, defeating
a communist led coalition. The Tito-Stalin struggle of national communism opposed to Moscow, had broad results from  Eastern Europe to
Communist China.  The Marshall Plan began Western European
reconstruction. North Korea with Soviet support launched the crucial
Korean War. Iran precipitated a mideast crisis by confiscating British
oil assets, while the U.K. froze Iranian oil sales.  America used the
National War College and the separate Armed Services' colleges to
understand our role and interagency national security responsibilities.
After home leave, I was detailed to embassy Rome to report on the
communist sector of the national elections. Thereafter in State, I was
successively Bulgarian and Yugoslav affairs officer, where I helped
develop our policy in the Tito-Stalin communist rift, acted in charge of
Balkan Affairs, was assigned to the National War College, and then to
embassy Tehran as head of its political section.*

Fogbound in a London crowded with sightseers for the royal wedding of
Elizabeth and Philip, we were shunted into a little suburban hotel.  Each of three
days we groped toward the airport, but air traffic was paralyzed, and only Air
France, audibly referred to as Air Chance, flew at all.  Despite the dense fog,
British spirits brightened as the lengthy London program for the wedding
unfolded.  My depression, caused by the ongoing Rumanian tragedy and the fate
of friends we could not aid, also lifted somewhat.  I coped with reality in learning
how to use a succession of shillings to fuel the bedroom gas heater that seemed
to stop at inconvenient times.  On Guy Fawkes Day the customary neighborhood
bonfires burned, and with our baby asleep, we had restorative drinks with our
fellow transients.  On home leave, despite long, calming walks, I still had a legacy
of the strenuous years.  The unfettered leave and rest did set me up, and restored,
I reported into the Balkan Affairs division.

It took time to understand that the postwar world would bring frequent organization changes to the State Department and to appreciate that our temperament would respond in this way to meet our world challenges. It meant learning a new bureaucratic argot. In the first of these changes, the Office of European Affairs was now the bureau, headed by an assistant secretary instead an office director. Within the new bureau were regional offices, such as Eastern European Affairs, each with a director. Our Balkan division, headed by a chief, was a segment of the latter. From observations and talk with those more knowledgeable, there was no decline in our bureau's authority from past practice, but personnel certainly increased with the levels.

We were so preoccupied in Bucharest we scarcely noticed that in August 1946 the president signed a bill to strengthen the Foreign Service by incorporating remedies for the great changes in scope stemming from the war's impact upon its organization. It was the first such effort since 1924, when the Rogers Act established the Foreign Service. While Secretary Byrnes, in his memoir mentions the congressional help of his close South Carolina associate, State Assistant Secretary Donald Russell, in the passage of that Act, a private account to me by a future chief, Loy Henderson, makes a more pointed story. The Budget Bureau and Civil Service Commission had their reasons for not being administratively friendly to the separate Foreign Service, so it was a familiar bureaucratic pattern when the pending Act was held, unsigned, at the White House. A few senior FSOs, including Henderson, visited Russell to point out the Service advantages of the Act and to enlist his help with Secretary Byrnes at the Paris Peace Conference. Byrnes got the import and called the president, saying this was crucial legislation he wanted approved, whereupon President Truman signed the bill. Later I found that Service memoirs from courtesy can gloss over marked bureaucratic differences and personality divisions, but I also learned from the importance of our foreign affairs issues and the interests of diverse agencies, that it should be unsurprising to find abrasive interactions of this kind recurring.

I expected to be named assistant chief of the Balkan Affairs Division when I reported, but instead was asked by our head, Wally Barbour, to take an unusual detail to embassy Rome for six months to work in its political section on Italian communist activities, in view of the upcoming elections there. These were to be the first free elections since Mussolini had taken over, and the communists and their allies were most active. We had no clue as to impending results and if, because of the war's demoralization and the lethargy created by the earlier fascist regime, we might not find Italy eventually in the communist or pro-communist camp. I took on the assignment, although it meant leaving Virginia and April to stay with my sister and her husband while expecting our second baby. When I returned in six months I had a new daughter, Lucy.

Our Rome ambassador, James Dunn, was a diplomat of the old school; socially amiable, handsome, educated, and wealthy. His counselor, Homer Byington, Jr., showed the Service's continuity since I had met him when he visited his father in Montreal. Building on this, he and Jane had me as their social extra at their home on the Appian Way, appropriately next to a golf course, for he was, in addition to the strong resemblance, a golfer like his dad. I also became friendly with an economic officer, J. Gordon Mein and his wife, and I enjoyed Gordon's spirit. Years later, as ambassador to Guatemala, he was killed by terrorists.

Each embassy has, in addition to other agency affiliates, functional sections labeled political, economic, consular, and administrative. Our political section had a top notch head in J. Wesley (Johnny) Jones, who was astute, knew Italy from before the war, and knew how to manage us. His wife, Kitty, was a first rate Service spouse. Jerry Greene was a most personable and informed officer, and there was Eddie Page from Moscow, who watched the Russian side of activities. The chancery, Palazzo Margherita, was a national monument, and we could not modernize it. So Johnny, Jerry Greene, and I with two secretaries, worked in the ballroom, where we shouted across a polished, wooden expanse. Presumably to help the acoustics, metal wiring was spread beneath the ceiling with no discernible results. Undeterred, we went about our work. Mine, as decided by Johnny, was to follow communist and Nenni socialist developments and make estimates of their political strength, while he and Jerry and others of the section concentrated on the non-communists.

An important source for me, suggested by Johnny, was the private secretary to Prime Minister De Gasperi, who had full access to the government's reports on communist electoral activities and strength. As we got to know each other, the secretary once took me to the most ultra men's club in Rome, where aside from elaborate dishes and courses, the waiters were outfitted in footmen's breeches and wigs. In contrast, a ship's officer mess was not in the running. My host pointed out various personalities, and I remarked a crusty old fellow ranting at a husky footman. He was Orlando, the World War I prime minister of Italy, the last of the Big Four of 1919 Versailles.

Again I resorted to familiar sources, the American journalists. My old friend, Frank O'Brien, turned up in the AP office, and through him I met the American coterie and some excellent Italian associates. They were into their assignment, and I arranged a regular office-social beat to learn their latest appraisals, done by Italianate custom in talks at cafes. Over the few months I became familiar with the city's more frequented cafes, outdoors as weather improved, and realized how much of Roman life existed on its streets. Most informative, reports came regularly each week from the consulates, oriented toward checking communist strength. In the long run they proved to be the most valuable, and I was convinced our people were doing accurate appraisals. Periodically I would take all of my sources, pool them, and do telegrams which Johnny would approve. An aspect of Johnny's supervision I appreciated was his confidence in allowing me free rein in my assignment, while at the same time following the tenor of my activities.

The time came for our final pre-election estimate. I did the communist-Nenni socialist coalition portion after careful thought and some discussion with Johnny. I was grateful for his confidence when he let my estimate stand as the officer most intimately acquainted with that aspect. This impressed me, for I began to recognize true professionalism as having confidence in a colleague to do the job he had trained for. It pleased both of us when, after the election, the calculation of the seats the communist and fellow traveler coalition would acquire was only four off the actual result. It was the Christian Democratic vote, however, that everyone miscalculated. This party had strong Vatican support and benefitted from the communist fears of the Italian people, who gravitated toward it in majority numbers. The wives of American officials were not surprised, for they claimed to have observed Italian wives' attitudes while doing their shopping!

The contrast between the spirit in Rome prior to and following the election was marked. The air of uncertainty and tension gave place to a spirit of optimism as Italy embarked on a democratic course. Then too, with the coming of steadily warmer weather, people seemed to throng the sidewalk cafes and the Via Veneto in greater numbers. Doney's outdoor cafe, the most popular and a barometer I passed every day in rotating to my pension hotel, began to display people more elegantly dressed, and the film colony, typified by Orson Welles, was blossoming. Rome had entered a new cycle. We celebrated this, my embassy friends and I, at dinner in a Borghese Gardens restaurant before my departure.

Also in Rome were Rita Hume and John Secondari. Rita and Sec were American journalists, and I had met Rita in Bucharest when Sam Brewer brought her to the house for a Thanksgiving dinner. Before Sec and Rita married, she lived on the top floor of a high, old apartment house (the poet John Keats died on a lower floor) at the head of the Spanish Steps with another young American, who supervised Pan Am stewardesses. From its balconies you had a fine view of traditional Rome, although it was a strenuous climb. Rita was a superb cook, and it was a friendly America away from home. Soon after their marriage she was killed in an auto accident, and Sec dedicated his novel of Rome, "Three Coins in a Fountain," to her memory.

There is something particularly attractive and friendly about the Latin temperament. The diverse Mediterranean has been my favorite area, and the

Italians fitted that predilection.  In Rome I met all kinds of people, from the so-called aristocracy, political leaders, labor men and journalists, and enjoyed the way they worked and lived.  Still, I found the old aristocracy difficult, for their rules were not mine.  The wife of an army officer I knew in Bucharest, recounted an incident during the couple's visit to Rome.  Mickey had gone to a European boarding school with a bright Italian girl from an aristocratic family.  Her family, for money and lineage purposes, had literally propelled her into marrying a Roman nobleman who was mentally defective.  This was made painfully clear to Mickey when she had tea with her old friend one afternoon and met the man. The poor girl was most unhappy, but was caught in old Roman traditions.

I have other memories: one is a homestyle picnic on the beach at Ostia with Johnny, Jerry, and their families and another, the Rome opera.  The Baths of Caracalla were an impressive backdrop to "Aida" and that most Italian of operas, "Cavalleria Rusticana."  The Latins could not get the hang of Wagner.  I roamed the town to see some of its ancient and interesting sites such as the Vatican and its museum.  On a curve of Via Veneto, down from the chancery and on a slight rise, there is a monastic order's church fronting the city traffic.  Its crypt has special religious significance, as a church tablet inscribes.  The reason is a series of small chapels and altars entirely covered, except the floor, by the bones of thousands of devout monks arranged in regular designs and with skeletal symmetry.  It is a bizarre sight, and makes one reflect on cultures, eras, motives, and symbols of worship.

My strong impressions of unrolling time up to the Roman period were habitually accompanied by a spectrum of popular music.  The jumbled sounds of World War I tunes had, by my California era, cohered into one, "I'm Forever Blowing Bubbles," followed in Bremerton by the waltz, "Three O'Clock in the Morning."  The east coast gave a song stream.  High school freshmen echoed "Valencia," and as seniors, "You're the Cream in my Coffee."  College seniors joined in several verses, some raucously improvised, of Cole Porter's "You're the Top," but as critics we came to consider the most memorable to be Hoagy Carmichael's, "Stardust."  The gamut of such songs was an unforgettable element of our generation's culture.  Into the Foreign Service, there were two, "So Rare" and "Deep Purple," as I became accustomed to these melody bench marks. Here in Rome the prime number was "Arrividerci Roma," which the orchestra was playing at the Excelsior Hotel in a formal benefit dance for the American school. I was the protocol partner of the ambassador's charming wife and having a predictably polite conversation when the lights went out.  What to do?  I carefully took the lady's hand, and with forced pleasantries, she following, groped in the blackness toward an exit, bumping into others en route.  I couldn't find it.   Off on a different tack and with other forced remarks, I sensed an exit in dim outline, and eventually the lady, in full light, was beside her husband.  To avoid a like episode, I stayed in the nearly empty hotel bar where I had a long restorative talk with another refugee, the FBI nephew of General George Patton. No later popular songs seemed to have the same personal impact.

Frank O'Brien was an alert newsman who helped in my work, and arranged my meetings with George Santayana. The famous philosopher, then in his eighties, was living in a convent, and Frank had interviewed him for an article. I was interested in the man and his writings, so Frank arranged for me to call. Sunday was the day Santayana preferred, so I was invited to tea, the first of several such Sundays. I found him remarkably keen, while from his great courtesy he found me bearable as a layman conversationalist. The scene was always the same. A nun took me to his neat and simply furnished room, where he sat, either reading or writing. Dressed in bathrobe and slippers, he rose to his gaunt height to greet me. Over tea we talked about his life and experiences as a professor at Harvard and touched on his attitude toward life. We found what he considered to be a common bond in that both of our fathers had been seafarers, and he talked about his travels and his great love for Rome. Although not a practicing Catholic, he loved the atmosphere of Rome and aesthetically admired the churches and their ritual. Once I found him holding a single sheet of paper from a thick pile on a side table. These were cut from a large paperbound book, since it was too heavy for him, and he read each sheet separately. It was a Vatican critique of existentialism sent by his friend, Jacques Maritain, the French philosopher and diplomatic representative at the Vatican.

I suppose this charming man found a diversion from his regular round by talking with me, for we discussed world politics and, a matter of interest to him, the Italian election. He wanted assurances that the communists would be defeated, because he dreaded the effects on his way of life and the culture he loved if they should win. I could reassure him, and he was delighted with the election result. In alluding to his works, he told me how he came to write his only novel, "The Last Puritan," a totally unexpected commercial success and named a Book-of-the-Month Club choice in its time. He was candid in saying that he never felt at home teaching at Harvard during many years there, and he had a poor opinion of its former President Lowell. The latter was not alone, since he expressed similar sentiments toward historian Arnold Toynbee. He thought Toynbee grossly simplified history and, in an attempt to assay a philosophy, was sophomoric in his ideas. Santayana could be pungent. He confessed he was working on what would be his last book and his first attempt at political theory. Calling it "Dominations and Powers," he was writing it with large grease pencils supplied by Frank O'Brien, and talked about some of the premises he was using. My memory is of a truly engrossing gentleman.

Of books and ideas which Santayana evokes, without fully realizing it I had early begun a basic library. In a New York Sunday school I received a small Bible and became well acquainted with its stories and parables. By chance in high school I got a Modern Library edition of the philosophy of Spinoza, the only book of a philosopher I continually reread and carried. In talking of it with Santayana, he told me, perhaps in exaggeration, "We (philosophers) are all Spinozists." These seemingly disparate books, rebound, joined college anthologies of American and English literature as a vital quartet among other old favorites.

Late that spring I gained a valuable professional lesson about subordinate ratings in annual efficiency reports. Johnny, his next assignment China, was being succeeded by Outerbridge Horsey. As we got to know each other, Outer confided to me that at about the halfway mark for the annual efficiency report, he took a blank form and systematically discussed it with a ratee, emphasizing his weaknesses or limits. The officer knew where he stood and could try to remedy weaknesses over the next six months. If he made no serious effort, he had himself to blame at the later formal stage. If he did, earlier weaknesses might need no comment or could even become strengths. The practice generally worked, and some of my later subordinates adopted it. For me it was a formula as professionally useful as the election analyses.

After the election, there was a June Eastern European regional conference in Rome headed by European deputy assistant secretary, Llewellyn (Tommy) Thompson. The two representatives from Belgrade, Cavendish Cannon as ambassador and Bill Leonhart as a junior secretary, highlighted the meeting for me by pointing out the tensions that were building between Tito and Stalin. With the conference over and I at home, on June 28 the Cominform made public its denunciation of Tito, which started the open Tito-Stalin conflict.

In view of my work in Bucharest I expected a promotion, but the list appeared that spring without me so, at the Balkan conference I asked Thompson what happened. Tommy said that my performance, while appreciated in his bureau, had been downgraded by the Selection Board because Burton Berry had been the man rating me. Berry told me later, when asked to meet with several senior Department officers, he had expected a commendation, but instead had been hit by an old opponent, Cochran, after a Bucharest inspection following a disagreement begun in Istanbul. While Charley Hulick, Lee Metcalf and I knew that Burton had his eccentricities, in Bucharest he had been zealous in concentrating on the mission at hand. I swallowed hard, and moved on.

Now at home I had a down-to-earth transition to domestic life. On my first night in Philadelphia, I had the unfamiliar role of propping our new baby daughter, Lucy, on my chest while sleeping in an easy chair, my feet on a footstool. Lucy had the croup, and the doctor advised keeping her upright. How tiny my second daughter looked, and how she fought to clear her lungs as I sought to keep her comfortable.

In Washington, again in the Balkan Affairs division, I became Bulgarian desk officer, meaning all public and interagency matters relating to that country were my concern. Desk or country officers were divided between Foreign Service and Civil Service, and in background over time I deemed both were equally reliable, for the Civil Service people stayed in place, but those in the Foreign Service were periodically transferred. Virginia and I found a suitable house adjacent to the Hulicks, so we settled into homeside living, with Charley and I car-pooling to the Department.

Donald Heath, Maynard Barnes' successor, was another capable minister to Sofia, but the pattern was still the same. The communists were resolute in stamping out any trace of democratic political organization or symbolic resistance. At home we tried to boost their morale by cultivating close ties with the national refugee committees, which included old friends on the Rumanian committee, as well as the Bulgarian, with its main representative, Dr. Dimitrov. We did all we could, given the political realities. Wherever possible, we tried to make clear what was going on in Eastern Europe as relations between America and Russia settled into their cold war phase. To some of us exposed to actual conditions it was hard to appreciate that Washington only slowly came to realize the scope and ruthlessness of the Soviet objectives. The public has forgotten that when Churchill made his "Iron Curtain" speech in Missouri there was a substantial body of American criticism he was overstating the case and seeking to enlist America in an anti-communist crusade. More than one prominent politician and cabinet member later known for strong cold war stances came to this comparatively late.

A pleasant surprise on entering Balkan affairs was to see, just down the hall, the newly arrived French desk officer, Elim O'Shaughnessy, my Service School classmate. Somehow he seemed a natural for the position with his urbane intelligence. Refreshingly original, he had used the entire furniture lift van to transport, as personal effects, a complete load of French wines and liqueurs. He was frank with Customs in saying it was all intended for official use during his several years assignment, and needed in entertaining the French and others in his home. Customs proved understanding, the Foreign Service had a good reputation, and the lift van sailed through. He was also a friend of Chip Bohlen, then the Department's counselor, who used to walk to the office. The horseshoe driveway fronting the Department on 21st Street was used for V.I.P. parking. Chip was agreeable, so Elim parked his Cadillac convertible in the former's place, thus bringing a little style to the prosaic area.

Our Eastern European sector had some interesting people. We got a new director for Eastern Europe, Fred Reinhardt, also of the Service School and of Caserta. Freddy, a Russian language officer, had a truly exceptional career. He was one with all the tools and was a great person in the bargain, so it was beneficial to have him as a supportive chief during the Yugoslav-Soviet struggle. Claiborne Pell too for a time was assigned as special assistant to our Eastern European office. He left the Service, always its strong supporter, entered politics, became a senator from Rhode Island, and eventually chairman of the Senate Foreign Relations Committee. Cavendish Cannon, who had shepherded us in Southern Europe before I left for Bucharest, was ambassador to Yugoslavia, and I enjoyed seeing him when he was home on consultation. His stories I always retained, and one was of career officers as ambassadors. He asserted there were two kinds: one got there by ability and the other through work because he didn't want to go home!

After six months on the Bulgarian desk, I was shifted to the Yugoslav desk backstopping Cavendish, and the assignment took on more scope. The struggle between Tito and Stalin grew progressively more bitter as Stalin tried every device to overthrow Tito, including assassination and subversion, without success. Finally, in the summer of 1949, things became heated. During August we received a snowballing volume of reports that the Russians intended to invade across the Danubian plain, take Belgrade, install a subservient communist regime, and reinvoke the military treaty of alliance which Tito had renounced. Tito and his supporters would be in Russian hands. Reports had it that this was to be done by Soviet troops in Bulgarian, Rumanian and Hungarian uniforms, who from these three countries would make the assault.

It was the biggest item the European Bureau had to worry about that month, and the reports came with ever greater profusion and confusion. I evaluated these reports and, as many times a day as necessary, passed evaluations to the assistant secretary's office. It was then the practice to pass these on to the Secretary and he to the White House. To make sense of the welter, I broke the information into three piles of intentions : 1) it is going to happen imminently, 2) it is going to happen eventually, and 3) it is not going to happen. Regardless of reliability and classification, it went into one of these three folders. Now there would be sizeable organizations in State's Operations Center and in the White House properly following such crises; all for the best assuredly. Intelligence labeled top secret, I also found, regardless of the reliability of the information, was what impacted on upper echelons. These harassed officials never questioned its quality nor that it must have a unique credibility, which sometimes was not true. Perhaps from a jaundiced view, some top secrets created more confusion, since these were the messages remembered.

By September the crisis had subsided and Stalin, while he may have considered invasion or attempted a psychological ploy, finally decided against it. When we put the matter to bed, the three files for my personal use were roughly the same size! This underlined the difficulties of winnowing meaningful intelligence of intentions for practical operational and policy use. Intelligence, because of the plethora of material, may always give you what you want to hear and be used to justify after the fact. The exercise also showed the importance of evaluating in measured terms the information being received on a crisis. Under such times of tension and crisis (to use an accepted State Department word for prolonged, important, and shifting situations) it can be argued that the top should receive raw intelligence only when accompanied by evaluations.

While the work was most demanding, at the same time Yugoslav affairs were the most dynamic in Eastern Europe, save the Soviet Union. One communist state had defiantly split from Mother Russia, creating at an international level the internecine struggles so prominent in communist party politics. The policy that we followed was not an easy one. Tito could not forfeit communist orthodoxy to the Soviets, for he was in a life or death struggle, and could not deprive himself of the ideological shield that Yugoslav communism represented. This meant that he could not openly request and receive economic and military aid of an extent and adequacy to maintain Yugoslavia's independence. Quantity help would open his regime to the charge that it had sold out to the capitalist West, so a quiet, staged development, essentially allowing the Yugoslavs to make approaches to the West with their own timing, was the policy decided. The struggle was not merely Yugoslavia against the Soviet Union, for the Soviet satellites were watching, particularly the national communists, as we had detected in Rumania. The Soviets knew this and began, in Stalinist style, a broad purge. There were trials and executions. Some Rumanian communists were victims, but we noted a very few with whom we had earlier contact survived to go on to bigger things.

At the time China went communist in 1949, it was, of course, an ally of the Soviet Union. We can calculate from Yugoslav cultural factors alone that Mao would eventually be more independent minded than Tito, and that the precedent trail had been broken for him whenever it might be needed. It is remarkable that the importance of such cultural factors was not more adequately recognized.

A major aspect was the effect on Greece, Albania, Bulgaria, and Turkey. Greece was fighting a major civil war with its indigenous communists, and heavy American aid and military advisers were involved. The mountainous border with Yugoslavia had been a main source of Soviet supplies, which, until now, it had not been feasible to cut off. Similarly, communist Albania was isolated from material Soviet help, and its rough border for supplies to Greece was out of action. The only communist state with Greek border access was Bulgaria, and here the terrain was more moderate for control. The Greek rebels, in a final phase of the action, were driven across that frontier and an effective defense against their return was set up that ended the costly war. As a last gesture, the rebels took thousands of Greek children as orphans on their retreat, a potential nucleus for future conflict. Bulgaria additionally was buffeted by an eventual rupture of American relations, and it is plausible that its border vulnerability did not encourage Greek rebel activity from that source. Turkey, of course, gratefully experienced a reduction of tensions on its Bulgarian border, which helped in the success of the Truman Doctrine to maintain its stability.

There is a diverse chain of interrelationships and international effects from any significant political event. The Tito-Stalin rift had further fronts. A featured one was the United Nations, where the two states were in conflict. Yugoslavia was seeking United Nations assistance, and the struggle was an embarrassment to the Soviet Union. Throughout, because of the stage of action, I closely worked with State's United Nations bureau and learned something of its methods of operation, different from conventional geographic bureaus. Another front turned on whether Yugoslavia would be accorded a steel mill, symbolic of western economic aid and a boost for the domestic public. The mill was accorded, and the Yugoslavs felt they could plan with more economic confidence. There was still a road ahead to military assistance for Yugoslavia, but it was to come.

During this assignment it was usual to have calls from reporters seeking clarification on particular matters. A journalist with a reputation called me after a lunch in which he had clearly over imbibed. His queries were not particularly rational, so I politely suggested he call me the next day for firm information, and hung up. The reporter later complained to the press officer who plaintively inquired about the matter. I described my estimate of the man's condition and my awareness of the policy needs to be as forthcoming as possible. The policy security risk he created for a coherent story had impelled me to take the only sensible course. My early visa inquiry training had come in handy.

In Balkan affairs I came to understand Wally Barbour as an excellent political officer and a judicious one, as well as to appreciate Tommy Thompson. Wally was a bit aloof and businesslike with me, perhaps reflecting unease at not earlier having made me his assistant chief. However, in fairness, he could have detected initially I had lingering Rumanian tensions. Hence, he may have done me a favor. We got along well, and I have an unusual recollection. Once on Yugoslavia I proposed a course of action. Wally disagreed, favoring another, but suggested we see Llewellyn Thompson, the Soviet expert. He put the case to Tommy, giving our contrasting views, who weighed them and came up with a tactic merging both ideas that Wally and I agreed was an improvement on either of ours. This, I thought, was professionalism at its best. It also was a graphic instance that showed Tommy's caliber, who when he retired was recognized as one of our best diplomats.  It could not have been easy for Thompson to operate as deputy to an assistant secretary who was a political appointee without European experience.  He carried the heavy burden as the only deputy, although getting progressively more weary.  For the first time I encountered a system in State whereby the asset top officials represented was intensively used.  This problem came to be recognized, but the Department later went overboard, I believe, with the number of deputy assistant secretaries and an increase in area or country office directors.

When I took over the Yugoslav desk, I suggested that Charley Hulick take the Bulgarian desk.  Wally needed no urging, for he knew Charley in Cairo.  Thus we two were working together again, at facing desks, sharpening our views on each other.  In Bulgaria pressures were against us, which became so great we had no recourse but to break relations after a decisive event, the arrest and trial of our Bulgarian legation employee, Shipkov.  He knew he was targeted, and left a statement that no credence should be given to any so-called spying confessions that might be extracted.  It was not an easy thing to do, and there was much hesitation before we made the rupture, but it did dramatize our repugnance of repressions the Bulgarian communists were taking.  We also thought this might have a salutary influence on like repression and anti-American measures in other Balkan countries.  It did not work out that way.

In the midst of my Balkan preoccupations, the idea of a completed doctorate thesis nagged me.  I had a full set of my old Istanbul despatches in the office, and qualified Rumanian sources had given me interviews and extensive material which, if found on them, would arouse suspicions by the new regime.  This time the thesis would be on the political forces and propaganda directives motivating the former pro-Nazi Rumanian regime.  My old university proved cooperative, so after long workdays, on weekends in a bedroom of our home, I carried on with the thesis, while Virginia did everything else, maintaining the house, shopping, and caring for our two little ones and me.  It is feeble to thank her for that.  Given my health, I finished it, passed the comprehensive exams, and finally got the Ph.D.  It greatly eased my mind to have an academic union card and an alternative, for early I was convinced the only route to Service operating freedom was an independent income or another satisfying profession.

Meanwhile I had demanding concerns to stay on top of Balkan matters but, with energy I cannot now grasp, there was also time to make an  experimental academic try.  In Washington before going to Japan and without area forethought, I had taken a graduate course on the Far East at George Washington University.  My former professor, now dean of the college, reminded me I wanted to attempt teaching and that he would give me the chance.  It was a sensitive time, with arguments over who "lost" China to the communists, but I received Department permission to teach two evenings a week for two spring semesters, a course on the Far East (China, Korea, and Japan) since 1850. I found the students enjoyable and proved to myself an academic life was feasible.

Wally Barbour had gone abroad and I was acting officer in charge of Balkan Affairs for some six months. There was a policy discussion at the time, when I met and saw President Truman at a meeting. My friend John Campbell, earlier on the Rumanian desk, returned to the Department and, as a civil servant, prepared to take on my role. I put it up to Tommy. I wanted the premier assignment to the National War College, which was the institution relating all elements of our national security in the cold war. The time in Rome and Balkan Affairs had given me a wider view of the cold war that complemented the Bucharest assignment, and I was on the way to becoming a specialist upon Soviet applications of cold war strategy and tactics from the invaluable exposure those years had given me. Now as a student I wanted to observe the military and other agency counters to Soviet actions and how our policies depended upon interagency cooperation. I said this to Thompson, who first thought I might stay another year to develop our aid policy to Tito, but I thought the program was set and it was a good time for me to attend the College. He finally agreed, so I was an EUR nominee, and in the summer I left the bureau and became a full-time student.

It was natural for those with my background on entering Balkan Affairs to have wanted, as Republican leaders in the 1952 election proclaimed, to roll back the Soviet Eastern European conquests. Dealing with realities, however, gave no ground for such a hope if this meant substantial direct pressures. My Yugoslav assignment had reinforced the conviction that our best course was aid, where possible, to national communists like Tito. In reviewing the situation, Charley and I had discussed one very troubling aspect of the cold war in which we were close participants. This obliged me to take a concluding action before leaving for the War College. Llewellyn Thompson and I had a talk. Citing history, I could find no instance of a prolonged ideological conflict that brought a clear solution with one side retaining its original values. As an instance, the European religious wars had left either side seemingly as culpable morally as the other. For democracy, the temptation to use totalitarian weapons might prove irresistible, such as subversion and covert assault. It therefore was requisite for the West to be cautious and aware of the dangers in actions that put our free values at risk while proceeding against its opponent. Little did we know!

The National War College, on the Washington site of the old Army War College, now in Pennsylvania, began after World War II and had its first class in 1947. It was the only Armed Services school directed by the Joint Chiefs of Staff and the State Department as founders, thus it had the broadest perspective. A

Commandant came from a Military Service for a three year term, while other Military Services and State supplied deputies. Over ten months we were to study the interrelationships between our departments, the cold war, and the environment of our world. The Korean War erupted before the National War College convened, and the Joint Chiefs decided that the session should be held as more relevant than ever. We had officers who resented being a year away from the action, so to salve their consciences and the Joint Chiefs as well, the study and work schedules were increased to reduce student leisure time.

The College had approximately 32 officers from each of the major Services, the Navy having a contingent from the Marine Corps, 15 of us from State, and one each from several other agencies. The officers were full colonels or navy captains, and the State group similarly was senior. By now an FSO-3, I was at 37 the second youngest member of the class. A feature of the School was the computer rotation of students into different groups of six each time we finished a phase of the course, and rarely was there more than one civilian with the military in these groups. We did our assignments together, made presentations, and had discussions in our home rooms, each of us at his desk, usually in the afternoons.

The mornings started at 8:30 or 8:45 a.m. with a lecture by a speaker-and we got the best and most distinguished-in the auditorium to the entire College. Many would be attended by our fellow logistic school, the Industrial College of the Armed Forces. There was a break after an hour, when we would reconvene to question the speaker for half an hour. Provocative questions were encouraged. As an instance, the British ambassador was asked what his government preferred to be the basis for its foreign policy: NATO, the Commonwealth, Western Europe, or others. He blandly responded that Britain was a member of several clubs and interested in all. The questioner bore in, asking when the club dues were onerous, which clubs were the British going to give up? We all had our turn. After hearing the speaker, who joined us in one of our separate conference rooms, we covered the day's topic, which would relate to the theme segment of the curriculum and its supplementary readings. Meanwhile, faculty members would observe how the men handled themselves. We had some provocative meetings as we sought satisfactory answers to the complex matters we were studying, involving U.S. strategy in the cold war.

Transportation daily to the War College meant car pooling, with our quintet being a happy combination of two army and an air force colonel, and the Cuban affairs desk officer and myself from State. The commuting was an education, as each of us had professional examples relevant to the current curriculum. One Army colonel, Bob Fleming, was on General Short's staff in Hawaii the morning of the Pearl Harbor attack, where prior to the bombing the general had received only what his staff thought of as a downscale, provisional alert. Early that afternoon, despite direct Washington telephone service being available, a Western Union messenger routinely cycled up to headquarters to deliver the crucial message.

One special lecture was given by President Dwight Eisenhower of Columbia University, who discussed military leadership. He cited three staff types a senior commander might possess. First came a very small group of top flight officers, the commander being lucky to have. Next came a large number of solid, dependable ones, with the leader similarly fortunate. The third group you had to look out for. "Those are the ones who are dumb but energetic," Ike concluded. "They will get you in trouble every time." The story returned to me at the time of the Iran-Contra congressional hearings and the troubles of Lt. Col. Oliver North. Eisenhower was impressive, and we speculated in the car on whether he would run for president. Army Colonel Jack Kilgore quietly contributed that in his Service the man had the reputation of difficulty in making up his mind.

One thing we State men learned from the military was the need to sharpen our departmental action documents and thinking, and to cut unclear or cloudy conclusions and recommendations. The military, on the other hand, admitted they had learned in dealing with political aspects of strategy that answers were not as clear as an operational field order. Only too often in the political sphere they found there was no simple right or wrong way of responding. Good natured joshing was also part of it. The military would ask how striped pants felt, and we would inquire of the Air Force men when they were rejoining Army artillery. With it all we came to understand each other and our organizations. Any distorted stereotypes just disappeared. Military ways of thinking and the reasoning involved were important to us civilians in this new era of inter-agency operations.

Most of the students were military men and military briefings are distinctly different from public speaking. Dr. Alfred Westphal recalls the previous year students making demonstration speeches. One student brought an ironing board and iron, and told how to press trousers. Another showed how to make a wide Windsor knot in a necktie. A third illustrated how a Chinese uses a firecracker to honor his ancestors. After two failures, the third firecracker made such a resounding bang that our commandant, General Bull, henceforth forbade firecrackers in the public speaking class!

As an austerity measure, the annual spring trip abroad was canceled. However, we did travel to various military installations and witnessed some firepower and amphibious demonstrations. We were aboard an operating carrier, went down in a snorkel submarine, and visited an Air Force equipment experimental station in Florida, where we entered a large hangar kept at 30 degrees below zero with the outside temperature at over 90 degrees.

As our final project, each student presented a paper to the entire school. A portion, I must admit, were boring as audience tolerance flinched on hearing every one. Mine was on Greek communist activities during the civil war. Being familiar with the communist-controlled side of the Balkans, I wanted to learn how the communists had been defeated in Greece, so I probed into it for personal satisfaction and a good result.

What I remember most about the informalities of the college year are the joggers and tennis players during the two-hour lunch break; the Officers' Club lunches; the afternoon bull sessions in our rooms that frequently were so apt for the curriculum; the swingers on the little Fort McNair golf course as hazards to parked car windshields; the athletic competition with the Industrial College sharing Fort McNair; and the sense of being in an unmatched environment within reach of, but removed from, the action.

Because it relates to mores at Armed Services colleges, I smile about a lecture visit I made several years later to the Air University. I was met by Johnny Carrigan, a War College classmate acting as political adviser there, in his resplendent white Cadillac convertible. I admired his car, and he rejoined that it was the most impressive symbol he could find for the military to pay attention to him as a senior FSO.

After the College year, on active duty I dealt with only two of my military classmates, and that briefly. Nevertheless, I have every good feeling for the ten-month class of 1950-51, and great respect for its professional competence. World War II had ended five years before. My classmates had undergone its tests, and surely deserved the rarified ranks a goodly percentage attained: fleet commanders, chief of naval operations, commander of the Strategic Air Command, army lieutenant generals, and many more. The State group of fifteen also produced six ambassadors.

My Service colleagues have been a constant source of interest and education, and at the War College some made indelible impressions. Tony Freeman was energetic and personable, an extremely likeable man, who was a Service loss to a heart attack after serving as ambassador to Mexico. Maury Bernbaum told me his feelings in going as an ambassador to a dangerous Latin American assignment. He survived with a fine record. Jeff Parsons also had a Canadian wife, Peggy, and in after years he was ambassador in Stockholm while I was deputy in Helsinki. Johnny Steeves, balanced and steady, subsequently was an excellent choice as director general of the Foreign Service. Then Cecil Lyon, a longtime friend and an ambassador devoted to the Service, responded to my later luncheon compliment on his fine physical condition (he practiced yoga), "Yes, but one day it is all going to crumble."

With the student year ending, our thoughts dwelt on next assignments. Burton Berry, restored to grace, was deputy assistant secretary in the Near East and South Asia Bureau, and he wanted me in Tehran with my communist experience because an oil crisis had erupted there. Fiery prime minister Mosadeq had nationalized the British oil concessions and refinery, and Iran's Soviet neighbors intended to capitalize upon what looked like a possible breakthrough into the Middle East. My old Bucharest associate, now Iranian desk officer, Vaughan Ferguson, strongly urged the assignment, but the decisive reason for my decision was the opportunity to serve with our incoming ambassador, Loy Henderson, almost legendary as among our best.

There had been other suggested assignments, which show the fluidity of the early postwar era, and as a coda they are mentioned. Our State personnel chief, Elbridge Durbrow, proposed I go to Paris as deputy NATO political adviser under Douglas MacArthur II. He was disappointed in my preference for Tehran, and I later regretted not telling him my main reason was Doug MacArthur. He and Durby did not know that his father (the general's brother) and Virginia's mother were first cousins, which might have caused staff problems. Then Frank Wisner, in charge of CIA overseas operations, in an interview explained that his agency was serious in a government commitment to the peoples of communist controlled Eastern Europe. He wanted me assigned to our embassy in Vienna and charged with controlling CIA personnel the length of the Danube. We knew each other well and I had too high a regard for him not to be open. My Balkan experience on the ground and in Washington had convinced me, I said, that our country by covert actions could not restore area freedoms. Thereafter I could not direct others to risk themselves. We understood each other's positions and retained our mutual respect.

As we prepared for Iran, I saw that it would be an exceptionally demanding assignment in a prolonged crisis atmosphere. Thus I used my annual leave that summer and we sailed to Beirut rather than flew. It was one of the most sensible steps I ever took, for in the two and one-half years assigned to Tehran I had only brief spates of leave. So in August all four of our family, clutching an indispensable ironing board, set sail for the volatile Middle East.

Elburz mountains from embassy compound

April & Lucy Melbourne, with friends and camels

Vice President Nixon visits Tehran.  Ambassador Henderson is second on the left.

# CHAPTER 9

# OIL AND REVOLUTION: TEHRAN

## September 1951 - February 1954

*The Korean war added ice to the cold war and Japan began its reindustrialization from American needs in that war. The McCarthyites charged the loss of China to U.S. crypto-communists and the Eisenhower Administration added security checks. NATO Europe was a success. Iran's nationalist movement, led by Mosadeq, expropriated British held oil resources, raising Western fears the Soviets would undermine Iran and control the world's oil jugular, the Gulf. Mosadeq, pressing the West, became domestically isolated, and increasingly communist influenced. This impelled the United States successfully to support, under no illusions, an indecisive but popular Shah in a mass action against Mosadeq. In the Mosadeq revolution I headed the Tehran embassy's political section. We followed developments, made appraisals, and recommended support for the Shah, feasibly the West's only alternative.*

It was a relaxing sea trip, and I was ready for work on reaching Beirut. My car was aboard and I meant to drive to Tehran, leaving the family to enjoy Beirut and a visit with the Harlan Clarks in Damascus. With our local embassy's army attaché and the counselor's son, we drove through Jordan and across the Syrian desert, following the pipeline to Baghdad. We climbed abruptly to the Iranian plateau from the Mesopotamia plain, and saw how the Iran-Iraq border followed that feature. Then it was on to Hamadan and Tehran. Such an approach proved a basic orientation. Most intriguing about Iran was the barren stretches between mountain ranges, the aridity, and the khanats, the underground irrigation flows formed by digging deep wells at periodic points and tunnelling between them. Such a pockmarked land feature would run for miles and was a remarkable achievement, preventing water from evaporating in the hot sun. From the air they looked like spaced bomb craters across long desert stretches.

We checked into the new chancery building looking like an American high school (it came to be called Henderson High), within a new wall enclosed compound covered with construction rubble. The compound also had an embassy residence, its garden, some staff bungalows, a commissary, and a large garage.

For family living the Darband Hotel, in the foothills of the Elburz Mountains, proved suitable, so Virginia and the two little girls joined me there. From that base Virginia combed for a permanent home, a search that took three months, given scarce suitable housing, while in the chancery I plunged into work. Loy Henderson had arrived a week before, and in his energetic way was building the embassy's organization and activities in his style. Typifying this was one item, a unique feature of his office. Behind his desk on a small table was a framed motto, "The three hardest words to say in the English language are: I was wrong."

The motto crystallized a part of my education in human nature, for a series of small events had made me conscious of official reluctance to admit substantive error, since this raised an embarrassing query about total judgment. There was variety in this, as conversely those making the greatest errors could even be given sympathy and undue credence. Sometimes error prone ranking officials, without serious question, could simply brazen it out. Currently I became aware repentant communists were telling all to Congressional committees, and their observations, even when far afield, were given full credence. Most recently a former Defense Secretary, author and director of the gradual escalation strategy in Vietnam, notable for its failure, told an attentive congressional committee prior to the Iraq war how we should comport ourselves in the Persian Gulf. Nevertheless, best epitomizing the major reaction was a story given to me in Istanbul by a nephew of Wendell Willkie, who was there with the Office of War Information.

Although Wendell Willkie became the Republican presidential nominee in 1940, he supported Roosevelt in the 1932 election. When his convention managers asked him to talk to party stalwarts, none more unbending than former Indiana senator Jim Watson from his hometown, Willkie began: "Uncle Jim, you've known me since I was a boy, and I confess that I voted for Roosevelt. But I've seen the light. I've got religion, and I'm a Republican now." "Wendell," said the inflexible Watson," what you say makes me happy, but it reminds me of the preacher back home when the town prostitute came repentant to church. He said, 'Sister, welcome; come to glory.' But at the same time, he didn't let her lead the choir."

Arthur Richards, the DCM (Deputy Chief of Mission) operated as Henderson's chief of staff. As a professional he was among the best, and I came to have great liking for him and his wife. Within a year, since he was the carryover, Arthur was transferred and my Service School classmate, Gordon Mattison, a mideast specialist, was his successor. My political section eventually consisted of seven officers and the Information Office's press attaché, an experienced newsman who functioned as the sole embassy spokesman and author of our daily press cables. In addition to reporting, the section became Henderson's liaison arm with other major official activities. My successive deputies, Bill Burdett, later ambassador to Malawi, and Mike Gannett, were the liaison points with our Point Four (technical assistance) organization, named after a point made in President Truman's 1949 inaugural address. Another officer was our liaison with the large American military training mission, headed by a major general. Then, of course, our press attaché served to keep us in touch with the U. S. Information Service (USIS). These three activities had sizeable branches throughout the country. Others of the section generally devoted themselves to Iranian politics, which given the times were complex indeed. We were aided by indispensable secretaries, including mine, Glenna, and another, Nancy. The latter the ambassador "stole" from me as his second on witnessing her competence.

An important member of the section was the resident regional labor attaché, Cliff Finch, who also was accredited to Gulf states. He visited the oil installations in southern Iran and frequently those in Saudi Arabia, where he reported to us on the oil development there. He also told us the American oil consortium in the peninsula was the area leader in government-employee relations and had instituted a 50-50 profit division between the Saudis and the company, temporarily to be a regional norm.

Every aspect of American society was affected by the influx of returned war veterans, and for me this aspect was most marked in Tehran. Several of the political section officers, for instance, had maturing war experiences with our air force. John Howison had been shot down as a crewman, another was a bomber pilot, and Joe Cunningham, who broke the exam record for the Service, had been a navigator on Tokyo raids. Mike Gannett had been an army combat officer. Chris Chapman was initially with the Free French Air Force, then with the American. I respected these men and others I would serve with later, who demonstrated the Service's continuing effort to be representative of the country.

While I had controlled the mission in Bucharest and for a period in Balkan Affairs, running the busy section was different. The officers had to be allocated work and responsibilities to keep the entire load even, as well as suitable to the capacities of those given spot assignments. If my in-box was over-flowing, it was a sure sign I was not delegating enough. It was detailed on-the-job management. All of us in the section regularly interviewed various Iranians, gave background information to American journalists, and I periodically would prepare evaluative cables upon aspects of our evolving situation. In the successive periods of crises and rioting that took place in the city, Tony Cuomo, also a war veteran and the most imperturbable, came to act as city editor, and handled the telephone calls from our officers and other sources as they fanned out to observe developments. In a management error, I acceded to John Howison, our Farsi (Persian) speaker, and Bob Melone, and allowed them to travel as political officers to eastern Iran and Kabul, Afghanistan, John's former post. They promised to use halizone tablets to purify water a half hour before drinking, but of course didn't, and on their return I had to ship them to Beirut for cures of serious dysentery. We had a long schedule, which meant working on the Moslem Sabbath (Friday), as well as on Sundays, ostensibly our day off. Nationalist feeling was high and xenophobic, which produced successive riots and prolonged days of tension whose cause it is fruitless to recall, followed by intervals when a curfew was imposed. In such an atmosphere, I would stay over within the embassy compound in the Cuomo bungalow guest bedroom and phone home daily, with every assurance from its location that the family was all right.

Our house was in Golhak, roughly halfway between the embassy and Shimran, and about a half mile off the main road, which removed the family from any fallout from anti-American agitation or other demonstrations which would take place in the city. It just meant the little girls would not go to the Presbyterian mission school those days, and Petros, our guardian and driver, would stay at home. Ranch-style Persian described the house, converted to some western conveniences such as a western toilet rather than the Persian version, and with a large garden and swimming pool purified by copper sulfate. Drinking water came from our chlorinated cistern, regularly supplied by an embassy water truck. Virginia had located the place, suitable with some repairs, and the owner, an accommodating man, agreed to do everything we wanted, provided we paid six months rent in advance. The slight pitched roof was covered by flattened jerry cans which, in a prolonged rain or snow, would leak through the nail holes. We resorted to hiring a small boy who scurried onto the roof after each snowfall to scrape it clean. After we got it in some shape we became attached to the place and lived with its frustrations. Electric current was erratic, not only because of the fluctuating power, but because others, untraceable, tapped into our line, so we bought a 110 volt transformer to regulate the power. Since it was 220 current, 110 light bulbs early gave a dull glow when there were more unknown customers. We would forget, and later at night the brightening 110 bulbs would blow out from the few users. Phone service too, had its peculiarities.

During the lengthy dry season, the back roads leading from the Golhak Road were dust and gravel, in winter muddy and deep tracked, where Chris Chapman's Jaguar regularly stuck, so to reach our gate we routinely spread donkey loads of canvas bagged gravel. We had other animals, for camels walking or resting along the Golhak Road were a common sight, and in nearby fields herds of sheep grazed when there was sufficient pasture. The youngsters, of course, delighted in all this.

When I arrived in Tehran, everyone advised a local driver for the car, and I was fortunate to get Petros. He was an older Assyrian Christian, spoke understandable English and French, was energetic, and a jack-of-all trades. He could drive, make car and house repairs, serve as houseman, and be entrusted with numerous errands essential in such environment. He and his family were the only ones to which I ever gave an affidavit of support years later when they emigrated to America. Ali, our cook, was Iranian, and he used to do reasonably well on our kerosene stove and with our kerosene refrigerator. Then we had an Armenian nursemaid for the two girls, who, with Petros, did cleaning. The one day, Sunday, Petros was off I drove down to the embassy, and an incident showed why a local driver was essential. The Shimran road was two lane macadam with dirt shoulders. On approaching a blind curve I slowed, whereupon a trailing car drew alongside and another paralleled him. I hit the brakes while the two cars careened around the curve. There were no accident noises, so the Prophet and Ali, his son-in-law and the first of the Shia line, undoubtedly saved them.

Before household routine was organized, Virginia fell ill. She was feeling unwell but determined to be in our home by our first Christmas. We moved in Christmas Eve, she was ill on Christmas, and the next day was diagnosed with infectious hepatitis or a severe case of jaundice. I was fortunate to get one of the Point Four doctors for her, since she had been infected by food or water at the hotel, and was in bed for a prolonged period. Petros, and I after work, would arrange the house, and the little girls were well taken care of. Virginia's recovery was slow. Told that she could not have a cocktail for six months, she determinedly outlasted the period. Lucy too, came down with a dysentery we met with another Point Four doctor. She still remembers the bottles of saline solution I had scoured Tehran's pharmacies for, hanging from the chandelier and the tube going into her arm. As we knew from our friends, these were accepted Foreign Service family hazards.

Our office hours started early and ostensibly went to 2:00 p.m., six days a week. There was a little snack lunchroom in the chancery, and we had our own itinerant barber, so presumably we needed few distractions from the work at hand. Frequently we went on beyond the 2:00 p.m. closing, but on Saturdays I established a rule. Unless we needed a watch officer, all our political section people who wished and those invited from other parts of the embassy, came to our house for a long lunch at mid-afternoon, a swim in our pool, and canapes and drinks beforehand while floating around on tire inner tubes. Petros in one of my old summer linen jackets would scoot around the pool keeping everyone happy. It was an interval in which we completely relaxed.

A feature of house and garden was the dogs. We started with a big, battle-scarred animal and departing Americans left a mate, a German shepherd. They produced puppies we could give away, and still when we left there were five large animals in the garden we fed for 10 cents a day on sheep innards.

Robberies were frequent among foreigners, and with barbed wire atop our garden wall and the dogs we felt comparatively safe. Once a robber did try a break-in, ingeniously distracting the dogs by tossing meat over the wall at the farthest end. Further illustrative of the lengths to which such robbers would go, the labor attaché and his wife had their evening coffee drugged, and while they slept their house was stripped of its furnishings.

On raising my sights from home and workplace I came to realize Iran is a fascinating collection of peoples and of colorful history. The disparate groups, still distinct, stretch in a great horseshoe on its borders; the Azeris, Kurds, and the Bakhtiari of the northwest, the Qashqais and Arabs of the south, the Baluchis of the south-east, and the Turkmen of the northeast. The Iranian core is the other half. In history Iran also exemplified the diversity of power politics. Long buffeted by an Anglo-Russian rivalry, it lost significant territories to Russia. In the south, Khuzistan, the British ran the great oil fields and refinery essentially for their own benefit. The country once had been divided (1907) into spheres of influence between the two powers and militarily during the exigencies of World War II. Thereafter British troops left, but it took great American pressure and some Iranian guile to impel the Russians to desert their puppet Azerbaijan regime and to evacuate the country in 1946. A 1921 treaty with Iran, however, could give them a future handle to return. Then, too, a secret clause of the 1939 Hitler-Stalin Pact revealed ultimate Soviet aims by giving that country a free hand south in the direction of the Persian Gulf, which the West came to see by this time as the oil jugular of the free world and of nascent NATO.

The environment I saw featured popular resentments toward foreign domination, erupting over Iran's oil. The highly visible British controlled the Anglo-Iranian Oil Company (AIOC), divided between a financially beset British government and private ownership, and refused to increase Iran's oil royalties at a time when the country was the world's largest exporter. When the smoke cleared, emotional nationalism was embodied in the 1951 coalition government, not surprising by later standards, and uncompensated oil nationalization was its policy. The Iranian-British standoff featured a boycott of Iranian oil and deepening financial depression for Iran. To international concern that the deteriorating situation gave fertile scope for communist subversion, Mohammed Mosadeq,[1] Iran's complex, elderly prime minister, merely replied, "Too bad for you." Time magazine started 1952 by naming him its "Man of the Year." The caption, "He oiled the wheels of chaos," delighted the old man. Years later, showing the durability of politics, Ayatollah Khomeini was similarly featured.

---

[1] Farsi into English had acceptable transliterations. The British preferred Musaddiq. Our embassy adopted the practical Mosadeq.

It may be to the credit of the American character that its contemporary officials were aware of ethical aspects that varying assignments thrust upon them. Earlier in Montreal and Washington, there were no issues other than to do a conscientious job. In Kobe and Istanbul, with war pressures, we wholeheartedly accepted roles in a tremendous national effort in which we had complete confidence. In Bucharest, first confronted by the reality of limitation and by the ruthless Stalinist dictatorship, no American could view death, disappearance, and prison as other than the negation of a birthright. Iran strategically was the most important and difficult assignment I had yet held. In a private moment Loy Henderson also admitted that our Iranian situation was his most challenging, and intuitively I sensed that it would be a complex personal and national test.

In the political situation, a literal revolution, the advice of my first chief re-echoed. He had firmly proposed that I avoid all political work, but above all, oil mixed with politics. In the changing facets of the current assignment I dealt with dubious types, both internal and external, as well as the clash of international politics. Ruefully I sometimes admitted my old boss had something. Iran was in a ferment as internal forces jockeyed for influence or were used for that purpose. The Iranians had a very poor life, so opium smoking, stemming from extensive poppy growing, was common and was one of the few pleasures that their bare existence afforded. Another interest arose when Mosadeq's coalition, by nationalizing the British oil interest, galvanized Iranian emotions. With no outlet because of an international boycott, the largest oil industry in the Middle East was at a standstill. The economic experts, including Americans, regularly predicted Iran's bankruptcy, but Mosadeq's regime confounded them by operating the industry and the country. After all, there was not much distance to fall.

Because the Anglo-Iranian Oil Company (now BP) was so conscious of Britain's serious financial difficulties, it earlier refused to recognize the nationalist trend in Iran. Even after production halted, there were colonial types who believed they could bring Mosadeq down through the oil boycott. The oriental counselor (the Iranians disliked the title) of the British embassy typified this. Despite his knowledge of the rocks, he was incapable of understanding the forces Mosadeq was leading. British deferral to his views was a handicap to Western interests, for this official could not grow or adjust in a local era of rapid change. He typified the mythical tombstone: born; died at 30; buried at 80. The period furthered my distrust of experts, who, until they proved themselves, did not have my full confidence. I came to feel a further hazard for the expert is that he may become emotionally involved in a situation through long service, which can impair his thinking and usefulness. I agree with a congressional witness, who testified that an official may be adept in a foreign language, but lacking other qualities (like FSO Dave in Tokyo), can alienate more people more effectively. By now I knew there was no substitute for sound experience and a whole personality.

The expert left and a British chargé, George Middleton, came who was receptive to looking at things with an open mind, bringing a more confident relation between our two embassies. Feeling the growing pressures, Mosadeq broke relations with Great Britain, and Loy, Gordon, and I watched the British departing caravan one late autumn dawn as it drove for Baghdad. I also was on hand at the airport to greet the British when, after Mosadeq, they returned.

Domestic politics revolved around two elements: the Shah and Mosadeq, meaning the military and the National Front. The Shah had not disowned the emotional xenophobia arising from the oil crisis. Prime Minister Mosadeq, controlling the Majlis or parliament, had taken care to govern in the name of the Shah and not to challenge openly his popular position as a traditional symbol of stability and, despite his youth, as a father figure. The Shah, personable and intelligent, found himself once more in a ceremonial position with the power wielded by Mosadeq, of whose extreme oil policies he disapproved. He was not trained to be forthright, since as a youth he had been intimidated by his tyrannical father. Credibly I was told that as a boy the future shah was gazing at a fountain in a palace garden when his father met him and asked what he was doing. When the youth replied, "Thinking," his father booted him into the fountain, saying, "This will teach you to think!". It is said his twin sister inherited the father's hard qualities.

The Shah was educated in Switzerland, and during the war was put on the throne when the British deported his father, who later died in South Africa. The new shah had been guided in his constitutional role by the British and some old line Iranian politicians, including the military. Now the nationalist hurricane, exemplified in the National Front, needed him as a substantive symbol of Iranian continuity and nationalism. It was congenial for the Shah to bide his time in his palaces with his court circle, keeping informed and in touch with military men. After all, by upbringing and training he had not been encouraged in positive action. While the man had courage and spirit, by temperament he was indecisive and hesitant to make decisions if there could be forked consequences. Foreigners speculated that he had dreams for himself and the Pahlavi dynasty, of being a strong leader and builder of Iran, thereby exorcising his father. Meanwhile he looked like a shah, enjoyed ceremony and the social life, was a nationalist by virtue of his position and memories, and had learned from his earliest years to play an appropriate role whenever on view. The people liked the institution of the monarchy, and to them he was as important a figure as Mosadeq. In the public mind they were still linked.

The military, so important a factor for any Iranian government, was quiet, but was looking to the Shah. Its officers took their oaths of loyalty and generally owed their promotions to him as their leader, not a transient prime minister. Of course, there were significant military numbers of communist (Tudeh) and Mosadeq sympathizers which time would reveal. True, there was a constitution which had aspects of parliamentary government, but the professional military felt themselves a breed apart. Further, their training proceeded under the aegis of an American military mission, and quantities of new equipment arrived to bolster the effectiveness of the armed forces, despite the oil embargo and financial difficulties. This shaping of the military Mosadeq hesitatingly approved, while at the same time watching the officers closely and by inducements getting cadre supporters there. Mosadeq could not seriously object, for Iran's strategic position, like Turkey's, made it a front line of the non-communist world. Russia, despite the raucous emotions and theatrics of the anti-British syndrome, was the country truly feared as an aggressive neighbor. For American policy too, there appeared small reason in strengthening Turkey if there was not an effort to block, with the cooperation of Iran's military chief and his forces, the road to the Persian Gulf. So most officers looked to the Shah, and in their large Tehran club, prominently displayed as a talisman in an upright glass case, was the Shah's bloody tunic, when wounded he had fended with an assailant.

Mosadeq was of the landowner aristocracy, related to the Qajar dynasty superseded by the Shah's rags-to-power war minister father, when the son was a small boy. He had a dislike and contempt for the Shah as a virtual usurper, and his plans, despite his age, admitted of no rival. French-educated Mosadeq eventually had become leader of the Majlis nationalists and, as an old man, prime minister. On occasion he could carry the entire Majlis, even opponents, by his emotional speech, crying and fainting. A doctor, who was a Majlis opponent, once reached him recumbent, grabbed his wrist and felt a full, regular, conscious pulse. The old charlatan was effective in knowing his country's culture. Pleading age and personal security, Mosadeq carried out his duties from a guarded home bedroom, which naturally restricted visitors and, if he played the invalid, the length of visits. There were no personal or financial scandals, for he lived simply, and in conversation could be witty and agreeable. Yet a realistic New York Times reporter, showing the divergence between cultures, after some interviews with him exclaimed, "Intellectually he is the most dishonest man I have ever met." As John Stutesman, a Service friend quite familiar with the Iranians remarked, "You have to understand that an Iranian is not lying. He believes sincerely in all he says and this is as natural as breathing...It's like dealing with a flowing stream." Such a cultural disjuncture could cause problems in negotiation.

The National Front, like most coalitions, had incongruous components: some wealthy landowners like Mosadeq; some reasonably competent foreign-educated ministers and senior bureaucrats; a Majlis majority; Tehran university professors and students; Dr. Baghai and his Toilers party; bazaar merchants; significantly, active Shia clergy such as Ayatollah Kashani, the most politically known and influential with the Tehran bazaar; labor figures like vice premier Makki, controlling the oil workers; the Tudeh (communist) party, and a large groundswell of the peasants, and city workers. Inevitably opportunists like the foreign minister rode the wave. Such a coalition, as long as it focused on the villainous British and Iran's oil birthright, could have a fragile unity, but eroding time, other important issues and consequences, differing political objectives such as those of the communists, and personal conflicts could break it apart.

Despite its convoluted, frustrating politics, there is a continuous attraction to Iran and its people that is not easy to shake. While I have described certain aspects and the oil politics of the troubled country, one cannot resist mentioning others. Tehran was a busy city, and as an inflation hedge in the declining economy there was much building steadily north from the city toward Shimran, which it has now reached. The great feature was the Elburz mountain range to the north, where as the seasons went by, we could mark the advancing and receding snow line. From our chancery windows we never tired of watching the magnificent sunsets and the colors these brought to the mountains. On clear days off to the east was the impressive cone of Demavend, over 18,500 feet as the highest mountain in Iran. In our midst was the bright sunshine, rags, and dust. It is easy to understand why the Iranians loved gardens and flowers, because they had to work so hard with nature to get them. On barren ground and stones, and with careful use of irrigated water, saplings and small bushes might be planted within a walled enclosure and be nurtured into a pretty garden. The Iranians said, "Unless there are trees, men die. Here, unless there are men, trees die." It was not unusual to see a poorly dressed porter or a shabby youngster on a bicycle wearing a rose over an ear or holding a stem between his teeth. Women would do likewise. Poets were the Iranian favorites, and their ancient heroes in this field were as quoted and fresh as ever.

Persian carpets were legendary and Iranians viewed themselves as experts. It was acceptable for guests to foot-flip a carpet corner and count the knots for quality, so they were always surprised when our Chinese living room carpet did not pass such a test. New home carpets were virtually unknown, for quality ones attained this by wear, so to break in carpets the practice was to place them in the roadway and for normal traffic, vehicular, pedestrian, and animal, to produce the desired effect.

Iranians, in another aspect of nature, had a belief that flowing water purifies itself within a comparatively few feet. It was fascinating to see the activity along the citywide water ditches (jubes) as I drove along the Golhak Road. At various points a car was being washed, someone might be brushing his teeth, and at still another, household laundry and pans might be given a cleaning. Finally, a housewife would be taking jugs of water for family drinking. Somehow, despite dysentery, intestinal parasites, jaundice, and other illnesses which doctors told us were endemic, the people survived.

Iranians and Arabs have a deep love for the spoken word, hence the poetry. An opponent of Mosadeq I saw socially the evening the old man delivered a speech. His opponent kept repeating what a marvelous speech it had been, so I asked what he said. "Oh," exclaimed this English university educated man, "it doesn't matter. It was a marvelous speech." There was something lively about the Iranians, whom I thought of as the Latins of the Middle East. We came to know many fine Iranians, and some could be most agreeable social companions after you came to realize they did not mean all they said. You could take this as rising from a precarious environment requiring nimbleness to survive. In general contrast to the Arabs, the Iranians could laugh at themselves and later appreciate when they had been carried away by rhetoric. Sensibly the Iranian New Year holiday, No-Ruz, was March 21, the first day of spring, when people sent their annual greetings.

Religion was the deep cultural exception. Iranians belonged to the Shia sect, whereas the majority of Islam was Sunni, and they took seriously what they believed to be the martyrdom of Ali, Hassan, and Hussein at the hands of the Sunni. Without dwelling on a religious difference, genealogy or leader selection, this originally was encouraged by Iranian shahs to maintain Iranian identity against the rival Sunni Ottoman sultans. Since the people annually commemorated the Shia martyrs, the period could be an emotional one when religious processions paraded. Every foreigner was cautioned not to take pictures of these or of possible flagellants. We recognized the influence of the mullahs, and we kept up with the most politically influential, Ayatollah Kashani. Tony Cuomo followed the Imam Jumeh (Friday imam) of the leading Tehran mosque, whom I found to be a discreet man, chary in expressing radical, nationalist opinions.

In a vein more diplomatic than religious, a formal requiem mass in the Italian embassy chapel was arranged by the Argentine embassy for Evita Peron, where Virginia and I represented our embassy. Being ignorant of the procedure, we closely watched a French embassy couple, the Girards, and followed their actions. Later I thanked him for being our guide, and we had a solid laugh when he exclaimed that they also were at sea. "We're Huguenots." My guide, Girard, was a fashion plate, his English excellent, his wife a striking redhead, and he was erroneously judged an aesthete. In World War II, a language liaison officer with a British division at Dunkirk, he decided as long as an enemy remained on French soil he would resist, and jumped into a boat. He fought in Africa, and his tank unit was among the first in Paris. From a garage where he stopped his unit, after an emotional silence he talked by phone to his parents. In public service he had a good career, here heading his embassy's political section, and was amusing and informative.

There was another commemorative ceremony, at the Saudi Arabs for their late king. Loy and I came to pay our respects, sat for a time against the wall in a heavily carpeted room, and drank coffee from cups served by a Saudi official. He was followed by his black servant (traditional in Arabia), who swilled the cups for the next guests and emptied the contents on the costly carpets.

In our social life we frequently visited Iranian and American homes. Again there is such a bevy it is pointless to outline, but I enjoy some recollections: Bill Warne, the Point Four director, and his technical study group's weekly study of poker's law of averages; Bob Parke, the fine commercial officer, the most amusing host in town; the CIA station chief the most interesting; Loy Henderson, host at a big Fourth of July reception, replying to Virginia's parting wonder at his still being genial, "How can you be civil at such affairs, Virginia, without at least two double martinis?" The servants always kept his glass filled, hidden behind a table V.I.P. photo. There were big occasions at the Gulistan (Peacock throne) and Shimran palaces by the Shah. Then married to Soraya, a beautiful woman who wore little jewelry in contrast to his first wife, he put on some elaborate evenings. One, to celebrate Soraya's twenty-first birthday, found Virginia and me in a Conga line going from the Shimran Palace to the gardens and back, the Shah in the lead. He liked a good time.

Continued personnel changes were natural in a large embassy, and I took time out for friendship when greeting Carl Norden, whom I had last seen before Bucharest. Carl was an excellent economist, number two of that section, but he dwelt on the political situation as the key, and he and I found a kindred viewpoint. On the personal side he took kidding as a bachelor, but his defense was that, as he grew older, he became more particular and had less to offer. Later he negated this by marrying a fine woman, formerly with the OSS in Italy, and they had three children (twins) in two years.

In an important embassy, beset by a major international issue, the numbers of foreign officials, journalists, and diverse visitors meant considerable social activity. I did have junior officers, who would handle as much as possible, but Virginia and I could not escape. A most misunderstood feature of diplomatic life, the cocktail reception, came to the rescue. It is obvious, when attention is called to it, that there is no device that can bring so many people of contrasting views together in such a brief period. This applies to people who normally would avoid, as too conspicuous, coming to the chancery or for dinner. Successive unobtrusive brief talks while circulating can be quite productive and are professionally unmatched for varied views. Another stereotype is morning coat and striped pants. For the first time since acquiring them in Shanghai, I found their use as an usher at formal Tehran weddings. Two FSOs, John Howison of my staff and Stuart Campbell of the economic section, married delightful young women from our chancery and information office. I was suitable accoutred.

During the oil impasse Mosadeq was still trying to sell his oil abroad and people were visiting Iran, as were our journalists to cover the big story or those seeking to arrange various settlements. We got our full quota ranging from the curious, adventurers seeking an easy dollar, oil company executives, technicians, and politicians. Just a few may be mentioned, such as Averell Harriman, Senator Claude Pepper, and our most decorated soldier of World War II, Audie Murphy, who seemed to have every decoration but the army good conduct medal. Toward the end of my assignment, when we were able to help toward an oil settlement, we had Herbert Hoover, Jr., then an oil executive sent by the Department. He was an impressive man, and we got on well. At my place we had a private talk about Iranian politics, followed by my raising the Republican inclination tacitly to accept Senator McCarthy's charges of communist subversion of American foreign policy by the Foreign Service. I stood up for the loyalty of the Service, citing a few facts, and from his reaction I hoped this had been helpful. For the way he handled the oil problem Hoover deservedly became Deputy Secretary of State. Still, he had an aloof attitude until he got to know you stemming from his hearing problems, which in new environments made him wary of new people and their views.

Among the senators and congressmen visiting Tehran was a young congress-man traveling alone around the world, quietly picking up impressions. I was his escort officer for a day during his brief stay, and I liked him. This brought about a good private discussion on similar problems in foreign affairs and domestic politics. I was preoccupied by our dilemma compounded of national interest. Viewing things politically, he thought that domestic and foreign issues were similar, in that most had disagreeable alternatives. The problem generally was not black and white, but the need to choose the least disagreeable; in other words, to decide which was the lightest shade of gray. His analogy made an impression and is one I have accepted. John F. Kennedy and I were in agreement.

After the Shah regained authority, Vice President and Mrs. Nixon also came through on a baptismal around-the-world trip. It naturally was a formal program, and my role was minor. I went with him on a couple of interviews and ghosted a Tehran University speech he liked. Nixon was a new vice president, and I had the impression that he, too, was retaining impressions and conscientiously learning while he was there. Although Kennedy and Nixon did not know a future opponent's identity, I am convinced that, as ambitious and far sighted men, they were girding for the 1960 elections.

Time off from the office was rare, and many are amazed we never got to Isfahan or Shiraz. Scheduled trips had to be canceled because of politics. However, I did get a few official trips; to Tabriz, in Azerbaijan, and to Meshed, near the border of Russian Turkestan, where we had consulates. Tabriz had a Russian atmosphere and a Balkan flavor, but Meshed was exotic. It was a religious shrine, its mosque with a golden dome, and was an outpost of Islam in which central Asian faces were common. In our Meshed consulate they were thrown on their own resources through isolation, and understandably welcomed embassy visitors. I sampled this one memorable weekend after coming on the air attaché's plane, and found myself playing badminton at 11:00 a.m. with a martini glass in one hand. That set the tone for the weekend. Later, showing a hazard of the post, our consul contracted polio and was evacuated.

Virginia and I did get two brief trips, thanks to a friend. The Service lived up to its reputation of old associates crossing paths, when Marie Chabot of the Montreal group came as consul to Tehran. With time, Virginia and I were able to leave the girls, when home from school, because Marie lived at our place temporarily. One of these trips, four or five days to the Caspian Sea, meant traveling through the Elburz mountains and coming down to a tropically lush area fed by rains off the large sea. The contrast was astonishing. It was a little less so in the hotel bedroom to mistake for mice what were termites noisily nibbling away inside the furniture. By no means a drinker, I still learned in a short Beirut leave that after a long period at high altitudes you can hold more when you go to sea level because your multiplied red corpuscles burn up alcohol faster. A colleague serving in Bolivia at some 12,000 feet underlined this by putting two friends to bed in Buenos Aires, while he remained cold sober. The Beirut experience, without his attempted capacity, confirmed this.

Business went into high gear during the year end holidays of 1952, when Loy Henderson returned from a trip to Washington. He had instructions to try his hand, after so many others had failed, in a final search to negotiate a viable agreement with Mosadeq. The United States, sympathetic to the financial problems of its ally, Britain, and aware of the effects upon other oil operations in the Persian Gulf, was not going to push for a debilitating, no-accommodation deal. It wanted a compromise. The outlines of the package have been publicly described as having Anglo-Iranian compensation set by an arbiter or panel, with the British dropping the oil blockade, while the United States ordered a large quantity of oil and gave a large advance to help Iranian recovery.

There followed two months of intensive negotiations conducted by Loy and Mosadeq alone, with only Ali Pasha Saleh, our senior Iranian interpreter and adviser, present. As Loy later told it, during one meeting he had a sign (the cane habitually used by Foreign Minister Fatemi for his limp parked on the banisters) that the fellow was in an adjacent room eavesdropping. Fatemi was controversial and I did not take to him because he earlier had tried to have me removed from Iran. He saw to it that inaccurate reports of questionable political activities, from the government's viewpoint, in which I was allegedly engaged were given to Mosadeq to raise with Henderson. Loy was able to confute the reports by pointing out their glaring errors.

Because of the heavy political content of the negotiations, I was closely associated with the ambassador, together with Gordon Mattison. We three, and sometimes I alone with Henderson, daily would have long sessions in reviewing Loy's tactics for future meetings and in analyzing those already held. It was a time when I saw Henderson at his best and gained an added education in political tactics and analysis. From positions as chargé and ambassador, he had an extraordinary personal knowledge of the Soviet Union, Iraq, and India. Since he had also been responsible for these areas in the State Department, he knew the workings of Washington. With it Henderson had a professional prudence, for he would not comment upon the Soviet Union despite his wide experience. As he phrased it, "There is nothing worse than an obsolescent expert." We certainly needed more with that attitude. Loy's mind was intuitive and wide-ranging, and he had an unshakable integrity. In brief, he was the finest Foreign Service Officer I ever knew.

A break at the end of February spelled failure for the talks and showed itself in a curious way. Loy was building a point with Mosadeq based upon something the latter had agreed at an earlier stage. Mosadeq denied he had accepted the earlier point and Loy persisted, reminding him of a careful notation in his small black book, the ultimate reference on items of importance. Mosadeq got out a little black book, shook his head, and told Loy that there was no record. Crucially, it was a different black book and, although unspoken, both he and Loy knew it! In analyzing the episode, we concluded that the pressures on Mosadeq from an unraveling of National Front support and from the extremists, such as the pro-communists, had forced him to draw back. From here on, while Loy persisted a bit longer, I lost all confidence that we could get realistic terms. As the last talks slowed and I returned to the operations of the political section delegated to my deputy, I found that the deterioration had become quite marked. Factual appraisals showed a mounting communist strength gradually enveloping Mosadeq as the symbol of the regime, while nationalists not sympathetic to the Tudeh were being shunted aside.

A natural query arises. How sure was the embassy in this troublesome period of its facts and analyses and how was it possible to be well informed? There were more than the Tehran embassy and the three consulates at Isfahan, Meshed, and Tabriz. Two other large operations scattered in the country were responsible to the ambassador: the military mission and the Point Four technical assistance mission. The CIA station was concentrated in Tehran and our military worked with the Iranian military throughout the country, being careful to keep that work purely professional. Point Four was the largest such technical aid program in the world, again very prudent in confining itself to agriculture, health, education, and like activities, with coordinating suboffices in major towns of the country. The leadership of both missions was excellent and had the full respect of the Iranians. These were particularly impressed that the Mormons in Point Four would not drink coca cola because of the caffeine. The shifting situation and operations generated regular requested and voluntary factual and analytical reports to Washington on varied subjects. In Tehran the political section representatives attended regular meetings of the agencies they were assigned to follow. Also, close liaison among the American elements included joint conferences and evaluations, each element from its respective sphere.

As the crisis deepened from 1952, Iranian antipathies and suspicions were fanned against Americans. At least it was not discouraged by the leadership, by some encouraged, and the Tudeh were progressively active, while the large Soviet embassy aided its rise. The United States was literally in the middle. Since the Iranians were not realizing their oil hopes through America, which was Britain's NATO ally, and since domestic tensions were growing, the visible Americans became the target. It varied in parts of the country, but there were hostile incidents and demonstrations of an organized character about them. Americans became cautious in public, while shouts, graffiti, and door stickers had the same message, "Yankee, go home."

Gholem Mosadeq was the English-speaking physician son of the premier and a liaison point. In early March, John Howison and I had a long conversation with him in which we probed areas of concern, but Gholem's answers were alarming, and ignoring of realities. They also offered no other prospect than to follow a course which was losing the prime minister non-Tudeh adherents by the day. It was time in mid-March, when I gave Loy a first memorandum on the subject. The memo pulled together all that the section had learned about developments, sought to put them into perspective, and concluded that, from the standpoint of communist infiltration and influence, the light for American interests was changing from amber to red. The conclusion hit Loy: the continuance of the Mosadeq regime was now contrary to our policy interests. We had a real discussion, with Loy his energetic and stimulating self, but he was not prepared to agree.

It is difficult, unless looked at from the time, to appreciate the situation. Here was Iran, the largest oil exporter in the Middle East, out of world markets for two years. The Korean war was raging, as well as the cold war, and Russia was making an effort through subversion within Iran to reach the Persian Gulf and take a front seat in Mideast oil with grave consequences for NATO. At home, Senator Joseph McCarthy was in his heyday, heightening his charges that pro-communists in the State Department had lost China to the communists. Dwight Eisenhower had been elected with a mandate to end the Korean war. On becoming president he did not openly oppose Senator McCarthy on his State Department accusations. Now it looked as if the Mideast could be up for grabs through the Tudeh in Iran. It was a difficult position for any ambassador, and we fully appreciated it.

By April, the signs to us in the section were clearer and I gave Loy a second memorandum showing this and reiterating the earlier conclusion. Because I was speaking with confidence from the variety of sources we used, I could do this. Further, in making the policy recommendation I recalled the private words of Averell Harriman to Burton Berry in Bucharest when I was present: "Remember always to stay this side of the horizon so Washington can follow you." Again we had an animated discussion, with Loy probing away, but still not prepared to agree. By this time I was more uncomfortable because, after all, he had unparalleled experience in dealing with the communists, although mine in the Balkans and in Washington was recent. It still did not make me happy that I had a fundamental disagreement with my boss. Late some nights I pondered the problem. Not that there was personal tension between us; it was simply the political disagreement on the situation. However, when mid-May rolled around, there was the job I had been sent to do. I gave him a third, a further reinforcement of my section's reports and conclusions, combined with the various American sources mentioned earlier.

My situation was clearly not easy. In coping with the dilemma of reconciling national interest and opposing the Mosadeq regime, somehow I struck the right shared note with the ambassador. In one of our talks I described the moral seriousness of the issue. I said that such an opposing action was not necessarily a sign of our national strength, if not being done openly, but in broader reality, if it were covert, could even be a sign of the weakness of power. Nevertheless it had to be done. It was a choice between disagreeable alternatives. With the third and last memorandum I finally understood Loy had been impressed by the earlier ones and that he was at his most searching whenever he was. This time, after a talk which was remarkably brief, he lightened my load. While there were some elements of the memorandum with which he did not fully agree, he generally concurred in its conclusions. Promptly I asked if he would be willing to say this in a covering dispatch sending the memorandum to the Department. He dictated it and sent the package on its way. As a result of this and comparable developments I learned later also were occurring in Washington, he was called home for consultations.

Before leaving, the ambassador called Mattison into his office. After he emphasized the need for utmost secrecy, he told Gordon, the only embassy officer to be informed, of contingency plans. We had pursued good faith negotiations with Mosadeq, Henderson said, but in the event of failure of those negotiations American and British Intelligence were preparing a covert contingency plan for Mosadeq's overthrow, to be made operative when all were convinced that diplomatic alternatives had been exhausted. The plan had the full approval of President Eisenhower and Prime Minister Churchill and was to be directed on the spot by Kermit Roosevelt of the CIA. The embassy was to give every appearance of normalcy and accord full cooperation, while the ambassador would go on consultation and leave, being absent when the operation was launched. Henderson said it was not easy to accept this last part, for if the plan failed he would disown it and Mattison, if not Melbourne, recalled or declared *persona non grata*. Henderson would return, hopefully to resume talks with Mosadeq. It was a bitter pill for him to swallow - as the president's personal representative to have his authority thus diluted - but he accepted his orders with good grace. Gordon confided all this to me when later developments made this necessary. It deepened my understanding of Loy's final acceptance of the Mosadeq challenge.

Things began to move; part of the plan's success was the embassy staff carrying on under difficult circumstances, particularly our political section. Friends of those days like Kim Roosevelt, the later-arriving CIA leader, long remain so. It was a stirring period involving Iranians and Americans meeting quietly and privately. Meanwhile, Loy, after his Washington consultation, could not return to Iran, and yet we had to keep him informed. He was scheduled to go to Rome and Beirut to check in our American hospital there. Fortunately our naval attaché, Commander Eric Pollard, was exchanging his aircraft at Port Lyautey, Morocco. This helped Gordon and me to decide that I should meet Loy in Rome, so I took off with Eric.

Pollard had a quiet gift for making friends. At this vital period he was the one American who had close ties with the disparate political elements. He was close to the Shah and his secretary, through whom I made some contacts. He used to gamble with the Qashqai leaders; was on intimate terms with two of Mosadeq's family and advisers; and even used to visit the future prime minister, an army officer who was in hiding. Without one circle knowing he was as close with the others, he made his way as a factual reporter and de facto member of the political section. With my assistants analyzing his reports, we credited Eric with his information. He and I became continued good friends, and the Navy Department and State were happy at the collaboration. It certainly showed the advantages of inter-agency cooperation.

Besides Eric and his air crew, were his French wife and myself. It proved quite a trip. From Beirut we flew to Rome, where I briefed Loy, who was eager for our news in detail. He decided not to go on to Tehran, and approved my continuing to Port Lyautey and Spain to pick up the returning plane. Virginia did not come because Janice, in the midst of all the domestic turbulence, recently had been born at our little U.S. Army hospital. She was still tiny, and we both could not leave her. When I described the new scenes of the trip to Virginia, I realized this was a poor substitute. Foreign Service wives have their own tests of character.

After Morocco, including picturesque Tangier, I crossed to Spain and went to Granada, where I fulfilled an old wish to see the Alhambra. Then I was in Madrid as a frustrated Spanish language officer, my first solid contact with a Spanish-speaking country since induction. There I renewed ties with Johnny Jones of Rome, now deputy chief of mission there, and in Majorca I rejoined our Tehran crew. Engine trouble out of Beirut obliged us to land overnight in Baghdad, Iraq, where Burton Berry was our ambassador. He put me up, and we talked area politics and our Iranian problems. The brief trip proved a helpful way to regain perspective.

The State Department rule, barely relaxed, still existed to the effect that an officer might resign if he married a foreigner. During the trip I sat at an outdoor cafe with a promising young officer, later an ambassador. He frankly described his Catch-22 situation. He was single, occasionally dating interesting local girls, but blocked by the solid cultural practice that more than two dates signified an engagement. Sympathetic, I knew his calibre, for the young fellow resolved his dilemma successfully.

In Tehran, Mosadeq was still losing support; Makki of the Oilworkers was gone; Ayatollah Kashani and the important, militant clergy, as well as the influential bazaar, were in open opposition; Dr. Baghai and his coterie were estranged, as were many of the professors, students, and bureaucrats. Essentially, only opportunists, Tudeh, and some unquestioning followers remained with Mosadeq, who maintained the facade of authority. Dissatisfied groups within Iran and the army and landowning circles began to press the Shah for some action against Mosadeq. It became clearer that his nationalist supporters, secular and clerical, were becoming alienated and the Tudeh elements backing him were gaining greater influence.

Our consul at Tabriz, Jack Iams, was being reassigned and leaving a remarkable legacy. He had earned a doctorate at M.I.T. in electronic physics, and at Tabriz with his own receiving equipment, his hobby, he heard an intriguing prolonged sound. After continued checks he decided the sounds were missiles in flight. Accorded more sophisticated apparatus, he detected, the first foreigner to do so, the large Soviet missile test center in Central Asia. From a little acorn, a great radio monitoring project grew. In a subsequent contribution, Jack was charged with developing the project a generation ago which gave certain of our embassies, for their time, electronic-proof meeting rooms. So valuable was he that a distinguished ambassador once told me if he could have Iams alone as a substantive officer at any specific embassy, he would be satisfied.

The day after Iams flew home, a group of Iranian army officers with the approval of the Shah finally moved when he replaced Mosadeq constitutionally as his right and named General Zahedi. The move was a fiasco. Mosadeq was aware of their plotting, and on the eve, arrested the ringleaders. The Shah fled the country, and Ambassador Henderson, in Beirut by then, promptly flew in. It looked as if failure was complete. Before then, at Mattison's suggestion, he and I joined in sending a cable praising what had been attempted, and stating the result was not to America's discredit. The CIA group was professional and had done its best. There proved to be a second plan by those seeking Mosadeq's overthrow and, as Kim Roosevelt told me at the time, everything was to be attempted, this time benefiting from the earlier surfacing of key Tudeh elements and allies. This second caught fire in the Tehran bazaar. There the respected body building clubs, the Zirkaneh, in their practice dress demonstrated for the Shah, and proved to be the spark. Combined with further efforts by the Iranian military and popular support which was unquestioned, this ultimately succeeded during the course of a day in August. Kermit Roosevelt who headed the CIA operation, has published a record of the eventually successful action, in a volume called "Countercoup." It was confirmation of an American understanding that no covert action against a leader and even a rump regime that would contend to the end, could possibly succeed unless there was sufficient approval within the country for the change.

It was a bright and hot day. The demonstrations started in the morning and gathered momentum. The political section was deployed as usual, and we kept our fingers crossed. As support rose in behalf of General Zahedi, who had been in hiding, my officers became more impatient to tell the Department that Mosadeq was out. While I delayed, we kept sending factual operational immediate messages to the Department. Only in the early scorching afternoon, when the public customarily napped after lunch and when the fury of the pro-Shah public continued to mount, I authorized a draft telegram saying that Mosadeq was being overthrown. I took it to Loy, advised him to inform the Department to this effect, and gave my chief reason. This was the first occasion in the two years he and I had been in Iran when a so-called popular demonstration had not stopped or slackened after lunch for people to rest in the hot summer. It was gaining momentum, and I was convinced that the movement was genuine and would replace Mosadeq. Loy laughed and said, "I agree with you, but we certainly can't tell that [as the reason] to the Department." The message went.

Popular enthusiasm for the Shah was unmistakable. The public had finally made a choice, which up to that time it had refused to do. People also had become very disturbed when, in the interval between the first coup effort and the second, the Tudeh had come out so blatantly behind Mosadeq with speeches and threatening activities. That day all cars ran with lights in celebration, and each had to have a windshield picture of the Shah, even if on a banknote. There was an air of celebration and of relief throughout Tehran, which we learned from the consulates and our other official offices was reflected in the country. A Point Four doctor years later described to me his long trip at the time from Tehran to the far south, where he invariably met in the villages the same scene of rejoicing and relief. It was recognized by the Soviets as a strategic defeat. In the days that followed, as I said to Loy, it was great for the first time to see a road in front of us rather than a roadblock. Years later some analysts evaluated the situation and concluded that the Tudeh could not have taken power successfully. However, the world and regional environments, growing evidence of Tudeh para-military moves, our extensive reporting coverage, and the fragile infrastructure of Iran, made it a realistic possibility, and thus an unacceptable risk option for the United States.

Mosadeq and Nasser were contrasts in their approaches to Moscow. Nasser met Soviet diplomats in the most favorable and friendly way, while enjoining them from talking to Egyptians. Since Mosadeq tended to be stand-offish with Soviet diplomats, they were more fortunate, since this allowed the Tudeh free rein. If the U.S. had moved more slowly, our intelligence showed, the Communist organizational arm would have been a greater threat, even though the Tudeh did not have wide success in influencing mass opinion. Disturbingly there were mounting reports claiming the Tudeh also were preparing a coup effort.

To share the trial of a major international crisis with an ambassador for whom I had great respect and regard, and to see a successful outcome of our efforts, was fulfilling. I gained further experience in analysis and sufficient confidence in evaluating my political staff, our sources, and our inter-agency assets to persist in a key policy recommendation. I saw how a man of principle wrestled with the stages toward his eventual decision, and how that very character influenced me. There are few such assignments which could give a Service professional conviction that he had made the right career choice.

There are numerous post mortems on how the quarter century given the Shah was squandered, for invariably an iconoclastic revision arises to reconcile the past to accord with current concepts and actions. It is facile now to decry American policy,  yet a ranking State official of the period asserts that if we could have been assured, regardless of whom we supported, of twenty five years of a stable non-communist Iran, we would have leaped at it.  Aside from Iran, the problems in the Mideast for nation building were underestimated.  Under a weak Shah, a lengthy, idle period was followed by the so-called White Revolution, with mangled agrarian reforms, steps toward women's emancipation, and military and industrial development.  These brought great strains and a traditional backlash that eventually ousted the Shah and created a clerical state.  Like all self-indulgent men, the Shah for some years kept secret from the United States his terminal cancer, an unforgivable act when one realizes the area stakes involved and the unwavering American commitment to him.  This made his decision paralysis traumatic for his unknowing ally and brought incalculable suffering to his people. From such instances history may be regarded as a chronicle of leaders' human strengths and weaknesses.

Unaware of the future, with the new regime, the return of the Shah, and the prospect of economic life renewed,  Iran rapidly revived.  It was exciting to be taken with the fresh prospects for the country and the changing political situation. Oil negotiators like Herbert Hoover, Jr., and others came and went, and we worked with them all.  It was a busy time.  The United States pumped critically short rice and sugar into the Iranian economy to generate local currency to meet essential government obligations.  Iran's oil nationalization was recognized, but production and marketing proved the temporary responsibility of an international cartel, which assured the gradual reentry of the oil in world markets to avoid cutbacks by other producing counties.

Throughout this period we had been too occupied to think about doing the officer efficiency reports, due in July.  A few days in seclusion produced those for my section, and one late September day Loy called me in to talk about mine. He was brief.  He was not going into what he was saying, which I knew would be favorable, but he did want me to know that he was saying one thing: I was not a yes man.  We both grinned in understanding.  Henderson's comment had a personal impact, for I knew earlier he had unhesitatingly placed his career on the line over at least two major policy issues involving what he believed to be American national interests.  When he died at ninety three, he was known to all colleagues as Mr. Foreign Service.

Efficiency reports are the determinant in the career of an officer and an amalgam of the factual with the personal, so there is much truth that the reports often reveal more about the rating officer than the one rated.  However, a lukewarm or unfavorable report could trail an officer despite an origin which may be quite irrational.  Up to now my career and advancement gave no cause for complaint.  I was moving along in good rhythm, had interesting work and responsibilities, and was well regarded by my seniors in the field and in the Department. Tehran was in a group of capitals known as Class 1 missions, consisting of places comparable to London or New Delhi. Through the grapevine, I understood that I was on the recommended promotion list to FSO-2, so it was a compliment when the ambassador sought to have me formally designated as his deputy in Tehran to follow the promotion.

When Arthur Richards left, I was not the most senior officer, but at Henderson's request, because of the political situation, had acted as such until Gordon Mattison came. He left after the coup because of some problems with the ambassador's wife. Let there be a brief digression. Personalities in a close embassy circle are important, and it is natural that differences can arise. This is as true for wives as for husbands. For example, none of my chiefs was unscathed in the view of at least one subordinate. The subject of ambassadors' wives and women's clubs recurs in any Service conversation. Because of the important role the lady plays, her personality can contribute to making a post difficult or congenial. One such (with whom we thankfully never served) ordered all the officers' wives to appear at the residence at 9:30 a.m. to be given their daily instructions for social work or what not. There were more than the usual number of pregnancies. As well, women's organizations can be friction points. Once Virginia, as a senior wife, had to become president of the local American women's club, since the lady normally eligible might have caused an eruption.

A new Administration had taken over and Secretary Dulles announced there would be no promotion list until all FSOs had gone through another security clearance procedure. This took all year. Loy had persisted in wanting me as an 0-3 to be his deputy, but Elbridge Durbrow, as head of Personnel, with customary Service practice in mind, insisted that the deputy chief of mission at a Class 1 post should be at least an 0-2. The new deputy was Bill Rountree, an excellent man and a friend, who later held several embassies.

Meanwhile I had soundings about a new assignment. Virginia and I thought it would be a fine idea if the next were less strenuous. Then the welcome news came that I was being assigned as deputy chief of mission (DCM) and consul general at Bern, Switzerland, and supervisory consul general of Geneva, Zurich, and Basel. This was accompanied by a private assurance that I was expected to be there no more than two years. After strenuous work and farewells, which made a hard schedule, the Melbournes, now numbering five and including Janice, our Tehran-born baby, in February prepared to fly on a direct transfer for Switzerland. First there was a morning request from Loy to prepare a general political appraisal. It was my departure day, but I could not refuse. I have never left a field post so tired.

Ambassador Willis with
Protocol Officer

At the Matterhorn

Secretary Dulles arriving at Geneva Summit

# CHAPTER 10

# EUROPEAN INTERLUDE: BERN

# February 1954 - January 1956

*The Korean armistice meant the United States lived with the cold war. Domestically tension decreased and was viewed as one of happy times. Buttressing this was the first international atomic energy conference at Geneva, and American assurances to provide detailed atomic information. A summit meeting with the leaders of the United States, the Soviet Union, Great Britain and France, had "the spirit of Geneva" blasted a month later by the Soviet arms sales to Egypt. Under our first career woman ambassador, I was DCM at Bern, Switzerland, and supervisory consul general of Geneva, Zurich, and Basel. From that European center I watched developments and participated in protocol aspects of the Atomic Energy conference and the Summit, while gleaning much from the international environment.*

After a difficult trip and arriving in Bern with a sick baby, we were greeted by the ambassador, Frances Willis, and, most timely, by Teta Strasser, our nanny from Bucharest. Thereafter she was our family aunt-housekeeper until she retired.

My new chief, Ambassador Frances Willis, was our first woman career chief of mission, recently arrived as ambassador after serving a quarter century in various European posts, her last as DCM at Helsinki. There were other firsts. Miss Willis was the first diplomat in Bern to be an ambassador. Previously our office, like others locally, had been a legation and the chief ranked as minister. A further Swiss first was Frances Willis herself, the first woman to head a diplomatic mission in Bern, and that in Switzerland, the only European country in which women did not have the vote. For the burden described, the ambassador was creating a new body of protocol, as with intelligence and forethought she advanced carefully, proving to be a professional diplomat.

Miss Willis had one advantage in Bern. Too often Switzerland had seen American political appointees who at best were mediocre. Her predecessor came from the theatre world and was popular socially for showing first-run movies in his residence. After being there six months, that ambassador became irritated with the Swiss and promptly told his deputy to cable Washington temporarily to cut off

American aid to the Swiss - this during the Marshall Plan rehabilitating Western Europe. His deputy gently reminded him that the Swiss were not getting any aid; in fact were extending some.

I had early noted the hard road for women officers in the Foreign Service, but a few active training years and the war and its aftermath had dimmed the initial observation. Now the movement for women's rights was gaining hesitant momentum at home. I realized that in Bern we could point to our chief. Since Swiss women did not vote in cantonal elections, it created a stir when Frances was named as ambassador. She told me that at a press conference shortly after her arrival the newsmen asked what she thought about the vote for Swiss women. She had responded that she had her own views, but if she announced them she imagined that she would not be remaining in Switzerland very long! The lady had a sense of humor. Frances, later at another mission as a career ambassador, the top rating of the profession, cabled the Department in irritation at some business. Lee Metcalf, then in Washington and deputy director of her area, read it and remarked in a "David Copperfield" inversion, "Willis is barking." I believe she, too, would have laughed.

Miss Willis was a personable, energetic woman who knew Western Europe intimately from long service. Earlier she had been an assistant professor of government at a leading woman's college, and in the Service had to prove her ability time and again to skeptical males. She had served more than her quota as an embassy administrative officer, considered in her career period as a less desirable assignment, and in self defense learned the Foreign Service regulations thoroughly. While Miss Willis had a detailed knowledge of diplomatic practice, it still was surprising that she did not treat me, her deputy, as a true chief of staff. For example, she might have seen, as customary, that I had a copy of her daily appointments list, so I could offer a helpful suggestion or two beforehand. Upon a naturally gracious personality, a defensive overlay of detailed professional knowledge showed itself by difficulty in delegating responsibility and in freeing herself from painstaking attention to detail. Lack of full confidence in subordinates is understandable for her era. For me, however, it had implications as her deputy after years of substantive experience, when I had come to regard perceptiveness of the latter rather than the form as what counted. I like to think that we both learned from each other.

Meanwhile the family was ensconced in the Bellevue Palace, the posh hotel of Bern, and after the first week's bill I pleaded drastic economies. We did not know it would be a long stay before finding an apartment, but with Teta aiding Virginia I was able to turn full attention to the chancery. It was an extension of the Silvahof Hotel in a pleasant residential area adjacent to a large public swimming pool-skating rink. The ambassador and some from the Department used to fret about security arrangements, but for the time it seemed to work out, and the quarters we used were suitable. It was a small conventional office arrangement, with consular and general public information services on the first floor. A Swiss male receptionist directed traffic, with one of our marine guards standing by. The second floor, as usual, was the heart of our operations. This was the embassy and, together with its three constituent posts, I assisted the ambassador.

Since the ambassador wanted me to live within Bern rather than the suburbs, which were but a few minutes more away, this restricted housing prospects. By three months, always in a hotel and despite the good food, we were tired of the life. April and Lucy had so thoroughly explored the corridors and stairways of the big, old hotel in its quiet season that it held no further surprises. Eventually, Virginia and Teta did track a lead to an ample apartment in a building a few minutes from our chancery, having a Swiss judge below and the Danish chancery above. It worked out very well, and after Teta got another Austrian maid, who lived with her small daughter on the fourth floor, we were set up. I was amused at being surrounded by women. It was unusual though, to have a woman chief and then at home a wife, three daughters, and two women servants, one with a daughter. I did not succeed in getting a male puppy as I threatened.

One great blessing was given us: it was the only European capital without direct airport connections. This meant our visitors came from the Geneva or Zurich airports and by train or car to Bern. We were the one post in Europe which knew when these visitors would arrive. Swiss trains ran on time or our visitors would arrive by car at the chancery office or embassy residence within a predictable space. The chancery was less than 10 minutes from the railroad station, so this meant no waiting for people either going or coming. The time saved meeting and speeding visitors was incalculable. What a contrast with Geneva and Zurich, whose people had long tedious drives to and from airports and, only too frequently, prolonged hours and waits if schedules were not being met. I had seen something in Tehran of trips to and waits at the airport, but it was nothing like Western Europe. The consul general in Geneva or his deputy seemed to spend half their time going or coming from the airport. It was a necessary function for ranking officials frequently to meet various visitors, which only too often could not be delegated. We were alert that it could pique the traveler, who might consider he should be met by the principal officer or his deputy, and there were stories of those who considered they should have this courtesy.

One of my duties encompassed new staff arrivals. It was my practice to meet them and, aside from generalities, to give some informal guidance. The young marines I especially wanted to see get off on the right foot, so there was one unvarying comment. Given Switzerland's accessibility, if the young fellows wanted to kick up their heels, not to let the home town down, but go to another city.

Typifying our role in assisting Americans was the instance of an American fundamentalist minister and his wife who were brought to me by the vice consul. They needed help to remain in Switzerland, for their residence in a Catholic canton was jeopardized. Naturally they had sought adherents there, and this conflicted with the Swiss, who were always careful not to upset the religious balance between cantons. They proved to be a good hearted couple, easy to talk to, and they had not understood their problem was, for the Swiss, political. We spoke of home. The minister was from Germantown, Pennsylvania, and had attended high school there. We looked at each other more closely. I said, "Francis," and he, "Roy." We were high school friends, Francis Schaeffer and I. We helped them get residence in a Protestant canton, from where they went on to establish in Europe and the United States a group of religious shelters called L'Abri, which has done good work. His wife, Edith, has carried on.

Two episodes concerned our staff. Lew Bowden, a political section officer, was engaged to a charming and very pretty Yugoslav girl from his previous post. The procedures were in course for the bureaucratic approval of their marriage, and the young fellow was sweating it out. It continued still later in her taxing formal interview with some security people in Washington when I was there, after which I joined the successful fiancee in bar lounge scotches. I was drinking for Virginia and myself as well. Another political officer, who did not seem representative for labor reporting, I thought needed to broaden his horizons. He would have been more comfortable in dealing with the Political Department, but he took on the job, made his fresh contacts, and did very well with the new field.

In the office I built a good relationship with various components of the embassy because of our size, and followed their workings easily. The economic section was the most important and its head, Doug Henderson, very competent. Still I found myself serving as a buffer between the staff and the ambassador and in helping to relieve some of the strains which arose from Frances's application to details. One section chief plaintively confided whenever he heard the ambassador's cheery voice on the phone he had a sinking sensation with the accompanying thought, "What have I done wrong now?" Because of Switzerland's size and the ease of transport, it was simple to have our consular officers traveling to or from Bern. Certainly the three principal consular officers were different types. Our Geneva representative easily handled the mainly protocol matters and representation affairs (official-social) there. Zurich was run by an old-line consular officer, who ran a tight shop in the economic capital of Switzerland. A non-career vice consul headed our Basel office, which was of declining importance and shortly after my time was closed. I remarked the diplomatic turn with which Geneva would stamp its affairs contrasted with the sometimes abrupt but effective style out of Zurich. Both were good size offices, and it required some attention and visits to keep things running smoothly between us all.

Under the travel grant program our excellent Geneva public affairs officer nominated an editor deemed somewhat anti-American, arguing we should not only accept the converted, but dare to name independent minded grantees. The ambassador was not convinced, but after my investigation with the political section and our clearance, the editor had his American travel. As Garnish later reported, it was one of the best grants we proposed, for the editor saw our country and became strongly pro-American.

At Frances's residence we were there often with her diverse guests, when at such times she accorded my request to sit next to her mother, a lively, really amiable old lady, which meant on one side I had assured good company. There were congressmen, singly and in groups, and private and public figures. Dr. Milton Eisenhower, for one, was an intelligent man who had moved to Johns Hopkins as president to be near his brother to give regular advice.

Like other peoples, the Swiss have two facets, one seen by tourists and the other by foreign residents. It was a surprise to learn that no diplomats then used the Bern cream or butter, because some came from tuberculosis infected cattle. Swiss farmers had stubbornly resisted having any of their suspect stock destroyed to make their herds fully certified, so we found ourselves using only Danish butter, boiling milk or using it powdered, just as we had in Iran. We heard of two instances of children of diplomats who were said to have contracted TB, presumably from local dairy products. This practice we could not understand. Being preoccupied with the tourist trade, the Swiss sometimes went to great lengths to hide what might be considered normal information. In the coming summer of our arrival there was a major polio epidemic in Bern which crested when we were in the U.S. on a delayed home leave. As told to me, there was not a line about the epidemic in the newspapers, the swimming pool adjacent to the chancery continued open, and the number of patients grew in the hospitals.

The Swiss have a deservedly good reputation in other areas, so this serves to round out what is either good or undesirable in their society. There is no doubt that they are well-ordered. Bern is a quiet town, so quiet that apartment house dwellers then complained to the authorities if someone drew bath water after 10:00 p.m. Naturally, loud radios and things of that sort were under a similar ban. It had its good points when our baby, Janice, escaped from the side yard and wandered down the street. She was picked up by a Swiss lady, who called the authorities, and we retrieved her at a station house surrounded by intrigued police.

Bern had a well-established old aristocracy built upon the long history of the canton, at one point the most influential in the Confederation. A sign of this was the club in which ranking diplomats were welcome, called La Grande Societe. Only in Bern could it be so named! The city itself was an attractive town, particularly in the old quarter with its centuries-old buildings and covered walkways as protection against the weather. The hardy geranium was the favorite flower, found in boxes along windows and on street lamps. Then by the Aare river, which curled around the old town, was the bear pit with several bears kept as symbols of the origin of the city's name. Swiss weather in the great central valley, the heart of the country, was notoriously poor, and it was frequently overcast and rainy in Bern. However, some days through the summer the clouds would roll away and there would be the magnificent spectacle of the Bernese Alps stretched white and jagged across the blue skyline.

An interesting aspect of the Swiss federal system is that the people are not citizens of Switzerland, but of the cantons in which they reside. If a Swiss moves from Geneva to Bern, he must get residence approval from Bern Canton, and to vote there must become a citizen of that canton. Each country has its singularities, and Switzerland has its share.

Naturally I got to know many official and private Swiss and to learn the workings of their government. The apex was seven Federal councilors, each of whom controlled a major department and on a seniority basis served as Swiss president for one year. The Political Department handled foreign affairs and Max Petitpierre was its head. He was a fine man, and throughout Frances Willis' tour of duty we had excellent relations with him. I was later told, when Frances's tour ended and in an unprecedented gesture, all seven councilors came to the farewell lunch given by Petitpierre. She had a keen personal sense of dedication in pursuing American-Swiss interests, and in being able to do and say the right thing that gained her their regard.

Finally the summer arrived, when the family could take deferred home leave. Virginia and I and the three girls stopped first in Norfolk to see my folks. Here illness hit us. First Janice, and then April and Lucy came down with bad cases of chicken pox, each at intervals of some 10 days. At any rate, we were immobilized for 6 weeks, and there went home leave. We saw much television and on occasion got to the beach, but it was hard on the girls. By the time we regained Switzerland, Virginia and I felt relieved. There was compensation, an uninterrupted year in Switzerland, which saw our fourth daughter, Hope, born. Virginia was overeating during pregnancy, and her Swiss doctor made no effort, such as an American would, to put her on a regime. When Hope was born, the doctor gave an unnecessary shot to hasten delivery and promptly left for a Zurich meeting without notifying his assistant, who belatedly rallied around at the clinic-hospital. Subjectively and perhaps unjustly we had a mixed opinion of Swiss medicine.

At the time of Hope's birth, I searched for a special gift for Virginia. As I passed a jewelry store, I saw a gold soccer ball strung on a watch chain in the window. Struck by an idea, I entered and asked the jeweler if he could outline the continents on a gold ball and embed four diamond chips in appropriate locales. Intrigued, he took the assignment and marked Bucharest, Philadelphia, Tehran, and Bern, the birthplaces of our four daughters, on a charm bracelet for Virginia.

Traveling in Switzerland was a pleasure, especially after our home leave debacle. In the more relaxing environment we were tasting, Frances, Virginia and myself took a few trips together. One was to Glarus canton, when it was having its annual open assembly of citizens to pass on local laws. It was a colorful ceremony in the little town, the nucleus of the tiny canton, and all the male citizens participated, dressed in their Sunday black, while we watched from windows and balconies in the hotel across the street. I enjoyed Geneva as a cosmopolitan city, which at the same time had all the advantages of a reasonably small town. There were the mountain resorts and the drives up remote valleys with their rocky watercourses, high bluff waterfalls, and chalets. In the spring and summer it was refreshing to take the funiculars, ski lifts in the winter, to see the flowers, and the mountain distances. In the winter there were locales like Zermatt under the Matterhorn, reached by cog railway, where winter scenery was at its best. Such places as Lugano on a hill-ringed lake in the Ticino, with its mild climate on the southern slopes of the Alps and palmettos the year round, came to be one of our favorite spots. The trips were on weekends, with an extra day thrown in, but we did have one leave before Frances left for a United Nations General Assembly session. For about a week we traveled in northern Italy, especially Venice, where a then-pregnant Virginia was given solicitous attention by the gondoliers, and extended this to some Po Valley cities and Trieste to see my old Tehran deputy, Mike Gannett. Rarely we might take a long weekend in southern Germany, where we were aware of the small size of western Europe and that, pleasantly, we were at the hub.

Skiing was a passion. The Swiss, no matter how many injuries, would come back for more. At lunch the attractive wife of a Swiss banker once regretted to me that she had finally given up skiing after having broken the same leg three times. I was impressed. Others were not so fortunate, for there were stories of inadequate care at some of the resort areas. Our Americans, of course, tried it every free weekend. A torn ankle ligament skiing in the Japan Alps years before impelled me to forego, and Virginia felt no desire to attempt it. It was just as well, for in the winter there were so many legs in casts hobbling around the chancery that the ambassador and I were on the verge of declaring an American ski moratorium.

Swiss hospitality, when they came to know you, was genuine. We also came to identify temperament with the area of Switzerland. Generally, German speaking Swiss were more reserved, the French cantons more open, and the Ticino, the Italian canton, very Latin. Somehow, despite their own internal quarrels and regional dislikes, which they freely admit, the Swiss kept together in such a way that some of us came to consider the entire country as a single working corporation. The Swiss pointed with pride that they had no trade tariffs, but omitted that none were needed. If, for example, you wanted to sell American shirts, you accepted the rules of the Swiss shirt association. These, not mysteriously, meant that there was no price competition. When one economic interest was adversely affected, the others would circle. In all, it was a remarkable achievement for a state without natural resources other than the abilities of its people and the scenery.

To point the difference between our activities in Tehran and Bern there was the issue of American duties on Swiss watches. It was the main problem in our Swiss relations, for they feared a possible American tariff on their watches could seriously impede the industry. With the revival of Western Europe, the result of the Marshall Plan and its accompanying initiatives, the Swiss did not want to have their most important industry so handicapped, and they took the matter seriously. Frances understood their predicament and, honestly deeming it in our mutual interest, brought her abilities to bear. Her efforts were successful, and the Swiss government knew of her attitude and work. There was one night, however, that put international affairs in domestic proportion. Very late I was awakened by an embassy call reporting a NIACT (night action) cable, which meant I had to go the chancery. Virginia got the drift and sleepily remarked, "In Tehran being aroused means something like a coup. Here it means watches." I did not attempt in the pre-dawn to explain this as part of the Service's diversity.

In Tehran, I had noted a minutia of protocol. At some receptions, a senior officer's wife dispensed coffee and a more junior handled tea. Coffee ranked tea. From Miss Willis I learned more. After installing her in the senior car place, the right rear, I would walk around to mine, on the left. Similarly, the right side of sofas was hers. These diplomatic niceties seemingly served in our nationalist era. Representatives of mini and mega states, using seniority symbols, had the same status. Not only nationalism, but human nature was pacified.

National day receptions are the featured method of establishing an identity within a diplomatic community, and in Bern there were an unusual number of diplomatic missions. Such occasions were marked by a receiving line headed by the ambassador, the deputy, and senior military attachés, who welcomed the guests and received their congratulations on the holiday. Frances Willis, invariably punctilious, made her one protocol error. July 4th fell on a Sunday, and she changed the reception date. Inadvertently it was the national day of a Latin American mission possessed of Latin pride. Too late, her reception set, Frances learned of the mistake and it was here I added another to my miscellany of duties. Our reception started earlier than the other, and Virginia and I broke off to hurry to the Latin celebration. It turned out to be quite a party, with plenty of verve, and to show our goodwill, we were among the last to leave in the late hours. Our national reputation, in measure, was redeemed.

A frustrating aspect came when the ambassador insisted upon preparing detailed separate instructions for the guidance of the staff of the embassy and the information of the consulates, which ranged through such varied topics as security and protocol. My fellow sufferer was the administrative officer, John Crawford. He was most effective in the same position in Helsinki, and the ambassador had asked for him. We became good friends, but the details frustrated him too. Our officers in Geneva and Zurich, however, greeted these efforts with smiles.

One early Saturday evening, Frances, John and I had worried the draft staff instruction on protocol for five hours. On leaving the residence, John was groggy, and for the first time I came down with the symptoms of a migraine headache; proof that it can arise from containing stress. In the most trying days of Bucharest and Tehran, I never had one. Totally unexpectedly, I found that I was more engaged in what might be termed busy work rather than substance. Office detail tensions of which Frances was not aware could not be removed, because it was her working style. Mulling over that period I can see a fine woman as my chief, but in my position one difficult to work for.

The occasion came when I had the opportunity to sit down with Frances and to talk in open and reasonable terms, for she was such a person, concerning my frustrations as the middleman. Some Rumanian exiles to dramatize their situation had raided the local Rumanian communist legation, and it had taken Swiss army tanks to get them out. We were attending a small dinner when we heard the distinctive sounds of tanks, and recognized these from Tehran. Subsequently I learned the raid had been done under the leadership of some exiles I had known in Rumania. I was in a position to give an evaluation and, if Frances decided to be helpful, to the Swiss as well. However, the ambassador handled the whole business herself, perhaps welcoming the change and forgetful of my Rumanian background. It was the aftermath that brought our discussion. This proved helpful, and I could see a better attitude and more regard for speaking up. In her lifetime we remained friendly.

Among the many good things about Switzerland were the embassy friends we acquired. Col. Howard Burris, the air attaché, and his wife were most congenial. As everyone knows, there is a CIA segment in an embassy led by a station chief, in this case known to the Swiss and others. Both he and his wife had been educated at the Curtis Institute of Music in Philadelphia, she studying piano and he voice, and later he became a music critic. War and its aftermath found them in Europe. They too, were interesting companions and, with the Burrises, we six got around. Through his wife, my friend was awakened to jazz and became an enthusiast, reflecting attitudes then strong among European youth. When we heard Lionel Hampton in Bern, it was a mild surprise that we six were the oldest in the hall. We had virtually the same sensation in Zurich, listening to Count Basie, when it was fun having homeside talk with the jazzmen. Lionel had told us after his concert, as an old rhythm and blues man, "You've got to have the melody and the beat. If you don't, it ain't jazz." When my music critic friend in his exuberance exclaimed to Basie over drinks that one of his selections reminded him of a Bach fugue, the Count looked puzzled and said simply, "I think I'll just let that one pass." He didn't know what the man was talking about.

We had a variety of Swiss associates, ranging from the heads of companies like Emmenthaler cheese to Oerlikon anti-aircraft weapons. However, a youngish Bern businessman and I had a common interest in jazz, and he mentioned that a small, well known European group was appearing at a local nightclub, which by Bern standards had a reputation. After a formal male dinner at La Grande Societé and on Beat's signal we left for the club. I was then chargé and using the ambassador's driver, so I gave him the destination, which he acknowledged in a deep tone. Then I told him he need not wait, which he acknowledged in a still deeper tone. The jazzmen were excellent musicians, but I suspect I earned points as a playboy of sorts among our Swiss staff.

While on entertainers, I should mention Americans like the Martha Graham Dance group (she was, from her manager's privately declared tribulations, and to use an old phrase, a caution), the "Porgy and Bess" company, and the New York Philharmonic; all in Switzerland under official sponsorship. When as chargé I gave an obligatory post-concert reception for the orchestra attended by ranking Swiss, the latter were dressed formally from the concert. Our American musicians were so informal some appeared to be race track touts; their way of relaxing and getting out of uniform. Dimitri Mitropoulos, the New York conductor, featured as a final selection the last Shostakovich symphony, not known for tranquillity. In the small Swiss hall it reverberated, and I saw Political Department people wincing. When later I asked about his choice he reaffirmed the artist by saying, "I like it."

It is satisfying, after seeing Foreign Service people serve with you, to hear of their behavior in later settings. Joe Mendenhall, here a political officer and later an ambassador, shocked President Kennedy and his National Security Council by reporting that we were losing the political war in Vietnam. Lew Bowden, an Oklahoman, was a multi-linguist and later expert on Russia. A quiet and steady first post vice consul, Bill Edmondson, proved to have a later career as an ambassador. Mavericks, the unconventional ones, I came to believe were the salt of the Service, and wherever possible I tried to support them. I could have been put off partly by what I saw as the growth of bureaucracy in the Service, and I had some successes.

Again I refer to my diplomatic colleagues. The first was a Scot, a former fighter pilot who couldn't stand cold, and who spent a wartime leave at home in his warm flight suit. The Frenchman, a former colonel, was one I would want in my corner in a difficult situation. The Spanish minister was an amiable type, who gave us a story. Like many of us, he was not relaxed about the Swiss cost of living, which the prosperous burghers undoubtedly felt justified by residence in their country. The minister had a family, and after recounting some practical problems, concluded with a sigh, "This means I'll have to sell another Goya."

There were two major conferences at Geneva in which we were involved. The first international atomic energy conference directed much attention to American activities, and because of the scope of the meeting the ambassador and myself had essentially protocol responsibilities. It meant being present at proceedings, particularly when the Indian representative, Dr. Bhabba, impressively urged international cooperation. At its close, Chairman Strauss of our Atomic Energy Commission told me he was especially pleased with the conference's success.

The second big event was the political summit meeting with Eisenhower, Bulganin, Anthony Eden, and the Frenchman, Edgar Faure. Given the cold war developments that preceded it, there was what might be termed hype over the declared changed atmosphere, labeled "the spirit of Geneva." which evaporated in a month with the announced Soviet arms sales to Nasser's Egypt. I met President Eisenhower twice, in the conference flow. Still, Frances Willis, from our own and Swiss protocol participated in some top social affairs of the Summit and made an excellent impression as the sole ranking woman official there. Virginia was technically the next American woman, and attended dinner with top conference ladies. Some were so bejeweled (one wore an orchid brooch in diamonds) that Virginia was dazzled, but she did create a congenial topic when it was known she was pregnant.

In September the ambassador left for the UN General Assembly in New York, and, aside from earlier short periods as chargé, there was a stretch of four months until her return in January. Things went well in the office and constituent posts during her absence, and I think that morale was better, since the staff could figuratively catch its breath despite the fact that we in Switzerland were undergoing an inspection.

A Foreign Service inspection can vary with the inspectors and posts. Three posts at which I served had been scrutinized by Washington inspectors, and Bern was the fourth. An inspection at that time was usually conducted by two officers, one on the substantive and one on the administrative side. Here the substantive head of the team had been a classmate at the War College, but we had moved in different circles. The ambassador arranged to meet him and his assistant a day before her departure, when they were to start with a constituent post, and I took over from there to see they got everything needed. The gratifying result of their final report was that, thanks to our joint efforts, we were a model of a small embassy. We saw the inspectors off, and the administrative officer and I were glad to have come through so well as a team. However, I was in for a surprise a year and a half later when I learned what the inspector had written on me.

Frances Willis had a brief holiday in California after the General Assembly, and then, dedicated as she was, flew to Bern just before New Year's to be present for the typical Swiss custom of the induction of the new president on New Year's morning. Only in Switzerland - and I went through the procedure twice - did the authorities expect the diplomatic corps to turn out to congratulate and to be received by the new president at 9:00 a.m. on New Year's morning in white tie and tails. Our custom was to assemble at the residence at least by 8:30 a.m., go over at 9:00 a short distance to the government building, join our fellow diplomats, many bleary-eyed and still in their New Year's Eve clothes, return to the residence for a glass of champagne, and then go back to bed. Just before the UN General Assembly session ended in December, however, the ambassador had phoned me urgently from New York. She had just heard from Loy Henderson, who was back in the Department as under secretary for Administration, to say he wanted to take me from Bern for work with an interagency organization in Washington. Distressed, she plaintively asked if I had requested a transfer and if I knew the change was coming. I, of course, was able to tell her I had been perfectly happy, especially since our frank talk, to continue serving with her, and had indicated to no one that I wanted a transfer. She could take this at full value, and sounded better and only a little disturbed at the prospect of having to break in a new DCM.

What she said quickly proved true. A telegram requested my prompt arrival in Washington for assignment to a garbled position and organization I could not recognize. Then after an exchange, the Department agreed I should wait until the return of the ambassador. The ambassador returned for New Year's, had a few working days, and gave a good review of what she intended to say on my performance. I left the post with two suitcases, while my family remained to pack and to follow. It did strike me that I was leaving in the 23rd month of my assignment, and only then I recalled the earlier informal forecast that I would be in Bern no more than two years. Nevertheless, it was a curious business, the need for haste, and this unusual sounding Operations Coordinating Board for which I was destined.

NSC-OCB, Defense-State demonstration cruise on U.S.S. Franklin D. Roosevelt

# CHAPTER 11

# OPERATIONS AND POLICIES: WASHINGTON & THE OCB

## January 1956 - July 1959

*The domestic calm of the Eisenhower years continued. The Soviet Union made its Sputnik launching a space challenge and Castro's Cuba became a Latin American irritant to U.S. policy. The two 1956 crises of Hungary and Suez showed the U.S. unable to roll back communism, as well as the disruptive dimension of the Mideast question. Communist China endured Mao's Great Leap Forward, while in South-east Asia there was a rebuilding of communist energies and, almost unnoticed, U.S. political-military activities. Two U.S. staff organizations, policy and operations, worked in tandem to handle national security issues: the National Security Council (NSC) and the Operations Coordinating Board (OCB). For three and a half years I was deputy and acting executive officer (staff director) of the OCB, including two years as operations adviser to the NSC Planning Board, which prepared NSC policies. This gave insights into top level treatment of foreign policy and national security.*

State Department people knew something about my new organization, but Loy Henderson, who had talked to Frances Willis, was away. The OCB was on Jackson Place, a side of Lafayette Park across from the White House. I went there directly and met its staff chief, Elmer Staats, who briefed me. The OCB evolved from an Administration organization with a more formidable name, the Psychological Strategy Board. Transmuted into the OCB, it backstopped our national security policies by coordinating specific major operations in their behalf and developing interagency operations plans, which aided our international affairs in the jump from policy to operation. The Board followed the effectiveness of policies and usually advised the National Security Council semi-annually if any major changes were needed. It all seemed quite logical.

I also was encouraged by the seeming calibre of Elmer Staats, called OCB's executive officer. Later I learned he had been deputy director of the Budget Bureau (later the Office of Management and Budget) under President Truman and had been named by Eisenhower to the present position. Still later, I found him a serious man, outstanding in negotiating patience and in careful handling of agendas, initially reserved but excellent to work with and unsurpassed as a staff executive. In the future he was to be Budget Bureau director and then Comptroller General of the United States. At that interview, I learned why I had been named deputy executive officer. My State predecessor, a very good man, did not have a compatible relation with Deputy Secretary Hoover, the OCB chairman. Since he was being moved, Loy Henderson proposed me.

Personal security clearances for comparable positions had multiplied and Elmer had already begun actions for mine. Every Foreign Service Officer after investigation is accorded a top secret clearance, but this position had at least four more, each requiring an investigation. My old college friend, A.K. Bowles, was with the F.B.I., and to simplify the investigative drudgery, with each obligatory clearance form I added his name. Now when we met in Washington, in pure curiosity he asked where I was working, for it seemed every time he turned around there was an agent inquiring about Melbourne.

The Board had State's Deputy Secretary as its chairman, while the others included the Deputy Secretary of Defense, the Director of Central Intelligence, the Director of the International Cooperation Administration (ICA- economic aid), the Director of the U.S. Information Agency (USIA),the Special Assistant to the President for International Security Affairs, and with time, a presidential Special Assistant for Operations Coordination. This meant five national security action agencies and two presidential staff agents. Very quickly I was told about the financial emphasis of the Administration and the strong influence of Treasury Secretary George Humphrey upon the president, so it was not surprising that the Treasury Deputy Secretary and a Budget Bureau representative, initially observers, grew to be de facto Board members. Like the National Security Council, when an issue was a major interest of another agency, illustratively the Department of Commerce, it would have a representative at Board staffing stages.

As I settled into my office next to Elmer Staats, it was a unique environment for an FSO. Our organization had regular inter-relations with the national security agencies at all substantive levels, from agency heads and deputies to office directors and country desk officers. The scope and variety of American government international activities and the ways policies were formed initially seemed diffuse, but this was the American government in action. Gradually patterns appeared and meanings clarified. The OCB had tremendous range, for national security policies, aside from those for covert action, generally were assigned to it. This meant the Board could go from outer space policy to Antarctica or to a particular area or country. Because of the dimensions of the mission, its organization and channeling of priorities were important. An outline of the OCB's activities, I came to recognize, was a picture of American decision making in a vital and long neglected aspect of policy-operations, the systematic follow-up. As any veteran bureaucrat knows, the most difficult aspect is the unremitting pursuit of an agreed policy objective. Unless there is a means to require full attention, such activities can lose impetus or become distorted. The span of the Board's operational net was intended to avoid this, and to be done through three levels: the Board members, their staff assistants, and the interagency working groups of full time officials involved with each policy. State almost always chaired these groups, aided by our staff people working with the chairmen in drafting operating papers, identifying issues, and handling schedules and distribution.

The Board Assistants held weekly meetings, which Elmer or I chaired, as a preview of the Board's agenda the following week. They not only cross-checked with each other if they sensed impending operational issues or policy review needs, but they interviewed their agency working group people, saw how the interests of respective agencies were projected, and, fully knowledgeable before Board meetings, briefed their members and made staff recommendations. The chairman of a working group, from agencies directly responsible for implementing a policy, usually was a State office director or sometimes its deputy assistant secretary, and the operations plan it devised with Board approval served as a practical document. Over time, there came to be at least forty-odd working groups and committees backstopping the variety of NSC policies.

Our OCB staff held steady despite the increased volume of work: twenty officer/professional positions, half Civil Service and half national security agencies people, with Elmer from the top of the Civil Service and I from State. There were four State FSOs mingled with those from Defense, the CIA, Information Agency, and occasionally the International Cooperation Administration, who were assigned to area, functional/scientific, and intelligence sectors. At first, the OCB and NSC staffs were separate, but a reorganization which proved beneficial placed us within the NSC structure, meaning both staffs were jointly served administratively. The NSC had its executive secretary, while the OCB staff was led by Elmer.

Initially our Jackson Place offices were two old residences abutting the rear of Blair House, but when we merged within the NSC, we moved across Pennsylvania Avenue into the old State Department quarters known as the Executive Offices Building. It was familiar ground to be in Old State and to pass where I worked nearly eighteen years before. The ceiling fans were gone and air conditioners were in the windows. The barroom swinging doors remained and the heavy mahogany doors with their pressed metal, U.S. seal doorknobs. Fireplaces were rarely used and generally blocked, but a few in ranking offices were open, such as Nelson Rockefeller's, who as a presidential aide fed cellophane wrapped fireplace logs. Despite the changes, I always felt at home there.

While I had followed Senator McCarthy's assault upon alleged State Department crypto-communists and had much commentary from friends, the wounding impact upon the Department was clear only when I served in Washington. We had been aware of the high stakes involved in our Iranian actions from the dimension of the cold war. A misstep could, through Iran, lose the Mideast for the free world, with inevitable accusations. Our success in removing the Mosadeq imposed challenge gave small comfort when the McCarthy campaign was unabated. I was in Tehran and Bern, with only a brief home leave, during the worst of these excesses. Now in Washington I saw the effects upon the Service of McCarthy's ravages. The high morale of the Foreign Service was shaky. Respected officers had been branded as security risks, notably those in the Chinese language specialty, and it was years before their vindication. Reactions were serious or pathetically absurd, for I noted several years passed before red neckties reappeared in State. Of graver consequence, the Foreign Service, without a constituency and with a role grossly misunderstood by the public, acquired a varying presidential distrust and a reputation for being soft on our policy interests. Some see other plausible reasons, but I believe the phenomenon was one contribution to the long range decline of the policy importance of the State Department.

Soon I was caught up in the OCB schedule, whereby every Wednesday, after a sensitive agenda and private luncheon meeting, the Board met in a conference room on the executive floor of the State Department. Behind the members at such meetings were the Board assistants, where at my first meeting I was delighted to see the State assistant, Arthur Richards, my old Tehran DCM. Arthur had two FSO aides, others normally one, for State was heavily involved in a leadership role. In assignment changes, three of the State side, including Arthur himself, became ambassadors, and another, Jerry O'Connor, who became a good friend, was only stopped by lung cancer. As we worked with our own staff, we also coordinated with the Board assistants, and naturally I was close to Arthur Richards and to Jerry O'Connor when he succeeded Arthur. Together we sought to discourage unnecessary paper work, but the volume of policies and operations plans and reviews had a schedule not fully attendant upon priority needs.

When the Board moved into its open meeting, the sequence went like this. An operation plan, its semi-annual review or a proposed policy change would have been developed by the concerned working group. The Board listened to a working group chairman, discussed the issues, and the staff made a brief recorded action decision. A weekly Board agenda item was a record of all working group activities, done by our staff men consulting with the chairmen. Christian Herter, Mr. Hoover's successor, used to say if a working group did not meet at least monthly to handle a substantive question there was no need for the working group, or very possibly the policy. At the Board either Elmer or myself, sitting opposite the chairman, would direct his attention to the agenda, later prepare and get approval for the record of actions, and keep the process moving to cover all that was projected.

I am not sure how Mr. Hoover viewed the OCB, for I was not in formal briefing proximity to him. He conducted himself and the Board's agenda well, as I saw at the meetings and at the few luncheons I attended during his term. I was more familiar with the system by Mr. Herter's chairmanship, and I had more briefing contacts and luncheon meetings, aside from regular meetings, which aided me in knowing him. He believed the OCB was an essential national security tool, and supported it whenever necessary. As well, he asserted the foreign policy leadership role of the State Department. Mr. Herter was Board chairman a good while before becoming Secretary of State and I came to admire him as an intelligent and perceptive gentleman. He had a quiet manner, but there was plenty of firmness in his makeup if this should be needed. Earlier governor of Massachusetts and a longtime congressman, I believe all his associates were gratified to see him become Secretary of State. He became ever-more crippled by arthritis, until he had to use metal canes, but this painful condition was never reflected in his temperament.

A regular State inspection found our office being surveyed in its State aspects, and here fate caught up with me. The congenial inspector in informal talk hinted that I would be well advised to check with Personnel about my Bern inspection report. The personnel officer, an old acquaintance, was a civil servant there since my Service entry, so he let me read the Bern inspector's report, while shaking his head over its contents. After all, these matters are highly subjective, but I could not recognize my personality and the effectiveness of my operations from the report. I still wonder about the man's motives. One, a conjecture, was that he had resented my wartime marriage with half-American Virginia, while he in London waited until the war's end before marrying his English fiancee. He underestimated my penchant for logic over bureaucracy. Frances Willis, of course, had given me a good final evaluation. The personnel officer, as concerned as I, said that even at this late date I should file a rebuttal statement. Without illusions as to its short-term benefits, I prepared one carefully that he thought satisfactory. Thus I had to cope with a first bump in what I had come to recognize as a good career. I never met the Bern inspector afterwards, although I saw him once distantly at a large reception, but awhile later, traveling on a passenger liner, the troubled man disappeared in a quiet sea.

The incident made me see the Service's vulnerability to bureaucracy. With my Ph.D. I had another profession. Yet the Foreign Service was my career, and as long as I derived personal satisfaction from the work I intended to remain. Time might produce a sufficient number of good reports as an overlay. My promotion to O-2 ironically had been announced the day after my arrival in Bern, and I could now expect an interval before another. There is some truth that adversity can have its beneficial side, whereupon I took a personnel course in Washington to give me better tools and turned to the OCB, my current assignment, as I put the bump behind me.

The private luncheon meetings preceding the formal Board meetings were the highlight of the week. Invited were only the Board members, Treasury's deputy secretary, an occasional guest concerned about a special matter, and either Elmer or myself. The members discussed sensitive items, munched salads and sandwiches, enjoyed the company, and felt at ease. Elmer and I briefly recorded the actions taken and strictly limited their distribution. To see these men under such conditions, to learn what to remember and when to forget, was illuminating.

As the holders of these top positions changed over three and one half years, the gallery became fairly numerous, providing snapshots of American politics and politicians, and of bureaucracy in action. Illustrative of the many professional stories told at the luncheons was one by Mr. Herter. He was a congressman when World War II began, and the committee on which he served was setting war production goals. It pulled "out of the hat" the figure that we would produce 50,000 aircraft yearly. President Roosevelt seized on the numbers, and Mr. Herter and the committee were gratified when that magic figure was reached.

Given the size of bureaucracy and the many issues stemming from an American decade-old, post World War II position, it is not surprising that our staff operations failed to affect some major activities such as arms control. A leading Foreign Service figure once confirmed that in this important field there was no OCB guidance. There were other instances, one cannot doubt, notably in Latin America, whose assistant secretary, with other help, steadfastly discouraged it. As a staff organization the OCB sought to fulfill its assigned responsibilities. On adjusting to the home working environment and accepting government issues as part of the landscape, I grew more comfortable with our variety and my staff role gained in depth. It was accepted, for instance, for me to cross check with the State men on significant matters and get their perspectives on issues, which I discussed with Elmer Staats. We could never forget that it was our staff responsibility to do all we could to expedite business and not put sand in the gears, so this tactic was valuable.

State and Defense were the linchpins of national security operations. Both departments knew it and were judicious in interacting for good results. The problem of getting other agencies to differentiate between the substantive and mainly editorial was not easily overcome, but as the Board assistants sought more action, this defect was generally remedied. Offhand, although there were natural differences that arose, given the variety of policies there were remarkably few significant issues that I recall between the two main departments. The CIA moved in synchronization, and in general so did the economic aid and information agencies. This is not surprising, if one considers the issues that were threshed out in elaborating the NSC policies. As I survey it, the headaches Treasury and the Budget Bureau sponsored appear as the most significant. Each Administration gave different emphases to the power and authority of its major agents. Theoretically I knew this, but reality gave it a visible cast. When at the OCB the Deputy Secretary of the Treasury or the Budget Bureau deputy expressed views, the table participants gave these due weight. Our next president regularly had the attorney general at his NSC meetings, congruous or not, but who incidentally was his brother.

How fortunate we were to have major international issues centered upon domestic financial questions. There were however, some serious challenges to the free world and to American international leadership. One major issue emerged when the Soviets launched Sputnik and stirred our media into charges that they were ahead in the space race. There were scientific committees that said otherwise, although we had been too financially prudent in meeting what the Soviets were intent upon making a space race. It was for America a fortunate era - the mid and late 50s. In adjusting to the financial emphasis, the OCB initiated an order of magnitude financial annex as standard practice for each operations plan. It was logical, but was distorted into a device for Treasury and Budget to monitor and criticize the national security agencies. The implication was that these spendthrifts had to be closely checked, else our international commitments would escalate beyond reason. Subjectively I assigned this as exactly what influential Treasury Secretary Humphrey wanted, for he also was the major voice over Budget. As a policy staffer my impression of Mr. Humphrey, once removed, is of an Administration figure who projected in simple terms the strategic atomic defense concept of more bang for the buck; reckoning atomic weapons as cheaper and thus better policy, omitting the rigidity and lack of flexibility this imposed. The Treasury secretary never appeared at the OCB, but his representative was an active presence. The latter was personally pleasant, but followed the policy line of his superior, as did his Board assistant and working group representatives. It was an impressive lesson on the influence a major personality could exert upon a key portion of our government.

Years later in a quiet evening in Baghdad, my guest, John J. McCloy, a prominent Republican adviser and a man with an outstanding record of bipartisan public service, asked what I thought to be the chief deficiency of the Eisenhower Administration in foreign affairs. From my OCB lens I indicated that it seemed Treasury and Budget were really insisting upon one hundred percent "gold coverage," in that any prospective activity or potential commitment should not cost money unless clearly available or in prospect. In foreign affairs normally there would be enterprises in which a large bill need not be a foregone conclusion or in which strategic benefits outweighed balance sheet costs. In their stand the financial twins were violating their own banking code, which insisted upon only a minute percentage of gold coverage for a transaction. If American activities or interests suddenly swelled in cost beyond what the operating agencies held feasible or effective for a policy, this signified a major change in the world picture. In turn, as in finance, this meant a reexamination and reappraisal by those with the responsibilities. The argument made sense to Mr. McCloy.

It may be the financial inhibitions on operations impeded the OCB and encouraged what I came to call "home and mother" language in operations plans, which could replace real substance with paper generalities. While this was capable of reform, one of the later Kennedy Administration complaints of the OCB was to brand it a paper pushing outfit, so its reformers unwisely threw the entire organization overboard. From then on it was improvisation. Still, with sufficient occasion to be heartening, there had been Board initiatives that materially aided our national interests. My attention is drawn to major issues, when operations plans were devised to see urgent problems through a definable time. The most successful means was to assign an agency full responsibility under those conditions, with the others expected to extend the fullest cooperation. In my memory these always worked, as an encouraging signal of the impact of single agency action with supervisory control.

During my assignment there were four relatively anonymous special assistants to the President for national security affairs, of whom the last two, Bobby Cutler and Gordon Gray, served longest. (Henry Kissinger later dropped the "special" and the anonymity.) Bobby Cutler was a Boston banker and worked earlier on national security questions for the president. He was articulate, a bit of an actor, intelligent, and I liked him. Sometimes volatile with his staff, he would calm down quickly and get to the topic at hand. There was an echo from an old Service classmate. Bobby once asked me to come see him, and when I did, said quite seriously that his niece had recently become engaged to an FSO named Elim O'Shaughnessy. The family knew nothing about him, and he was asked to make government inquiries. I gave a glowing background, which should have helped ease domestic concerns, for Bobby seemed more relaxed. I never mentioned this to Elim, but smiled as he went his way. Gordon Gray was from a family in Reynolds Tobacco, who had been president of the University of North Carolina and Secretary of the Army. He was soft spoken, but knew his mind, and I thought actually got more accomplished than Bobby. I came to have a very high regard for him.

The second White House staff Board members, for operations coordination, were successively Fred Dearborn, an excellent man who died suddenly, and Karl Harr, competent in following the Gray lead. Defense Deputy Secretary Quarles was replaced by assistant secretary Manny Sprague, a man I had rapport with, pleasant and informed. The CIA director, Allen Dulles, I enjoyed. He was always alert and helpful with OCB objectives, and over the years we were friendly acquaintances. Of course, in the OCB his major agency actions were untouched, although certain operations plans could include the CIA. Economic aid was embodied in Director John Hollister, who had two top flight assistants. The information side, initially headed by Arthur Larson, was later led by a Foreign Service career ambassador, George V. Allen. I knew him from Yugoslav days, where he had been ambassador, and welcomed his genuine friendliness.

Our staff personnel after three and a half years made strong impressions, and a major personality was Ken Landon. He came from State when a personnel commission sought to bring all State Civil Service officers rapidly into the Foreign Service. The commission head recommending this was President Wriston of Brown University, so the process was known as "wristonization." Ken had been a missionary in Thailand, a professor at home, and during World War II organized a Thai intelligence and resistance organization. Thereafter in State he had been Thai desk officer, and in charge of Southeast Asian affairs. His wife, Margaret, a delightful woman, wrote the best selling book, "Anna and the King of Siam," from which the musical, "The King and I", was made. Unfortunately she had a rheumatic heart and could not live abroad. No exceptions being allowed, Ken could not take the conversion step. He was keen and articulate, sure of his ground, and a stimulating companion. Butt of jokes was his tender care of a tubbed, good sized avocado tree in his office, reminding me of Pat Kiley's banana shrub in Montreal. He was, in brief, good for our morale. Other staff men from the Civil Service and agencies were unquestioned assets. I cannot forget Charley Taquey of the economic sector, who remarked one day that he had discovered the key weakness in American policy. Unlike the British who merely wanted to be respected, "We Americans have political nymphomania. We want to be loved by everybody."

Government organization never stands still, but the continuing flux during my time made a clearer pattern. The President's special assistant for operations coordination, when established, was associated with Bobby Cutler, but he tried to focus on OCB matters. Elmer and I came to have a dual responsibility before each weekly meeting of briefing him and the Board chairman. There was a little tugging between State and the White House concerning the OCB after Mr. Herter became Secretary of State. Gordon Gray succeeded him as chairman and State's political undersecretary, Robert Murphy, became State's representative. The maneuver brought no personal problems, for I worked well with both men.

Bob Murphy was one of the finest diplomats and a man with an extraordinary record, who held the third slot in State as undersecretary for political affairs and shared a trait with Loy Henderson, in that he was very warm. Both got their career starts from World War I, when each had been ineligible for military service because of teenage injuries; Loy an arm and Bob an ankle. Just working for Murphy was a lift, and I remember his sensitivity some years later when my eldest daughter died. In a talk with Loy a few months before his end, he said he always considered Bob Murphy to be the better diplomat. There can be no more informed accolade.

Unmentioned until now was my two year coincident assignment for the OCB as operations adviser to the Planning Board. This latter was the last policy stop before the National Security Council, and its weekly meetings were chaired by the president's special national security affairs adviser. Others were the State representative, Bob Bowie, head of Policy Planning; an admiral from the Joint Chiefs; a Defense man; Bob Amory, deputy CIA director for Intelligence, with Bob Komer, a Lake Barcroft neighbor, as his staff man, and others from concerned agencies. It was most relevant for our OCB assignment to observe how the policies were developed and to alert our staff on future issues. Immersed as I was in operations, where we had similar problems, I fretted with bland language when it surfaced in policy drafts. This tended to express U.S. desires rather than realities and to use stock phrases for our objectives; again, "home and mother" language. When a policy was approved and assigned to the OCB, the practical situation might be out of focus with theoretical policy bases.

It was a cliche that bureaucracy avoided contentious issues, which in my intensive staff years came from complex causes. The money aspect has been referred to. There also were the unelaborated policy parameters of an Administration. During a review of a draft Basic National Security Policy at the Planning Board, there was a discussion on a policy point. Consultant John McCloy said softly that it was, of course, not feasible unless you had price controls. There was a silence until Bobby Cutler resumed the thread. In an OCB occasion under a Chairman Herter not intimidated by contentious issues, there was an important but forgotten division between State and Defense. In seeking clarity, both departments identified this and pressed through the special assistant for a presidential decision. I could sense a downcast Board when, at the weekly meeting, Bobby Cutler announced that the president had returned the issue with the request that the two agencies come to their own accommodation. I recalled Jack Kilgore's War College comment on the Columbia University president.

There still were major crises. In the autumn of 1956, October-November enfolded two major foreign policy issues for the United States. The first was the Suez crisis, when the French and British cooperated with Israel against Egypt.

Contingency planning in some instances can be valuable. We early knew that the situation was dangerous between Egypt and Israel, so in concert with high level intelligence, the Board, at a luncheon meeting, agreed to a working group consisting of the Near East director of State and his counterparts in Defense and the CIA, who with an OCB staff man would prepare a contingency plan for use in the event of an Arab-Israeli conflict. Contingency plans are a long standing Pentagon feature, but we had no idea, it proved, of the future dimensions of this one. It was kept quite close. When the Israelis invaded the Sinai, the plan surfaced and reportedly was accepted by Secretary Dulles for twenty four hours as an outline for actions, including draft Washington and UN statements. Then, as is the case with emergency contingencies, an upsetting element appeared. The plan was premised on UK-French cooperation with us, but they were working with the Israelis. It was a new ballgame. As we know, President Eisenhower was outraged at the concealment tactics of the British, French and Israelis, not least because the operation was occurring on the verge of the American presidential election, the first Tuesday in November wherein he was a second-term candidate. Strong action was imperative, and his harsh notes to America's NATO allies achieved a ready result.

The second coincident major crisis was Hungary, when the Soviets invaded the country and destroyed a newly dissident communist regime. This was a great shock to the West, since it threw down the gauntlet to any concept that the communist states of Eastern Europe then could be liberated from Soviet control. There was a very brief period, from OCB-Planning Board vantage points, when the Soviets seemed uncertain how to act. A mass exodus followed of Hungarians into Austria, where as refugees they were succored by various European governments and the United States.

Since my return to Washington I had maintained my friendship with Frank Wisner. As mentioned earlier, he and others in the Administration believed sincerely in the possible freedom rollback of European communism, and he had tailored his actions accordingly. The shock of inaction during the Hungarian uprising had been so severe that I believe it caused Frank's breakdown, which after an recuperative interval resulted in his later tragic death as a casualty of the cold war. Feelings ran high elsewhere in the West over the Hungarian crisis, and in both OCB and Planning Board meetings prominent members, although unclear of the means, voiced strong views on the need to support the Hungarians against Moscow. Clearly America was bogged down because of the Suez crisis and since we were at odds with both Great Britain and France. This forcefully exemplified a truism of American foreign policy, learned at that time by a future career ambassador, who told me our government machinery is geared to handle only one major crisis at a time.

Through constant tandem association I became convinced it is impractical to consider policy and operational planning in separate compartments. Given the pragmatic nature of American foreign policy and its response to stimuli on a shorter range basis, it made more sense for policy to be rooted in operational feasibilities, not only policy generalities. After seeing policy and operations in the form of working papers, I also radically concluded it was worth a trial to have a single basic national security policy document containing major, and more extensive, segments of realistic, regional and functional priorities, principles, and objectives. Operations plans and consequent agency roles could flow from these major segments. An objective of acting to "eliminate" a major ideological influence in an area or country could be treated as unrealistic, as the environment generally showed this to be. Time and effort expended on lengthy preparation of separate policy and operations papers might clash with the dynamics of foreign affairs, so that they might become partially obsolescent. If so, operators could not have full confidence in referring to them. An amalgam looked better.

At the NSC Planning Board, I listened to a lengthy debate around the immense table over the preamble of a regional policy paper. Its verbosity had all the pious generalities I detested. This time I commented that the Planning Board should have no illusions when the finally approved policy document was given as guidance to the operating agencies. The preamble could be expected to be completely ignored. There was a short period of silence and the Board resumed wrestling with the preamble! I should add that the forecast was accurate.

Having said the above, I must point to a signal contribution of the NSC in its elaboration of basic national security papers for Administration guidance. In the Eisenhower years I witnessed one in full cycle. To the handicaps of unclear general language, there were offsetting benefits. The most important was setting our national priorities by region and subject in clear terms, combined with general financial estimates for these priorities. These aspects alone made it worth while, as interests were debated and major issues decided. The completed document, presidentially approved after Council debate, served as a future policy benchmark of value. A crucial weakness when our government lacks general policy guidance is that it is obliged to improvise in a series of major fires. It should not be forgotten that there was no basic national security policy in the years 1961 to 1969. If Vietnam had been displayed as a priority with other U.S. policy interests, the discrepancy could have been apparent, despite the American psychological need to respond. Thereafter in the Nixon Administration's first eighteen months Henry Kissinger, for his reasons, made a great contribution in obliging the government to assess its priorities and return to basics.

As State sought to maintain its policy leadership, there were times when complaints that it was not doing this arose among the Board assistants. One vulnerable area was Latin America, where I mentioned that State succeeded in avoiding OCB assigned policies in the belief it retained greater freedom of action. This in the long run was dubious, for State's Achilles heel in Latin America, as elsewhere, was its lack of program funds, contrasted with the other relatively well financed operators who could have been harnessed. Here was State, chairman of the Board, the poor relation at the table. Its budget was small, with over half devoted to salaries and expenses. Program funds for operations produced influence and power, and State simply was not in the running. Illustrative of the funds problem a generation ago, I was told (not by Jack Iams) that when money for the high priority project of an electronic proof room in certain embassies was urgent, Secretary Herter made a decisive private decision. He deferred home leaves for some months to obtain the needed funds. As the cold war held its vigor and as policies expanded, particularly later, the louder came the cry of State's inability to lead in current needs. The personal influence of Secretary Dulles or of Bob Murphy temporarily masked this erosion, but it had some of us concerned. I raised this in my departure talk with Bob Murphy, who was hopeful that his regular White House association would help keep State in a suitable position.

In at least one policy instance the OCB was ahead of its time. With Southeast Asia in mind, and sparked by Ken Landon, we prepared a regional study of Buddhism in its nationalist, political aspects. Religion in politics was a new subject to secular minded Americans like our Board members, who did not grasp the subject's value until Buddhism came to be appreciated as a major political element in Vietnam. Islamic fundamentalism even later demonstrated how far in advance we actually were. It is characteristic of secular America that religious, let alone clear ethical, references were unmentioned within the OCB leadership. This is apart from the comfortable exception of the free and communist worlds. Frequently principles of American policy were met in various forms, were tacitly accepted, and people moved on to operational questions. The strength of the system I came to understand. We Americans were agreed on the factors that gave our country its fabric, and although many issues were charged with energetic argument, the cultural underpinnings were intact. It may be remarked that the main strain on values, dominated by national interest thinking, was in covert operations, not the OCB's province.

As in any part of the national bureaucracy, a major bane was the clearance process by those sectors most concerned. This began when our staff man sought inter-agency agreement on a draft working group paper. I discovered that in our government the clearance difficulty frequently could be inversely related to an agency's responsibility for the subject. One agency, one vote, was cumbersome and not necessarily related to the agency's operational role. Getting agreement and reconciling differences, even with practice, could be trying at working group and Board assistants meetings, as we spanned the arc of our nation's foreign activities. Elmer and I were so engaged, for the efforts required persistence, a hard seat, and knowing when to press for decisive action. These could be called years of intensive negotiations. It can be sensed that I am not an innate staff man, I admire Elmer for that quality, but in my urge toward tangible results, I am not notably patient when the substance for compromise appears lacking. Nevertheless, the OCB was where there was much action, and this drew parties attracted by the intent and accomplishments of the Board. This spectrum of policies and operations gave participants an appreciation of its complexities and worth. It made people look at operating problems systematically and with continuity, where the follow-up objective was most valuable. Although some would complain, the organization could focus on key issues. When the Board assigned full responsibility to an agency, with others as auxiliaries, I noted there was no problem in pressing ahead. The success of this method induced my query why the Board did not do this more often? The fragmented responsibility of too many participants seemed to cause intermittent problems on some significant operational issues.

A diversion came when my classmate, Aaron Brown, as director of Foreign Service Personnel arranged my two week assignment on an oral examining panel of successful written exam candidates for the Service. There were three of us; a competent Wristonee chairman, a retired Commerce officer, and myself. The locale was a federal floor in New York City, and the candidates were from Yale to Princeton. We reviewed the records and each interview lasted half an hour. After a discussion we made our decision. Shades of my oral baptism! A young man, all personality, we failed, but another from New York was much more interesting, although noticeably defensive. We approved him while suggesting that our chairman use the occasion to emphasize that he was approved for the American Foreign Service, and that this was not dependent upon a candidate's ethnic nor religious background. The young man was delighted, and we, having our vision of the Service, felt better.

There was a drawback in staying too close to paper, for in the assignment our staff had only two scene changes from Washington. In each case, the combined OCB-NSC staff group made welcome trips to defense installations. We found it very useful to see the layout of the North American Defense Command at Colorado Springs and to visit the underground headquarters for the briefings. In another, we stepped off at Mayport, Florida, and onto the carrier, USS Franklin D. Roosevelt, for a three day sea exercise. Night landings by twin engine jet bombers at 120 miles an hour were stirring to witness. It was an exhilarating experience also to land on a carrier in a two seater jet at 90 miles an hour and to stop abruptly when the landing gear catches, for your head seemed to roll down the deck. To see a carrier and its escorting ships from a low flying helicopter was unforgettable. As part of our education, on the carrier we learned three things - all British. Our navy had acquired three major technical advances from theirs: the steam catapult for takeoffs, the angled deck, allowing landing planes a second go-round, and lastly, the meatball.  This was a red light disk within a spotlight that guided pilots into landings - so long as the disk remained centered.

After I had been with the OCB over two years I was restive to work in one of State's geographic bureaus or to return to the field.  Every day I had observed the importance of individuals in the shaping of foreign policy and witnessed the sources of government operations.  I saw how things were done through systems of agency and personal alliances and compromises.  The places were rare, I recognized, for an officer of my grade and background to acquire all this.  The people I worked with, Elmer, the Board members, and the State people, considered that I was on top of my responsibilities, and there were various written statements to this effect.  Meanwhile, in a surprise move, Elmer left the OCB and returned to the Budget Bureau as its deputy director.  Pending arrangements for further reorganization within the NSC structure, I accordingly acted as executive officer for six months, and then backstopped Bromley Smith of the NSC staff, a superb choice, when he was installed in Elmer's spot.  I had mastered the techniques of OCB work, Bromley appreciated my help, and we became friends.

It was my practice to follow developments in previous assignments, while aware of Loy Henderson's injunction about obsolescent experts.  Despite this, an assignment for me was never wholly relinquished.  Undoubtedly the intent of the National Security Act of 1947 was a entirely staff oriented NSC.  Sadly over time it became an operating agency without the congressional accountability of executive departments and agencies.  With acts of NSC staff leaders on record and charges of illegality rampant, any informed observer must have expressed dismay.  Hopefully, the operations oriented garb of a chastened NSC staff has been fully divested, but as I left this combined organization its troubles were in the future and its personnel had my fullest respect.

The OCB proved to be my longest assignment, three and a half years.  When my departure came, and in accord with annual Foreign Service rules, those I worked for, including Board members, made statements on my performance.  I was touched, as Jerry O'Connor recounted, that after preparing a statement for Secretary Herter's signature, Herter drafted his own in even warmer terms.  Loy Henderson believed with my background I should be on the Soviet periphery, so he recommended, as undersecretary for Administration, that I be assigned DCM and consul general at Helsinki.  Ambassador Jack Hickerson was soon to be replaced by a political nominee and he wanted me there with this development in mind.  Jerry O'Connor, knowing of the transfer, even suggested how I might get to know popular Finnish athletes! In the early summer, I got the assignment and had an orderly transition with my OCB successor, Ridgway Knight.  It would be a change of scene, but the familiar Russians would be next door.

Protocol. President Kekkonen departs for America.

Virginia lights candles for another dinner.

# CHAPTER 12

# NORTHERN PERIPHERY: HELSINKI

## August 1959 - June 1962

*Kennedy won the close 1960 election, and the missile gap issue was found non-existent. His Administration successfully created domestic support and prosperity, while its reactive handling of foreign crises focused on U.S. - Soviet relations. The 1961 Berlin Wall crisis, with no significant Western reaction, was followed by the U.S. fiasco of the Bay of Pigs. Mao smarted from the failure of the Great Leap Forward, and communist China and the USSR experienced severe strains. Western European economic recovery and NATO development progressed, countered in Eastern Europe by Soviet efforts to build their satellite region. The Finns, bounded by geography and political reality, evolved a unique policy of cooperation with the Soviets and full preservation of their parliamentary institutions. For nearly three years I was DCM and consul general of our embassy in Helsinki, and acted as chargé in a happy assignment. I visited the Soviet Union, Scandinavia, and Western Europe, which gave insights into the Finnish-Soviet relationship and Northern European views of the east-west struggle.*

We drove into Helsinki through the pines, very tired, and feeling ill, for it was a rugged trip. The departing DCM, a knowledgeable man on the Soviet Union, and his wife, both heavy smokers, met us in the ambassador's car with its power windows permanently locked. His wife told Virginia of a meeting at 9:30 the next morning for Mrs. Hickerson to introduce her to the staff. Virginia, feeling worse by the minute, responded that she would not be there. After a silence, the DCM, originally Civil Service and now Foreign Service as a Wristonee, asked how long I had been in the Service. I replied, and there was a longer silence. We got to the hotel, some of us to bed, and two days later, without discussing the office, the DCM left. Mrs. Hickerson, learning Virginia and some of the family were having health problems, could not have been nicer. Jack gave us a big welcome, privately expressing pleasure at having a career trained deputy.

Our building was an attractive design of brick colonial Williamsburg in the shape of a U, with one wing and the center comprising the embassy residence and the other wing the chancery. The ambassador's office and mine had our secretaries between. After the waiting room came various commercial offices with local clerks, and a reading room, while the basement had some administrative offices. On the second floor, as convention, were our economic and political sections, and our files and communications center. It was a good building, designed for business of an earlier period, and with a garden between the wings. Next to the residence-chancery was a large space used as a garden and parking lot, including a converted apartment house, whose first floor housed the budget and fiscal office and consular section. On the second floor were the armed services attachés, while the upper floors had staff apartments. The information office was downtown with its library.

The area was a quiet residential one on a hillside giving us a view of the outer harbor and the Gulf of Finland, and down the street were the French and British embassies. The main harbor was a distinctive sight. At the foot of a low hill was the large market square, all magically cleared away each afternoon. Behind this, the presidential mansion fronted the scene, and on a hill was the impressive Orthodox cathedral, built in a traditional Greek cross for its ever-standing parishioners. The neatness, the symmetry, the moderate size of Helsinki were engaging.

A long hotel stay, the search for quarters, and high living costs were all familiar until we found a large apartment on the top floor of an old apartment building near the embassy-chancery with a rickety, eccentric elevator. Continued use during a social affair would cause it to blow a fuse, so later guests trudged up the long flights. Before we found a solution, I recall a British ambassador, who was as they say, a bit of a stick, furious at making the climb. The solution was a janitor standing by to fix the apparatus when the blowouts happened. From our windows we could see one side of the Soviet embassy compound, windows always shuttered, and when we moved after the sale of our building, by chance we found a good one facing the Soviets on an opposite side of its square. We kept that embassy covered.

Now with quarters, the family adjusted to Helsinki, although April, our eldest daughter, asked why we were there, for everything looked so western and so like home. Education for April and Lucy became a problem, one that can haunt Foreign Service families, but a sign they were growing. We had little choice and finally settled on what was called the English School run by American nuns from St. Louis. It never was clear how the Order got to Finland, but they were teaching a grammar school and partial high school curriculum in English for Finnish children.

Ambassador Hickerson I knew when he had been in charge of European affairs, and he and his wife were old hands in Helsinki, but for the first time we were closely associated. As a professional he was a joy to work with and an easy and friendly chief. An initial small step with Hickerson's approval was to reorganize some space and working allocations for us and the political section, in which the latter, wanting this for some time, was made happy. Meanwhile the ambassador continued my Finnish education for the two months he remained, interspersed with stories, for he was a natural, and I was sorry to see him go to his next mission, Manila. Jack gave some parting advice worth remembering. Whenever a new ambassador arrives, it is an error to mention that the previous ambassador has done things in one way. Even the best, he claimed, feel the urge to change and do it in another. I had reason to think about this with his successor.

After my period as chargé, the new ambassador arrived. He was prominent in his state's political party and a wealthy industrial engineer, fresh from being deputy postmaster general, where he started postal automation. He and his wife were miscast in their roles, for by attitudes and conversation it was clear they considered Finland too small a place, the work and society not that interesting, and the climate onerous. It was my first direct work with a politically appointed chief of mission. He confided to me within a week of his arrival that he had made his fortune in private business by not trusting anyone, and now in the State Department he did not aim to change!

As an executive, the ambassador used the harpoon method, that is, he would prod one officer for several days or a week, and then shift to another. Apparently in private business he had done this to keep subordinates on their toes. As his deputy and knowing the officers, I would try to act as a buffer for both and simply see that the work got done. I had no illusions over my eventual turn for the harpoon. After two months a petty episode arose, a pretext he privately elaborated. He concluded his deliberate lecture by saying that thereafter he was uncertain he could have full confidence in me. To this planned thrust, I responded formally that it disturbed me as much for him as for myself. He had a mission from the president, and his staff had the responsibility to aid its success. It was vital he have people in whom he could have confidence. Therefore, did he want to write requesting my transfer or should I? The matter was above personalities, since it was essential that he be satisfied. When he was in Washington, he undoubtedly was told that I had a good record, and I would have no trouble in getting another assignment. The important thing was for him to have a man with whom he could work. He looked at me quizzically, remarked that we would see how things went later, and dropped the subject. I had no further such trouble, but if I had not taken with some forethought the tack described, no doubt my hide would have been regularly punctured.

Helsinki gave evidence that the most difficult position in the Foreign Service is to be a deputy chief of mission. The best, I might add, is to be consul general at a post distant from the capital. I envied Milt Rewinkel, my classmate friend, for he had two: Bombay and Vancouver.

Given the compact American staff, we got to know each other very well, and I have good memories and clear vignettes. A smart economic officer I advised to work for a law degree when he had a Washington assignment. He did, and upon graduation promptly accepted a very good offer from a prominent law firm. Bill Miller and Harvey Nelson, succeeding Grant Hilliker, heads of the economic and political sections, were most competent men, aided politically by Ted Sellin. There was Wally Pedersen, a knowledgeable commercial attaché. The naval attaché and I both liked jazz, so we had some interesting listening sessions, while his predecessor and wife became lifelong friends. A benefit of our social life was its homeside relaxed and friendly nature, which included the Finns, of course.

Secretaries are a secret to the success of any operation. I have advised young officers if they have to choose between increasing staff with another officer or a secretary, to opt for the secretary. She is the one who gets the work out for Washington, and it doesn't help to have officers with information to transmit if it can't get there. Also it seems to work better and morale is higher if an office is slightly understaffed. The secretaries in Helsinki and all other posts would work unselfishly for long hours if needed to get the job done. As well, these women added much to the post through their own personalities. My attractive secretary, a nice young woman of Swedish descent, wanted an assignment to Stockholm after Helsinki. The marines of our contingent and other single men generally dated the Finnish girls, and I knew it would be the same in Sweden. On my suggestion, Laverne took Karachi, having our then large military mission in that Moslem state in mind. She married an FSO in Pakistan.

The Finnish Foreign Office was naturally important to us, and its secretary general, Jaako Hallama, and the public affairs director Max Jakobson, were the ones I saw regularly and knew best. Both were energetic, young in Finland for their jobs, and very cooperative. In our time I believe our association was mutually useful in exchanging perspectives on issues. After my departure Jaako had a tragically incapacitating malady, and Max became the leading foreign affairs expert for his countrymen. In foreign affairs, however, the key domestic decisions were made between President Kekkonen and his foreign minister, who had earlier been his private secretary. On behalf of his country, nothing was going to trouble Finnish-Soviet relationships if the president could help it. Nevertheless, Kekkonen's predecessor as president had once mentioned that it was good for Finland to have educated Russian speakers - but not too many. I think he privately subscribed to this, for, after all, he valued Finland's independence.

From Kobe days I have gotten along well with the English, for I think I understand them. The French and ourselves were congenial, too. Officials of important countries are informed and judicious, and the trading of reliable information is a necessary part of an assignment. Here the French aided what I claim to have been my most effective morale contribution to the post. Advised by the French DCM, I located the agent for a Scotch whiskey trying to break into Finland's market through the diplomatic community. Since we paid the bill for the tastes of local friends, his terms were attractive. For our people on the diplomatic list (and informally for some of those perhaps who were not), I arranged twelve-bottle case orders of fifths for an unbelievably low price - delivered. That action made my reputation.

The Finns, of all I have lived among, I have most enjoyed. English is the second language in Scandinavia, and I felt an empathy toward them, developing a variety of friendships in all walks of life and, save the communists, in all political parties. They have a word for fortitude, which is "sisu," and it characterized them. They are sports conscious, love sauna baths, and delight in hieing to the woods (usually on a lake) in the brief summer, where they rough it. Many sided, they lead the world in books read per capita, and this is not solely due to the long winters. In the arts, such as music, architecture, sculpture, and ceramics, they have an exceptional record. One need only cite composer Jan Sibelius, the architect Saarinens, and artist-designer Alvar Aalto. They are also drinkers, and at the time, after the United States and Great Britain, the third largest importers of French brandy.

On a week's trip the ambassador and I took with the hard-drinking Foreign Minister to industrial plants in the north and into Lapland with its deer herds, the former retired early each evening, and I was left as a prudent drinker to uphold the capacity of the embassy. Each morning I had a headache, but the Foreign Minister was ready for the day. Because of drinking customs, control laws were very strict. Police cars would lie in wait to test customers exiting bars or night clubs and seeking to fly on their own. A test failure to meet the standard meant an automatic six months in prison, which in my day meant six months of labor constructing the international airport. There were no exceptions. If a known figure was absent at various affairs and you inquired, a simple response that he was at the airport told all. How many Finns gave of their time to finish that airport!

Diplomats were particularly popular socially since they were not stopped by the police. Discreet Finns would see to it, if not chauffeur driven or if not leaving by the rare taxi, that a diplomat would drive them home. Still, liquor was a problem in Scandinavia. In Copenhagen a few years back, I saw several groups of drink boisterous youths on a Saturday morning. Ted Sellin, one of our political officers and fluent in Finnish and all Scandinavian tongues, spent his college junior year in Sweden. He said that before the introduction of liquor rationing in the 20s, a large pitcher of *aqua vite* was set on the breakfast table for the students. A Finnish doctor claimed that heavy drinking markedly decreased in his country as conditions improved, which we could see, and attributed the cultural condition to subconscious depression over the long winters, as well as the hard times Finland had gone through during and after the war. However, for the area, aside from the regionally improving economy, it was a culturally embedded custom requiring control.

A typical social-business event would be men gathering after work for a sauna, the natural recreation, followed in the dressing room by drinks and snacks, which would progress to a home or a restaurant for a meal interspersed with drinks. Following a vigorous sauna, of course, you had a greater capacity for liquid intake. I found it true that after a winter sauna you could walk outdoors without a shiver and jump into a chopped hole in the ice for a quick cooling off. It was indeed stimulating, but you had to wear flimsy slippers to avoid your damp feet freezing to the ice! Another social practice was crayfish parties in the season and, a ritual which I successfully evaded, to drink the local liquor with each small crayfish. The national drink, *koskenkorva* (not *aqua vite* as in Sweden), allegedly came from wood. This was of two kinds, said the Finns, one with the bark on and the other with it off!

A tangible sign that economic conditions were steadily improving was accompanied by a growing buoyancy in outlook. The number of parked cars along the harbor steadily grew, the shops acquired a greater variety of goods, and prosperity became evident. With this development I used to joke with the head of the Finnish National Bank about the Finnmark-dollar exchange rate, which, as the economic tide turned, did not favor Americans.

An invariable function was a monthly meeting of the Finnish-American exchanges committee to decide on suitable nominees for leader, professorial, and student exchanges between the two countries. The money came from the Finnish repaid war debt fund, which our Congress had voted to be used for this purpose, and because of the amount involved, the program was large. The ambassador chaired the group, and in his absence it was my duty. The Finns, who we knew well, took the responsibility seriously, and over a tasty lunch and coffee we would integrate their judgments and ours on pending choices.

It was well that there was an active social life in Helsinki, particularly in the winter. A Scandinavian winter may find the sun technically rising at mid-morning and setting at 3, with weeks and even months of grey light. Snowfalls were sprinkles and there were no blizzards, but they were constant throughout the winter. The main streets were always ice covered, and it was a sensation to winter-drive in the city. Sometimes all you could do was hold the wheel, gently tap the brakes, and hope. The Gulf of Finland, of course, was frozen over, and it was a festive sight in the spring to see the ice break-up, although something was lacking; the water was not salty, being far from the ocean, so you missed the familiar sea tang. A contrast to the winters was the brief summers of long sunlight, when in midsummer for a period of three weeks it was the practice not to have street lights turned on. No matter how late you left a social affair, there was ample light in the sky, so bedrooms usually had dark double curtains. Fortunately we did not experience a "green winter," the name for a disagreeably cold summer.

The beginning of spring was May 1, when the sun-starved Finns celebrated. This was a great holiday, which started with crowds massing at the fountain mermaid statue of Havis Amanda on the harbor. The students came in their white caps and paraded, and every restaurant in town was filled for a day and two nights with celebrants. After a pre-May Day evening affair with Finnish friends, we were home at 4 a.m., and at 10:30 a.m. were back in a large restaurant for the height of the celebration, the noon lunch, complete with balloons. Finland is where people can have fun at any hour.

To know a country you travel, so I went, always with an embassy language officer, from the Gulf of Finland to the Arctic Circle, and got to know the almost invariably English-speaking officials, local news editors and politicians, on their home ground. Then I would see them when they came to Helsinki, which was frequently. In our travels, the countryside appeared monotonous except toward the southwest with its richer farmland, for the rest was pine cover and lakes. As a phenomenon, on the western, Gulf of Bothnia side, every generation the farmland would be resurveyed, as the still rising Finnish peninsula acquired more land. Large paper and pulp mills, dams and other industries were on our itinerary. The towns themselves, always well appointed, generally had a cultural center including a modernistic theatre and concert hall, and facilities for teaching various musical instruments. Each town also had a book of photographs, which traditionally a visitor received, and my collection was large.

Everyone knows Finnish as one of the world's difficult languages, but its original distribution, etymologists say, covers northeast Russia and Estonia, across the Gulf, while linguists told me it is more difficult than Chinese or Russian, accounting for its constricted use. We had language classes at the embassy, which

I attended, but I could not adjust to the grammar case system, where the root of the word also changes.  A prolonged sound was simply written in double letters, so the government alcohol monopoly, *alkoholiliike*, we jokingly translated as "alcohol I like."  Thankfully, the Finns preferred English, of which a high school graduate generally had a working knowledge.

One handicap for Finland was its place off the accustomed European tourist beat, so those who might visit Stockholm and Copenhagen would fly to Leningrad.  Similarly, that extra day each way made for more planning whenever we in Helsinki took a short trip.  My vehicle for this was the air attaché's plane, on which I made several flights to Air Force Headquarters in Wiesbaden, Germany, on business and for a change of scene.  Virginia, our two oldest girls, and I visited Copenhagen (our favorite as the Paris of the North, and its fabulous Tivoli Park), and then Frankfurt, and Heidelberg, as well as traveling through some impressive Norwegian fjords.  Oslo, to us, became Helsinki with hills.  In our car, we visited Copenhagen, Hamburg, and Bonn, but where we lingered longest was in the picturesque town of Bruges in Belgium, maintained in the style of several hundred years ago.  Europe, as we discovered in Switzerland, has numerous attractions.

Because of the good eating and full social schedule there was a problem the Service creates when we take insufficient exercise and have a heavy business load.  Since Japan I had never exercised, so under a doctor's advice I began a double regime of food watching and systematic exercise that came to the stage when Barbara, my secretary, remarked that it gave a straight silhouette.  There have been variations, but its great benefit was to retain fitness for energetic assignments.  Fitness conscious the Finns certainly were.  When I once remarked to a friend that President Kekkonen had, according to the press, done some extensive skiing over a weekend which I though worthy of remark since he was in his 60s, my friend rejoined that it was only some 45 kilometers (30 miles)!

When one speaks of sports in Finland, the first image is of track and field and the legendary runners, Hannes Kohlemainen and Paavo Nurmi, both of whom I met.  At the time I recalled to Nurmi seeing him run at the Penn Relays, with his ever-present wrist watch timing his rhythm.  Those who attended the 1952 Olympics in Helsinki tell of the moderation the Finns exercised in holding the successful Games.  To sports lovers it was memorable, they say, to see Nurmi carry the torch to the top of the Olympic tower, marking the beginning.  When the Soviets annexed Finnish Karelia, they dispossessed 400,000 people, one tenth of Finland's population.  These were resettled in Finland with remarkable effectiveness, and the extrovert Karelian personality remained intact.  One of the big winter sports events, skijumping, took place in Lahti, resettled by Karelians, and I cannot picture a more risky sport.  A Finnish friend drew my attention to the youth of the jumpers, adding they had to be that young with the nerve to do it! *For a later Olympics I was not surprised to see a 17 year old Finn win the gold.*

For us outlanders, there were two distinctive cultural aspects to the country. First, like Sweden, on ceremonial occasions there was formality. Until Helsinki, I had worn striped pants and frock coat a few times as usher at weddings. In Finland they were in frequent use for attendance at openings of parliament and various dedication ceremonies. Particularly notable was one for the dedication of the statue of the great World War II leader, Marshal Mannerheim. By the time I left I began to get used to wearing the items, for there are many events that an officer must engage in as his country's representative. Each year our president issues a Thanksgiving Proclamation, and overseas it is customary to read it at some American sponsored function or at a church service. Once the ambassador read the Proclamation at a meeting of the Finnish-American Society. As a chargé, I read it at a little English church on the ground floor of an apartment building which our family occasionally attended.

Open pro-Americanism was a Finnish feature, and the great function for the Finnish-American Society each year, known as "America Days," was held on a long weekend at a different Finnish town. Members of the Society from Helsinki and its branches would be there, and we would have a program including a formal dinner and dance, a luncheon, and a distinguished American speaker as a final attraction. It was the embassy's function to line up a suitable American for the capping address. Among these was the wife of Secretary of Agriculture Orville Freeman, who pinch-hit most effectively for her husband when a personal mishap made him unable to attend. Another occasion for "America Days" found us with *Representative* Lodge of Massachusetts as the speaker who, with his wife, were splendid. The ambassador and I arranged in advance, in view of the program, to split up going to functions when they overlapped. I represented him at the dinner and ball, since the plane on which his party was coming to town had been grounded by bad weather. One of our officers met the party at the railroad station at 6 a.m. since I had stayed with the ball, as customary, until at least 3. Returning on the plane, the weary ambassador complained that I had not got in touch with him before we went our early separate ways. I understood his state, but said that, based on our accepted private arrangements and his circumstances, if anyone had sought to awaken me before 9 a.m. I would have shot him. It was the only time since our original episode I received a personal complaint.

The atmosphere, the temperament of the people, and their widespread interests meant I acquired a variety of friendships among those in private life and in government. If I attempt names, the list would be long. There were men like Olavi Lindblom, vice chairman of the social democrats, Georg Ehrnooth, a young Swedish deputy, Aatos Erkko, director of the leading newspaper, and Paavio

Hetemaki, a conservative leader. At a farewell reception given for us, which my friends pointed out was unusual for the time, those from every political segment but the communists were present, and the affair was arranged by the managing director of the Finnish Industrialists Association, a conservative outfit.

Carl-Erik Olin, heading the industrialist association, was a Swedo-Finn. The Swedish speaking element, then 8 percent, was influential beyond its numbers, and was an important bridge between Finland and Sweden. We had known the Olins for some time, when they invited us for a weekend to their summer place on an island. There he made a standing toast to the effect that he and his wife wanted to extend their friendship, and asked to call us, and we they, by first names. It was so courtly and, from what we later learned, typical of custom that we were touched, since the Finns were not ones to give their friendship lightly. Illustratively, at my next post I reached the age of 50, which in Finland is a celebration landmark, and I received several telegrams from thoughtful Finnish friends.

One unusual associate I gained was Mr. Wallari, president of the Seamen's Union. After World War I, as an International Workers of the World member, a labor organization considered suspect in the Red scare of the time, he had been deported from the United States. He held no grudge, and was friendly to Americans. On acquaintance and on learning of my early merchant ship experience, he made me an honorary member of his union in a nice gesture.

We naturally had visitors, including cabinet members and congressional groups. Arthur Goldberg, Kennedy's Labor Secretary was quite active, and Commerce Secretary Hodges was a most congenial North Carolinian. He gave me the authentic version behind the classic comment of what the governor of North Carolina said to the governor of South Carolina. Various business men and tourists arrived (a shipload would come for a day), and the traffic to and from Moscow was persistent. Novelists like Erskine Caldwell were going to spend some of their blocked rubles, and another, Louis Bromfield, also came by. Marian Anderson, the famous contralto, was our house guest for a social evening.

An American cultural attraction on a European tour was a company headed by Helen Hayes, which performed three plays, and the lady proved to be very natural and a credit to our country. Another artist, Hal Holbrook, gave us his memorable one-man performance of "Mark Twain Tonight." Our musicians appeared at the annual Sibelius Festival, where Van Cliburn performed. The Helsinki symphony was a good orchestra, and any ceremony or concert had a special touch when it played the national hymn, the melody from Sibelius' "Finlandia," for every local listener was stirred by this symbol of Finnish nationalism against the Czars, as Sibelius intended. Then there was Leonard

Bernstein and our Bern visitors, the New York Philharmonic. Of equal interest to the Finns was the attraction of a half dozen American Olympic class track athletes. Finns crowded the Olympic stadium, and the group pleased everyone with outstanding performances.

In our first early spring, the promotion lists arrived, and short of 23 years I became an FSO-1. I thought of my first chief, Homer Byington, Senior, and that I had reached his old impossible number plateau. The Service had markedly changed in size and complexity, and there were now two higher grades, career minister and career ambassador. By a subsequent Foreign Service Act, the 0-1 grade became minister counselor, Senior Foreign Service, which the National War College, meticulous in such matters, deemed an equivalent of the military's two star rear admiral or major general. With a pensive smile, I thought how alien such concepts would have been to my old chief. At any rate I retained the grade for the rest of my career.

As a surprise and in a way not untypical, at a staff meeting after ten months the ambassador announced he had submitted his resignation and would be leaving in October prior to the presidential election. He never would have thought to tell me in advance. He had been having difficulties with people in the White House, and even our assistant secretary for European affairs had considered him a minor problem among his larger concerns. However, I knew from friends such as Milt Rewinkel, who was director of the area, that the bureau had been satisfied with the way I had handled the situation. In any event, out of sorts with the Administration and pleased to be leaving Finland, the couple took off on comparatively short notice. Before the ambassador left, I knew he was doing my efficiency report, but I never inquired nor did he mention it. Later his former secretary volunteered that he had done reasonably well by me, carping about a few things, but had finished by saying that I would be an ambassador within five years!

After a further period as chargé, we prepared for Bernard Gufler as the new chief. Guf, as he wanted to be called, previously had been an ambassador, and was an old time career officer with European experience. He was of middle height and heavy, with a florid complexion, so when his temper was released, his face would become markedly red. He had traits to which I accommodated, and we got along well with him and Mrs. Gufler, a nice, informal lady. She endeared herself when told there was no American women's club, by remarking, "This post has everything." Gufler liked the Finns and they him. He settled in, had sound judgment, was a good drafter, and our operations were more effective than before. Despite this, the vulnerability of being an ambassador is sharply reflected in his case. The European bureau assistant secretary later said when Guf was home on leave that he was very pleased with his work. The same day, Gufler was told by a more senior official that his post was needed for a political appointee, who also only stayed ten months. One example among others, was an ambassador to a major country awakened by a newsman to learn the surprising news that he was being replaced by a politico.

Developing office effectiveness was part of my job, so early in my assignment, aware of our small staff, I decided the officers should systematize their information contacts to avoid inadvertent loss. The most important in that environment were the political-economic, so initially I had those officers make lists of contacts in various sectors of these areas and, after study, decide on their comparative importance. The officers noted omissions of people it would be helpful to know, for they could judge where their present associates were not fully effective. After discussion, adding and pruning, major political and economic lists were achieved. This was difficult, for there were so many in these fields we liked and respected. The names were allocated, each with one officer as principal contact and another as secondary, having leaves and transfers in mind. The ambassador and myself shared in the allocations, and until I knew the fields, the listings proved useful. I believed it served a like purpose with the other officers. Then we expanded into other sectors.

Because of the release I felt in being in the field and in doing what I believed was constructive and congenial action away from Washington, I was ready to enjoy the country and the people, as reflected here. However, life was not all simple good times and camaraderie. We observed internal political developments closely, were on the sidelines encouraging democratic trends, watched communist tactics, and tried to develop cultural exchanges and trade. There were American business interests we assisted, including representatives of major companies, importers, and shipping firms. These were joined with Finnish businessmen in an organization called the Finnish-American Club that would hold regular lunches and an occasional social affair. As well, the Finnish-American Society had branches around Finland working closely with our Information Agency.

We knew the heavy indemnity the Soviets had imposed on Finland and the territorial sacrifices the country had made. There were less than four million Finns, and they had showed good judgment in stopping their military advance at the old 1939-40 Winter War boundaries. This was interpreted by some as the reason Finland and its parliamentary regime had been allowed to remain functioning. Others had a more realistic reason. If the Soviets had occupied Finland and established an Eastern Europe satellite pattern there, it might have driven Sweden into NATO and created a more viable northern Europe defense front. Through all of the instruments of an open society we had the opportunity to learn Finnish views and to follow country developments. Finland's politics of careful neutrality governed by the presence of the super-power neighbor, necessarily made the environment complex. The normally open and, on occasion, abrupt nature of the Finns was harnessed to a sophisticated politics which conditions inexorably enforced.

President Kekkonnen was an agrarian and tried to retain Soviet confidence in Finland's intentions, while maneuvering politically to retain a parliamentary majority for his policies. His was a dominant personality. Talking together after an opening of parliament ceremony I remarked that the newly elected President Kennedy had obtained a majority of one in a congressional committee for a major policy. Looking smilingly at me, he added, "But one vote is all that one needs." He knew that I knew he had been elected president by a parliamentary majority of one. His party was the Agrarian (center) and others ranged from the conservatives, the liberals, the Swedish peoples, social democrats, dissident social democrats, and communists. It was the Soviet tactic to retain a majority which would work acceptably to them. Simultaneously another one was to erode important opposition elements, principally the socialists, to control the Left. It was the communist tactical handbook I recognized in its application to other environments, but here it had added subtlety. On the non-communist side, including agrarians of Kekkonen's party, the object was to hold for the country as much political independence as it could, to avoid being too politically fragmented, and to maintain national values. Despite varying pressures, the Finns did this and owed their success to their own stamina.

There were several tense times between Russians and Finns. One arose over Finland's desire to have an association with the British sponsored European Free Trade Association (EFTA) composed of Western European states outside the Common Market. Finland, to make better economic progress, needed the EFTA tie, but the Russians were bent on keeping pressures on Finland through trade arrangements and long-range barter deals they could use as a lever on the economy. Fortunately for Finland, its trade with the West burgeoned in future years. Still another came, with the Russians planning their tactics on Kekkonen carefully. He was making his first visit to America and was relaxing on an Hawaiian beach, when the Russians announced they were invoking the consulta-tion part of their joint treaty to decide on mutual defense measures to be taken against possible German aggression. This put Finnish freedom of action in serious question. Kekkonen sent his foreign minister home, but completed his scheduled visit. Under great personal strain, which we knew of at first hand, he then went to the Soviet Union as required, to consult. He got out of the difficulty, but it was part of Russian pressure bargaining. Still, Kekkonen thereafter attended President Kennedy's funeral and made two official visits to Washington.

The cold war continued, based on Soviet adjacency and pressures on the Finns. We were sharply reminded of this when our security practices unearthed a Soviet agent among our Finnish staff. He was intelligent and personable, and had been led along by the Soviets with trips, unknown to us, to the Soviet Union. The man, from evidence we gathered, was getting in deeper, although his information was still unclassified, and he was being urged to more substantive production. Earlier I thought the Soviets have a point in employing only their nationals. We are faced by plaints that we cannot afford with a limited budget to follow such a thoroughgoing procedure. On the other hand, who can judge by a budget, not forgetting vulnerable Americans, the costs of intelligence obtained by pressure harassed nationals?

In Bucharest our wartime support point had been Caserta, Italy. Now we served as the supply and support point for our embassy in Moscow. While we had other contacts with that embassy, such as welcoming visitors on leave from Russia, we had never been there. This we remedied by traveling to Leningrad and Moscow in the spring and staying with our minister, Ed Freers and his wife, and seeing old Bern associates, the Lewis Bowdens. Both couples thereafter enjoyed Helsinki respites. On this trip, we took the train between Helsinki and Leningrad, and saw the contrast between the neatly appointed Finnish frontier station and the one at Viipuri, a first stop in Russia. We stayed around this last and were struck by the quiet and air of partial desertion to the town. It had formerly been part of Finland, and the people had evacuated on a few days notice to avoid coming under communist domination. When the Russians arrived, as the Finns said, there was not a dog in the streets to meet them.

Americans regularly visited the Soviet Union, but there were always differences, depending on observers. Tourists saw Leningrad, the old imperial capital, as a city of impressive broad avenues. We traveled by train in so-called luxury class with a samovar for tea in each coach. We could see the Kirov Ballet with "Swan Lake," and also an unusual circus. The big attraction, the Hermitage Museum, had every square foot of the walls covered with masterpieces, including a room of Rembrandts. The aroma of a first class Soviet hotel was not that agreeable, and we had the usual slow meal service, but we had a competent woman guide (working for the police, of course) who took us around during the day. A different feature was the Marriage Palace, an old mansion refurbished and used for civil wedding ceremonies and brief receptions. We watched one wedding in the stream, saw the woman official give the couple an ideological pep talk, and then she pronounced them married. I had a drink with the groom. The Freers' Moscow apartment in the chancery building was unusual since the building had Russian servants, and I was conscious of electronic devices, given the known Soviet sophistication. However, everyone living there had adjusted to it. As well, we had our chance to see two performances of the Bolshoi Ballet, but

Virginia, ballet trained, preferred the traditionally graceful Kirov. A more modern feature in Moscow and Leningrad was ostentatious subways, with chandeliers designed as showpieces and intended as a morale lift to the public. Their salient feature, however, was great depth. In and out were long escalators seemingly a hundred yards deep, which the Russians clearly prepared for use as entries to air raid shelters.

Seeing people I knew in our embassy and having luncheon with ambassador Tommy Thompson, my old European deputy assistant secretary, helped me see their environment. There was the striking Kremlin with treasures all tourists wanted to see, along with St. Basil's Church on Red Square. We had no interest in visiting Lenin's tomb, a secular shrine. Moscow, long before perestroika, gave an air of physical change, with building cranes then in profusion. From what our people told me, aside from the constant construction, there was an unsurprising frustration of artists and intellectuals. The town, despite the skyscrapers of Moscow University and other large buildings, gave an impression of facades, which off the main streets were not impressive. Even new apartment houses had catchments strung near the roofs to hold detached pieces. In the Moscow art gallery, officials at the time had only recently decided to exhibit paintings in the European style of the 1920s, for we were told the tractor school of art had been the accepted style. The changes of peristroika were yet to come.

Under glasnost I traveled in the USSR as a professor on the Semester at Sea program, and my eighty students gave accounts of their encounters with authority. We had respect for the people, but Gorbachev's effort seemed to prove cultural habits were hard to modify. None of the students was happy with acts of authority and intimidating restrictions, but there was an amusing instance of cultural lag. Two students in their city hotel room watched a small box TV, when one strongly objected to the subject. Suddenly there was a flip to another channel. The second student, in the game, praised the other channel, wanting to return to it, whereupon another magic flip restored the original! As comedian Bob Hope said after visiting, "In Russia the television watches you."

Not long after our Russian trip the Guflers took off for Spain to shake Helsinki's gloomy winter. As would happen, I received a new assignment telegram requesting me immediately to report to the Department before proceeding to Baghdad. I knew that before long I would be reassigned, for my three years were nearing a close, but, as always, it was unexpectedly random. I tracked down Gufler in Spain and we talked. The Department finally recognized that I could not leave while the Guflers were away, and they were able to finish the holiday. A few days after the telegram I got a letter from Jack Jernegan, our ambassador in Baghdad whom I knew, telling me things were getting difficult there. When he left to attend a conference he could not return, and the Department had decided there would be no new ambassador. The Iraqi Government had recalled its ambassador from Washington. Our relations were strained as the local regime had adopted an increasingly anti-American and pro-Soviet stance, erupting when we established an embassy in Kuwait, which Iraq claimed. Jack's DCM, Rodger Davies, also was being transferred to the Near East office in Washington. Because of my experience with the Soviets, he said, the Department wanted me to move as fast as possible. It was hectic to attend farewell social occasions and to pack under hurried conditions, but on June 19 we drove to the airport and had a final glimpse of fragrant fruit trees in full bloom.

Helsinki, through retrospect when I had the opportunity, was my favorite post. While there was the usual interesting work the Service provided, new elements contributed to my feelings as I gained more professional perspective. For the first time since Montreal I was in a friendly, fully open, pro-American society, that despite the handicap of geopolitics was devoid of a caution that sometimes flickered in pro-democratic, neutral Switzerland. This trait was a part of the Finnish character that I found so agreeable and relaxing. Then the people were the most complex with their diversity of interests and enthusiasm for sports. Friendship meant something to them, more so than I generally encountered. I felt fully comfortable with the direction and activities of our embassy, and the relations we maintained with Finnish officials and our foreign diplomatic colleagues. As the ambassador's deputy, this time to a suspicious, politically appointed emissary, I learned to get along with him by courtesy and honesty, and also keep an effective operation. Personally and professionally it was a great experience; so much so that in future years it was the only foreign post I ever paid to re-visit.

Baghdad embassy compound

# CHAPTER 13

# TIME BETWEEN THE RIVERS: BAGHDAD

# August 1962 - July 1963

*In America the civil rights movement gained impetus, while in Vietnam the numbers of U.S. military advisers increased. Premier Diem was killed and opponents held the U.S. responsible. The Cuban missile crisis, when the world faced the prospect of nuclear war, ended with Khruschev overreaching himself. The U.S. and U.S.S.R. established a communications hotline and suspended nuclear atmospheric and underwater testing. Sino-Soviet relations came to a public rupture aided by the Soviet strategic defeat over Cuban missiles. The French vetoed U.K. common market membership, Japan quietly developed its trade and industry, and the Organization of African Unity was formed to avoid national conflicts between its emerging states. Dictator Qasim's Iraq increased its Soviet ties, hammered on its long standing claim to Kuwait, and increased its hostility to the U.S. In Baghdad I was chargé of our embassy in a maximum hardship assignment. The Qasim regime incurred strong domestic resentments until a coup d'etat by the Ba'ath party overthrew the government and killed him. An American ambassador was designated and I was assigned to Washington.*

In Washington I learned of my selection as chargé because of the indefinite absence of an ambassador and in view of my mideast communist periphery experience. Qasim had been invoking, ever more strongly, a much disputed territorial claim to Kuwait that went back to World War I when the British and French had parcelled Ottoman territory, including the sheikdoms in the Persian Gulf. We had recognized a former sheikdom, now the state of Kuwait, and exchanged ambassadors, so Jack Jernegan had been told by the Iraqi government not to return when he left to attend a conference. Our government had responded by naming me its chargé d'affaires.

Adding to our difficulties was the Qasim regime's contribution to the east-west struggle through the strengthening of its military components, particularly the air force, with Soviet equipment. Qasim had developed a growing hostility toward the United States, which he labeled 'imperialist,' and found congenial ground with his Soviet military advisers and associates. Classically, the Soviets succeeded in controlling Qasim's personal security arrangements, playing on his paranoia, and furthering their efforts in other important sectors such as the police and military equipment and training. Qasim headed the Iraqi military leaders who, by coup, had massacred the members of the last royalist regime four years before. Fanatical and neurotic, he oppressed every modern political element in his governing of Iraq. His followers were subservient. The future regime of Saddam Hussein also had large numbers of Soviet personnel that included a military component. The ruthless actions between the two dictators are striking

For a week I was debriefed about Finland and did some business for Ambassador Gufler. Then came a week of briefings on Iraq in the Bureau of Near East affairs, headed by a political appointee of some area background. The country desk officer was competent, and I learned much, but I was ambivalent about the Near East office director, supplemented as in all organizations, by reports from trusted Service friends. I left for Iraq at the end of July, leaving my family to follow, when Virginia would enroll the two older girls in the American School in Beirut.

It was my first Arab post, and I sought a tangible sense of the environment by gathering informed impressions as I approached Baghdad. In London, my first stop, I saw our excellent Near East officer, David Newsom (whom I had met in Baghdad), and some Foreign Office people he recommended to give their perspectives. In Rome there were two of my old Tehran political section officers, who had relevant assignments there. Ambassadors Armin Meyer in Beirut, Ridge Knight (my OCB successor) in Damascus, and Bill Macomber in Amman had valuable combined insights. The unfriendly Iraqi regime would not hesitate to make life difficult, I had been warned, and there were various responsibilities, special and area related, to the embassy staff and American community.

One August day, the plane doors opened to the furnace-like summer heat of Baghdad. At the airport were the chief members of the embassy staff with their wives, and with that temperature I felt for them. The embassy compound was new since my previous visit, and striking in its modern architecture. As chargé I was to live in the residence, so as host I met them as individuals. The economic counselor had been in charge for two weeks since the DCM, Rodger Davies, left, and the head of the political section was going on home leave upon my arrival. This pending departure initially made me feel bereft, but I had been assured his deputy, Jim Akins, was excellent, as he proved to be. The other section heads I came to know later, but I was particularly interested to meet the administrative officer, whom I had been told was indispensable to cope with our special environment.

For the Department-designated maximum hardship conditions, there was an adequate official family. We had three political officers, the CIA station, four military attachés, and three each of economic, residual AID, information, and administrative officers. There was a consul. These had American and Iraqi staffs, and there were consular, communications, and file personnel, as well as our marine contingent. Each sector had reliable Iraqi contacts, and the American resident community, among which most official Americans lived, was helpful in reporting on its conditions. At the initial staff meeting I tried to set the tone for the way things would be done. Amid my few remarks I said that I was not an idea man, for to my mind these were rare. I could recognize a good idea when I heard it, so I enjoined the officers to keep their ideas coming. Privately I wanted them to be relaxed and uninhibited in any suggestions.

Our operations were organized so that I had a half hour meeting with all officers on Friday mornings, since the Moslem sabbath was the most convenient time. I felt strongly that large staff meetings should not be longer. At another point in the week I would have a small meeting of section or agency heads, commonly called the country team, to discuss more sensitive matters, or to obtain their views on pending operations.

To keep the staff informed, as customary, our file room had a small area with a current collection of all but the most sensitive telegrams and pouched despatches for the officers to see. It was the responsibility of each section that weekly at least one of its officers, who reported back, see the material before a new accumulation began. By this system each section was as fully informed as feasible.

It was a relief not to be concerned with getting quarters, domestic staff, and other distracting chores from the purposes of the assignment. For the first time I occupied government housing, and the compound was where my family lived and I worked. Housing was of the same modern architecture as the chancery, both designed for the Baghdad climate, each with an open space and a false roof, billowed and edged, that we called the flying carpet. Most of the ground floor consisted of an expandable dining room and a large living room area, all furnished in a style we called desert modern, featuring huge and elaborate Kuwait chests. Downstairs we had the impression of living in a modern hotel, with plenty of exterior glass sliding doors. Upstairs were ample bedrooms and baths and a private family area. My family would be comfortable. Outside, things could get rough.

The compound, including the residence, staff apartments, chancery, and maintenance shops and garage, was large, walled on three sides and fronting on the Tigris River with gardens and lawns watered by irrigation ditches filled by a riverside pump, where a sizeable launch, intended for emergencies was tethered. I quickly fell into a exercise routine, walked to the chancery, returned for a late lunch (office hours, 7:30 a.m. to 2 p.m., six days a week), and a nap before the evening schedule

A tennis court and a small swimming pool were in constant use, with the most frequent player our resident embassy doctor, Don McIntyre, who with a nurse looked after us, and lived with his family in a staff apartment. He had a regional assignment, and after visiting North Yemen described to me with gusto diseases, he said, not seen in the West since the Middle Ages. We swam in the afternoon, and the little pool was a popular place for the embassy staff. We could be on our own and have a change from infrequent visits to the Alwiyah club, the large British-sponsored club with its swimming pools and numerous tennis courts that served as the gathering ground for the foreign community. In the evening we could walk on the riverside terrace of the west bank, the Tigris flowing by. There would be the city hum on the east bank with its collection of colored lights, automobile headlights, traffic noise and other activities muted by the water. Our time thus was spent between the Tigris and the Euphrates, some miles to the west, and the two gave the ancient land its title of Mesopotamia, meaning the land between the rivers.

Virginia, Mrs. Strasser, and the two smaller girls (the elder two in Beirut school) adapted readily. Both girls attended a nearby school organized on an American standard, loosely interpreted, run by an American woman married to an Iraqi diplomat. This school had children of diplomats who wanted theirs to learn English, and Iraqi youngsters as well. Out of school hours our children joined others at home in the compound and pool.

The chancery layout, given the local situation, was helpful in making us self-contained, and for that is worth describing. Its first floor, the consular and administrative offices included the medical area, the snack bar, and a small commissary. It had offices of the closing economic-technical assistance programs making grants for technical study and travel in the U.S. The second floor had the ambassador's and deputy's offices, files and communications, political and economic sections, and army and air attaches.

Eight marine guards included a veteran marine sergeant. The young fellows were a good addition, although by the law of averages they were bound to get into a few scrapes. Their average was excellent for there were fewer distractions. My small daughters (attracted to uniforms) got to know them and had nicknames for each. The marines, aside from their professional competence, were a morale booster for our single secretaries. They had their own large communal apartment over some of the service and storage components of the compound, while the secretaries lived in the staff apartments building. There was some coming and going. In November at the residence I arranged for a social highlight, when the marine contingent gave its annual anniversary party, or ball as it is sometimes called. It was an enjoyable affair, with the great cake cut by a sword and a bit of other ceremony culminating in food and a dance. Time was moving, for all of the young marines, except the master sergeant, had been born after I entered the Foreign Service. In my light remarks I reminded them of the adage, new to the master sergeant, that 1 learned from my father: "A hundred gobs laid down their swabs to lick one sick marine."

Our personnel was generally excellent, and under the conditions I was thankful. Both Jim Akins, who headed the political section while Bill Lakeland was on home leave, and our pleasant station chief, had exceptional knowledge, of which I took full advantage. Jim was a fine officer, a born linguist, energetic, and a man of principle. In fact, when I view the FSOs most governed by principle, Loy Henderson, Charley Hulick, and Jim come first to mind. I welcomed his informed energy, but did convince him in cables a single noun or adjective was better than the combination. The station chief was a solid analyst with wide experience in the Arab world, while the air attache, having Baghdad as a one-time diplomatic assignment, had a steadiness I depended on as local tensions rose. Two new officers I felt had considerable promise. Michael Dowling was the son of FSO Walter (Red) Dowling, known for his wit. On Washington leave after his first six months as ambassador to South Korea, at lunch I had asked Red what he deemed to be his biggest accomplishment there. With a smile he replied, "Getting the military to extend diplomatic recognition to the embassy." Young Mike had a promising future, but later was discouraged by a mediocre supervisor, and resigned to enter international banking. Hume Horan, the other promising new officer, developed in a full career to be an ambassador. Again, the vagaries of the Service.

The economic section also was particularly competent, with its chief being my deputy. I had acceptable relations with him, but he had an abrasive personality. I had been warned of this, and there was a standing offer from Washington to transfer him if needed, for at this post we had enough concerns. We were subject to a vocally unfriendly, dictatorial regime, with harassments outside our mini-landscape that could escalate, so staff morale was all-important. After some episodes, including crying secretaries, and with the agreement of the Department's inspectors and the NEA Bureau, I arranged that he receive loose pack orders for his effects and be transferred while on leave. His replacement and his wife fitted well into our restricted life, and the Northrup Kirks became friends to the extent that Virginia accompanied Mrs. Kirk to Beirut when she was having her first baby.

To help maintain staff morale, Virginia and I worked with the embassy families to organize social affairs and general staff get-togethers on the lawn or elsewhere in the compound. Periodically we would have a purely American staff lunch in the residence for some dozen people, including those newly arriving or leaving. At such times we would sit back informally, talk of American subjects, and maybe listen to a little jazz or other music, and have a congenial afternoon. There was, of course, no distinction between officer and staff personnel, and the morale effect was good.

Despite the state of U.S.-Iraqi relations, we Americans still had friends. We would see, and I came to know and like, a small group of hardy souls in the professions and business who had long associations with Americans. One sad group consisted of American women married to Iraqis, quite like those we met in Iran. By local custom, these women rarely saw foreigners, let alone fellow Americans, and they were hungry for tangible American ties. The precedent had been established, which we gladly continued, of having an American women's organization meet in the residence at least once a month for some form of entertainment or lecture, conversation, and lunch. Obviously this event for some was a high point in the restricted lives they led. Again it emphasized the plight too often of an American girl who married into a completely different culture and who tried to assimilate into a life where a woman has such a subsidiary role. It is a shock when, in some families, a Christian American eats from separate crockery than her Moslem in-laws. When the children come it is harder since the father has absolute control over them. The young man with a car dated at an American university could, under family pressure, turn into something quite different in his homeland.

Because of the danger of demonstrations which could develop into physical attacks on the chancery, files were trimmed and kept as ready as possible for destruction, with my Japanese experience in mind. Certainly the files people deserved every credit for their work, and I visited their area often. Security precautions for the protection of the compound and chancery included special protective doors for the second floor and a plan for stationing our marine guards. To look after the safety of Americans we had, conventional in the Service under the circumstances, an alert and warning plan for the entire community. In offices within politically unsettled areas there were always American citizen evacuation plans. For example, when I was in Tehran, our goal was to attain the safety of friendly Baghdad. Ironically, our safe point now was Tehran. Our people had to be careful where they went to avoid incidents, and there were a few situations, but everyone cooperated in discreet actions, and lived quietly and inconspicuously. Around the city were mud hut communities, called sarifas, where the poorest lived. It was carefully calculated that if there was an internal uprising against him, Qasim would try to use the sarifa dwellers as popular mobs to loot and bring reprisals upon those who dared to overthrow him. Not far from our compound there was such a considerable settlement, and we had to count on the possibility of such a mob trying to overrun our compound. It was uncomfortable to consider this and our families, but comforting to note our ultimate escape hatch, the tethered launch.

Any head of a diplomatic mission has duties toward the American community, including their welfare. One of these duties in Baghdad was to foster an annual ceremony in behalf of the Americans who have died there. This was held in the area designated as the American cemetery, where I gave a short tribute to the predecessors of our grouped Americans. Each of us could react differently, but mine was to a sense of continuity.

Our citizens and American economic interests were typified by business representatives, oilmen, and missionaries engaged in education. Of these last, American Jesuits ran a good secondary school and a recently established college. These capable men, who I came to respect over the years in several assignments, understood the uncertainties of their position. As one said frankly, they had been thrown out of better countries than this. In time this was to happen. American companies had a percentage interest in the Iraqi Petroleum Company (IPC), which was British controlled and was the predominant revenue producer for the country. Between the company and Qasim there was a predictable running feud, as he tried to get as much as he could, while the company tried to keep the oil flowing and not have the enterprise disrupted. It was inevitable that a nationalist dictator, encouraged by the Soviets, would in the governing pattern of the country control its major resource, oil. To me, it was a familiar mixture of oil, politics, and the Russians.

Of course there was a goodly diplomatic community with which we had friendly relations, and it was protocol to call on the chiefs of these missions as soon as this could be arranged. The Spanish ambassador, a true gentleman, and the Yugoslav, an energetic man, I came to appreciate, but the most memorable of my protocol visits was on the Turk. A border episode had chilled Iraqi-Turkish relations temporarily to where, under government encouragement, hostile demonstrations were organized. On driving to the Turkish chancery I found a government-sponsored demonstrating crowd in front. My driver drove to the residential portion of the compound, where we were admitted by a jittery official, who escorted me into the chancery with the ambassador waiting. We had a passable talk under the circumstances, given the chanting crowd outside his second story window, while the ambassador (a former air force general) calmly considered more important matters. Because of the circumstances of our first meeting we got along very well thereafter, since he was pleased that I wasn't put off by the demonstration. The social-official relations I established with the foreign chiefs of mission were useful for their insights and the diversity of their information sources.

The British, with the greatest interests in Iraq, focused on the Iraqi Petroleum Company, were also being harassed and I expected to establish the closest possible relationship with their ambassador. However, Jack Jernegan warned me in Washington that, while he had visited the ambassador at his chancery in the British compound, he had not been able to get the man to reciprocate. I made a courtesy call on the ambassador, and then a second business call, during which I mentioned that we had certain documents in which he would be interested, but I did not feel comfortable in taking them from our embassy. He came along later, starting the practice of alternating visits. We became quite friendly, as did his wife and mine. A small, illogical contributing factor, I believe, may have been using, in informal conversation, a few discreet quotes from those early, bond-creating, English public school ballads.

It was significant that the chiefs of mission I called upon were able to speak English. Because of the strong British influence and the fortunate fact that English is a universal language, many Iraqis of rank also speak it. I evolved a personal technique when a foreign official speaks only his own language and I depend on an interpreter that is worth mentioning. You shift until the interpreter is barely off line of sight between you and the official. You speak directly to the official, and when the interpreter relays the message this gives further opportunity to watch the official's reactions as he regards you. Through his eyes, facial expressions, mien, and hand gestures, you note the silent language, an important accompaniment to the spoken. When the official speaks, you look directly at each other. Even when the interpreter turns, you still look at the official while the message is relayed. It needs use to show it can partly compensate for not knowing a local language. Use of an interpreter can have advantages in doing business, in that you have a double opportunity to judge the reaction of the official, and time, if you have even a sketchy knowledge of the language, to frame your answers and approach. Speaking the language of the country is important and one should try for even a cursory acquaintance, but given the era, many influential persons in a developing country (who generally acquire that influence through education) will speak English or French.

Into October and November we had a full-scale post inspection, since Department schedules must go on. The capable inspectors, Sam Boykin and Pete Skoufis, understood our situation and were helpful with advice. In personality we could not have two better men. Both men, with their wives, lived at the Baghdad hotel, while we saw to it that they had as much sociability as they wished with the embassy staff. Their report on us, they openly said, gave an excellent evaluation based upon the difficult tensions we lived under.

Just before our post inspection, there was the Cuban missile crisis, when we faced the prospect of U.S. - Soviet nuclear war. It had local repercussions. One night an operational immediate cable spelled out the situation, and I alerted key officers and requested a late night interview with the foreign minister, putting the gravity of the situation on the table. He saw its import, and I know after leaving him that he was off to see Qasim. Other messages, in and out, followed as our staff was prepared for anything. The foreign minister was troubled for its possible effects on the Qasim regime, revealing how such a major crisis can have wide international effects. The finale was a happy event for us, and we had felicitations from the democratic states and moderate Islamic representatives. In Iraq and the Arab world, where strength was understood, the result was salutary

Baghdad was expanding. Rashid Street was long known as the one straight street paralleling the river through the old segment of the city. Time had supplemented it by broader avenues, some of which extended into the desert wastelands, where there was as yet no sign of housing. As in ancient times, the houses had roofs where families slept on hot nights under the stars, and substantial homes had underground or cellar apartments with thick walls which served for cooler living during the summer days. I was driven around town on official appointments, on visits to the Baghdad hotel, which had the best such facilities, to book stores, and to the bazaar. The car was air conditioned, as was the residence and chancery, so living in the hottest months was bearable, but I mulled over the stringencies my pre-airconditioning predecessors had to endure. An initial hazard on official visits was being served a small cup of thick Arab coffee; powerful stuff. After several in the course of an hour or two, I was unpleasantly overdosed with caffeine, so I learned to request tea or the popular, very sweet coca cola instead.

In my excursions, the city's bazaars were always interesting with their color, bustle, exotic dress, and unusual items, as well as the most prosaic. Baghdad was improving its antiques museum, and there were many specimens I had seen in history and art books, such as the impressive great stone Assyrian winged bulls. Along the east bank of the Tigris, where the bulk of Baghdad was concentrated, there would be little shops on the shore that at all hours would sell fresh fish or cook it to order over a brazier. In driving or walking along the streets, one passed sidewalk cafes filled with berobed men watching the pedestrians and talking over their tea or coffee. One rarely saw women in such places, and they appeared on the street or bazaar in traditional dress. There were not many, and these foreign educated, in western clothes. The strange and exotic always had a strong appeal, and here it was our environment and life style - if one could only forget Qasim and his Soviet advisers.

I was acquiring more information about the Iraqi character. The Iraqis had their own traits as arabs. As a stereotype, they were known in the Arab world for being aggressive and unpolished. Despite the division between the Sunni and majority Shia sects, the regime since the demise of the monarchy through ruthless action would force a rough cohesion. Years later Saddam Hussein, as the Ba'ath party dictator and a known secularist, would show the power of such rule by extracting a half million casualties from his subservient subjects during the eight year Iraqi-Iran war, and still unyielding, take them into a catastrophic war against the UN-US coalition. For us, anti-American attitudes could lead to widescale violence.

We lived quietly, seeing those Iraqis and foreign diplomats we could, attending official functions when practical, and having social life among ourselves, but the day most American officials looked forward to was Sunday. That was the day to go on a telling expedition. Along the length of the two great rivers were small hills or large mounds called tells, which had been created over millennia as successive villages and towns on the sites had been destroyed or abandoned and new towns rose on the ruins. The settling of their surfaces yielded us abundant artifacts from ancient times. There were fragments and sometimes largely intact pottery, household talismans, and sharp serrated flints used for cutting chores. Virginia and I would arrange groups for picnic lunches in two cars, each with attached compass, and our drivers would head off across the barren plain by ill-defined roads, and even where there were none, for one or more tells to prospect. This could not be done in very hot weather, although some devotees then started before dawn and returned before noon. We simply used shoes or a stick to bring to light interesting manmade objects and fragments several thousand years old that we retained. Babylon was not too far off, and a trip there always was unusual, starting with the site of the legendary Tower of Babel. A machined, blue enameled tile fragment from Babylon's ancient walls made a good paper weight.

A signature of the area in ancient times was the ziggurats or towers of brick, built as city eminences stretching to considerable height, and appearing higher on the flat plain. These might have four sides of step back construction with a temple or altar on top. In another form they were circular towers with a road or footway twined around a cone-like shape and the ruins could form the nucleus of a goodly sized tell. Through the changes of architecture, the cone ziggurat became the Moslem minaret.

Our consulate at Basra near the Persian Gulf on the Shatt al Arab, the merged Tigris and Euphrates, was manned by two officers and an American clerk, who, aside from courier trips to Baghdad, led a pent-up existence in a tiny community. Yet the post had substantive utility as an observation point for relationships of Iraq with both Kuwait and Iran, their borders being very close.

Iraqi dates were a major export to the U.S., and American shipping frequented the port. Dates were a commercial problem in our relations since the Agriculture Department insisted on standards of fumigation which the Iraqis would not always observe, only to have some of the product condemned at the port of entry. Pitting dates was supposedly done by knife, but in some of the villages the workers merely bit into the dates and spit out the pits. I was assured that the date sugar sanitized them! The area was an essential outlet for Iraq's oil, in export volume approximating Iran's. I got to visit the south when travel restrictions were removed, and set up an interim procedure whereby the junior vice consul, eventually an ambassador, and clerk would have a first year in Basra and a second year in Baghdad, for unless these were absolutely congenial, friction could grow. Personnel were the Service's vital asset.

Unexpected was the natural advent of sand storms. The Iraqi sand is very fine grained, so when a heavy storm blew in the city it was comparable to a dust storm in our American southwest. Throughout Baghdad, the sand coated building interiors and seeped into cabinets. The following spring, our administrative officer and his wife made a trip to Ur, formerly a Gulf port and the birthplace of Abraham in ancient Chaldea. During their return, they were caught in a sand storm. Fortunately they carried five gallon water tins and traveled with another vehicle for further protection. As in a snow storm, when one vehicle was caught in a sanddrift, it had to be shoveled out to attain traction. Since any physical exertion resulted in dry throats and leathery skin, enormous amounts of water were needed to restore them. The danger from a lack of water was clear.

The political situation outlined in Washington was not changing for the better and there were some touchy episodes. Americans felt increasingly isolated from the Iraqis, and Qasim's unfriendly attitude toward the Western nations was more manifest. It reached the point where free world diplomats rarely accepted invitations to attend affairs where Qasim would be present, for they did not wish to hear his anti-Western tirades. Since I was to follow events and to gain impressions of the atmosphere at first hand, I rarely failed to go to the dedication of a small housing development or an amateur performance at which he would appear. Since Qasim and his henchmen knew I did not speak Arabic, it deprived them of the satisfaction of sting from his comments. It can be frustrating confronted by a non-Arabic speaking, poker faced American. It was at such times, confronted by hostility, that I had a sense of satisfaction in representing our country, disliked because of actions I believed were done for the right reasons. I usually had one of our Arabic-speaking officers with me, who would translate later, but occasionally I would go alone simply to sense the atmosphere and to observe.

It was instructive to watch the security arrangements for Qasim. At a housing dedication, for instance, there were soldiers with rifles on the adjacent roof tops and strategically placed in the environs. When all were in position, and never on time, Qasim would come under armed escort with his entourage, all in uniform. In appearance he was of middle height, lean, mustached, and with a burning or neurotic eye. Over time the security measures increased and you could sense the decreasing assurance of Qasim's main lieutenants. One of these, the foreign minister, was a slippery rascal, who had a background of an English education and professional experience. He was my natural contact point, and diplomats would call on him at the Foreign Office or his subordinates there. I used to mention, without pressing, that I would like to meet Qasim. He would agree, but failed to make arrangements. My instructions were to call on Qasim officially if at all possible. In this I never succeeded, but I could report I did meet him.

At the various affairs Qasim was difficult to approach because of security precautions, and those diplomats who did shake his hand were from the so-called radical Arab and communist states. I came to accept it as a challenge. If an affair was in one of the large government halls in his compound in the Defense ministry, it was a big reception. Prior to the late evening stampede to the food tables, Qasim under careful escort, moved around the large room speaking to those he recognized. The foreign minister once saw me at a point and deftly steered Qasim off. This time I suddenly planted myself strategically between some chairs and a sofa. The foreign minister was trapped. Thereupon I greeted him in friendly fashion, and he had to present me to his boss. The impression of Qasim given earlier was reinforced by close-up contact, which I managed to prolong in talk for a bit before dropping away. Qasim obviously had not wanted nor expected to meet me, so it was satisfying. At large receptions such as this, mounds of food were served as late as midnight, and after the meal everyone quickly drifted off. As you left, as on this occasion, you could hear the noise of the household staff, police, and soldier guards charging into the buffet rooms to finish off the remainder. Our diplomatic group ate sparingly being wary of the rice drenched in sheep fat.

In northern Iraq, spilling over into both Iran and Turkey, were the Kurds, who are Indo-European in origin (the hard fighting Carducci of Xenophon's "Anabasis"), and who were the perennial and often exploited source of international problems. As far as their relation to Iraq was concerned, the Kurds were engaged in a lasting struggle for autonomy, if not independence, because accumulated grievances they felt justified this. A Soviet radio station also helped keep things stirred up. The Iraqi military had waged and would continue sporadic, inconclusive campaigns against them, which the Kurds, under their leader, Barzani, earlier evaded in the wild northern terrain. Although there was a truce for the latter period of my assignment, the continuing tragedy for the Iraqi Kurds, in what over time came to be unwarranted government poison gas attacks, was one that seems incapable of any just solution. I did ask representatives of other American agencies who could send messages to their Washington headquarters, to forbear before discussing with me reports of activities involving the Kurds and any impending coup d'etat. These were subjects on which I wished no confusion in Washington. The request was respected, so prior consultation gave me the opportunity to comment either in the message being transmitted or in referenced State channels.

Once a Washington cable requested my prompt response on an action affecting the Kurds. I discussed it with the country team that morning and found all but the political section in agreement on my response. My recommendation was transmitted to the Department, and I asked the unhappy political officers to prepare a memo of their views by early afternoon. Puzzled, they did, and I exchanged with them a letter to the area assistant secretary for their drafted memo. The officers read that I sent my cable as requested, since it was my responsibility, but I wanted the disagreeing political section to have its views on record by outgoing courier that evening. If my cabled views proved in error, it could make my political section look awfully good. I glanced at the officers. We smiled.

Several times previously our embassy had tried to bell the cat in terms of predicting Qasim's downfall. Washington people had told me that they were dubious about such predictions, but this was a major assignment to follow and conditions in Iraq proved well suited to a type of reporting I have referred to earlier. The factual reports and at some locally opportune juncture, sector analyses, were capped by a general assessment, which I habitually prepared and discussed with the section chiefs. A suitable point came in January. We had done one such operation earlier, but the upshot of the latest indicated that difficulties were growing for Qasim. I reported that his regime had never been weaker in terms of hostility from non-communist elements, including secondary and university students, who were becoming united. The Soviet influence was expanding.

After the January estimate the situation continued to deteriorate. Our friends and some sources of information had to be almost conspiratorial in calling at all hours on the embassy officers living outside our compound. We began to mark Qasim was stepping up officer retirements among those of whom he was unsure, and he began to arrest Ba'ath civilians. The Ba'ath political party was an Arab secular-socialist-nationalist regional party that had its origin in Syria, in fact founded by a Syrian Christian, which had spread to other Arab countries. It was a political force Qasim could not control, so he suppressed it.

Friday, February 8, the Moslem sabbath, we expected our usual office work. I saw the incoming cables, already processed, and noted their routing. After a few phone calls, I glanced through the daily official wireless news not finished at breakfast. For two embassy officers, the air attache and a political officer, the street patterns en route to the chancery were disturbing. They saw groups of arm-banded men who, from a distance, seemed to be carrying weapons. They also heard unsurprising rapid fire, since the regime used rigid security measures, but it was worth checking. Phone calls were inconclusive, but the outside lines were clear, as if the bug monitors were inoperative. The political officer noted an erratic local radio carrying music, not talk. After an initial office interval brought the staff to speed, the weekly meeting began. As usual, I first asked if there were any non-routine or unusual items, upon which the two officers gave their observations. I adjourned the meeting, remarking we could be better occupied getting onto this.

Very shortly more concerted firing could be heard. We put our standing plans into effect, with each section pursuing inquiries of their sources. Drill or not, a buttoning operation began and I alerted my family in the residence. An economic officer, aided by the consul, readied the walkie talkie city network of district wardens charged with American citizen liaison. They could announce an evacuation alert or move to further steps as covered by our plan. They also checked our river launch for ready water access if the streets were closed. The administrative and general services officers alerted the marine contingent to take compound and chancery guarding positions, and vehicles were fully serviced. Within the chancery, protective devices, including the steel door to barricade the classified second floor, were workable. In the vault-like code and file rooms and other sensitive offices, rapid file incineration equipment was checked and readied, some of which could be taken to the chancery roof. A standby radio connection, activated after difficulties, brought in consulate Basra. Since it was a transmission within Iraq, the facility was available only for an emergency. News now traveled both ways, but slowly because of a special code.

By now Americans were being methodically located by phone, now surprisingly efficient. Information from citywide observers included the British embassy, uncomfortably close to a target, the defense ministry. Reports were funneled to the embassy's political section, which prepared operational immediate messages for my initialing and transmission to Washington and Mideast capitals. The armed services attaches and the CIA station naturally were sending theirs, and there were cross references. The Ba'ath plotters, we learned, apparently saw they had to move first against Qasim before their organization within the army would be made impotent by transfers and retirements. We also learned that they selected Friday as the best time, since senior officers were away from their units and many soldiers had weekend passes. We were told that armed green-banded Ba'ath led students were in groups all over town. The coup leaders took over the main military camp as their headquarters, and importantly, the radio transmitter there. The radio-TV broadcasting studios were taken later in the day. Again well planned, aircraft from the one large base dominating Baghdad had destroyed Soviet MIGS attempting takeoff from a local airfield having Soviet trained pilots and instructors. In a key action, the pro-Soviet head of the air force was killed at his home before he could assume command. The growing volume of fire, the radio station in rebel hands, joined with tank and fighter aircraft attacks on the defense ministry, where Qasim and personal units were besieged, showed a full scale revolt underway. Insurgent aircraft maintained rocket attacks on the ministry during daylight hours until Qasim's surrender later the next day. These we could follow from the chancery roof, spelling each other, and our air attache pointed out how the pilots were hitting only the defense ministry sector. Unfortunately, the nearby British embassy compound was hit several times.

The way the staff was organized, its morale, and its application to varied duties, put me at ease and sure of the entire machine. My confidence in our people mounted as I observed them doing their competent best. Somehow it was a vindication of professionalism and what this embodied in an action situation. Later I read novelist John Masters's "The Road Past Mandalay," where from headquarters he commanded an Indian army division for one day during the World War II Burma campaign. My feelings were similar. In brief, for me it was a field climax to a professional career.

Added to the chancery roof panorama of bombing and strafing was the hazard of Qasim regime anti-aircraft shrapnel from an adjacent former royal palace area, where such guns were located. They were firing at the planes and spraying shrapnel within our compound. It was dangerous to go hurriedly between compound points, with all under strict orders, except absolutely necessary, to stay indoors. Meanwhile our few marines, some understandably nervous, guarded our entrances. We kept a close watch by phone contacts on the currently undirected sarifas, quiet for the present, apparently due both to insurgent troops and armed civilians blocking them off. In thinking of the potential sarifa problem, our walls suddenly looked very vulnerable.

A Washington and Baghdad time differential of eight hours meant that the first operational immediate message reached the State department at night. The watch officer, as standard practice, phoned the Iraqi desk officer at home and gave the contents. Sleep forgotten, that official alerted his assistant to phone the bureau's duty secretary and to join him at the Department. He called the Near East affairs director who headed for the office as well. By their arrival, another message gave still more facts and showed a serious coup d'etat effort underway. These men were now an element in a Department task force or working group concerned with a crisis. With the safety of Americans in mind, the task force put the Washington Liaison Group (WLG) of administrators, including the Pentagon, on notice for standby logistics in a possible evacuation of all Americans in Iraq to the pre-selected safehaven, Tehran. The Near East assistant secretary had been advised, and he was kept continually informed. Pentagon officials received their attachés's messages with those of State, both agencies working together. The ripples rapidly widened, including State, Defense, CIA, Information Agency, and AID, as well as White House national security staff.

Within State and CIA, intelligence analysts were piecing the incoming information into a pattern that was supplementing the embassy's and geographic officials's analyses. This began to indicate the coup was sponsored by an alliance, including dissident military officers opposing the communists, an old Qasim rival, General Arif, and the Ba'ath (Arab Resurrection) party, with strong student and other civilian adherents. The military had outfitted the civilian groups as a militia with armband identities, and they were proving a valuable adjunct to the troops in controlling keypoints, traffic areas, and sarifa settlements. Baghdad apparently was the center of the revolt, and other cities would follow its lead. Meanwhile fighting was intense around the defense ministry.

News agencies, without private sources, were calling the Department, and the desk officers gave the information they had. Incoming messages were now time dated well into afternoon as the Washington winter dawn began. Thereabouts came a message that had been awaited: preliminarily all Americans appeared safe. The State press officer at the noon press briefing could be hopeful.

Over the two days naturally there was a curfew, irregularly observed, and the Americans we needed and a vital handful of Iraqi employees stayed in the compound, the others drifting off the first day to check on their families. People in the chancery and in the school were isolated from their east bank homes, and some moved in during the trouble. Aside from scattered private Americans, one of our unusual groups was the 40 odd children from the American School and their teachers, who were hurried "guests," a term later misused by future dictator Saddam Hussein. The snack bar was open until all hours, and the ladies pitched in to handle the care and feeding of everyone, with our housekeeper leading a bread-making brigade. The youngsters, teachers, and others were quartered in the residence, so when I came home at night I picked my way between blanketed, sleeping bodies in unusual places. I assumed financial responsibility for the feeding and maintenance of these guests, and was amused later when the IRS requested I show some higher authorization for this action!

Of our small cadre of Iraqis, an assistant to the political section was valuable in aiding our analysis of the regime's broadcasts and in helping to chart events.

We also had a spotter system organized throughout the city of embassy officers and reliable Americans, who gave us through telephone calls and visits, news of developments in their local areas. Foreign embassies also had our exchanges. An earlier report to Washington indicated Americans appeared to be safe, but now we could report that they really were.

Qasim and his chief aides surrendered early Saturday afternoon and were brought to the radio-television studio before military judges there, including General Arif, the announced head of the pending regime. Qasim had surrendered unconditionally, according to the reliable accounts we received, and asked that he be allowed to leave for Switzerland. His request was denied, and he and his aides were shot on the premises, with the radio carrying the announcement of his capture and death. That afternoon the TV showed pictures of the dead man to give public evidence, and in following days this feature was run several times, an updating of the spectacle of medieval heads on pikes at the city gates. East bank crowds still filed through the city chanting slogans in support of Qasim and "Death to the Imperialists" over that time. By the evening, TV showings of Qasim's body had their effect and the mobs began returning to their sarifas. As Adam, our houseman, said, "Now we know he's dead." The public was so bewildered by longterm propaganda that it needed the visual evidence, true even today.

All was not over. The fighting continued into Sunday in parts of the city as organized, armed communists put up a final resistance and still attempted to incite the sarifa dwellers. The Ba'ath won out. Then it was announced that the Soviet Union was withdrawing its mission from Iraq.

The attitude of the new regime toward westerners appeared friendly. Troops, tank crews, and militia at check points were helpful to Americans attempting to emerge. But there were questions needing prompt answers. What was the official attitude of the new authorities toward Americans? What commitments would they assume towards them and Iraq's international obligations? What was to be the regime's orientation?

With all due speed, by Sunday contact was made with officials in places of authority. The Revolutionary Council, wary of revealing all its members, had a designated foreign minister. Anticipating Washington, I requested an appointment. When we met later that Sunday, I found the young designated minister to be sophisticated and fluent in English. By now under formal Washington instructions, I put my queries to him. The Revolutionary Council, said the minister, would fully protect Americans in their normal occupations and in their property. It had complete control over the country and was accepted by the people. It intended to conduct internal affairs according to the restored legal code. It was determined to honor all Iraq's international obligations, such as specialized functional treaties and agreements and those with the United Nations. In orientation it sought good relations with all states without the bias that had been its predecessor's. It welcomed the prospect of diplomatic relations with the United States. To the successive statements I responded with the formula ingredients at such a time, expressing satisfaction at the minister's statements in the informal meeting and saying that I would report these assurances to Washington. As well, I would report evidences of governmental control by, and public acceptance of, the Revolutionary Council. I hoped the minister would continue to give me early appointments as conditions warranted. On my return to the chancery, I drafted still another operational priority message that evaluated the situation, contained the substance of the interview, and concluded that the new regime fulfilled American requirements for full and rapid diplomatic recognition. The British embassy had come to a like decision. An operational immediate brought recognition of the new Iraqi government late on Sunday, the third day. Formal notes were exchanged with that government and it was done.

By late in the third day, the embassy had another challenge, to size up the new government quickly and make recommendations as to American attitudes and actions toward it in all fields. Using the country team, I developed over the next day a message containing varied sector recommendations to meet the new situation, which gave Washington the framework of a proposed action program to consider. The embassy's sections estimated this turned off some inquiries and perhaps what they privately might have considered impractical suggestions from Washington.

The coup was an international news event, but there was little in the public media. Qasim's control over wire facilities, commercial airports, and frontier posts had sealed off the country. State's NEA bureau accordingly was beset by requests from the press, news services, and television for help in getting their correspondents into Iraq. The embassy was asked to assist, and the foreign minister said American correspondents would be allowed to land without visas, whereupon the first group flew in from Rome. It arrived on the fourth day, Monday, and came straight to the embassy, where qualified section chiefs gave briefings and answered questions, so they could know the ground. Then the correspondents were on their own. Each journalist appreciated our help, shown in letters to us and in one to the Secretary of State. Conditions, at least in Mideast terms, were returning to normal.

The Revolutionary Council, from experience, did not announce its membership. The foreign minister I have mentioned, and officers who led the coup were young men, supported by retired officers who joined them in uniform at the outset, like one of their announced leaders, General Arif. Quite a few of the ministers seemed qualified and persons with whom, given any reasonable chance, we could work.  I called on all of them to establish acceptable relations and to learn how each was viewing things, for the wider our relationships the better.

The regime made statements concerning its policy of non-alignment between the world power blocs, which suited us, but which, from communist screams clearly showed they knew it was a serious defeat.  In declaring for non-alignment, the new government made a customary distinction between communism in the Middle East and the Soviet bloc states, saying that it wanted to have good relations with the latter but would tolerate no communist activities internally.  The new regime came to power equipped with complete lists of communist and pro-communist sympathizers, and was energetic in tracking them down, so the communist organization and leadership were heavily damaged, at least while these were in jail or exile.  A leading Ba'ath feature of the post-coup period was the national guard auxiliary to the armed forces.  These youngsters in many cases were unfamiliar with weapons, but checked vehicle traffic and  helped patrol the city during curfew hours.  Generally they were polite to those they had checked, and especially to foreigners, a provisional sign of a better attitude toward us.

The foreign minister and I became friendly in the coming  months.  We had him and his English wife to dinner (always buffet, for you could never be sure who would appear), and I was impressed with what he was trying to do.  As I gained his confidence, and certainly with the full knowledge of the Revolutionary Council, he opened up with regard to Middle East developments.  Of particular interest was the strained Ba'ath relationship with Nasser, and I became reasonably informed on this and some other aspects on which we and my colleagues in other Middle East countries normally had sketchy or belated information.  The cabled reports were welcomed in Washington and, from messages I received, by ambassadors in the area.  For Americans the change and the advent of normal social relations with Iraqis was a relief, in some ways analogous to our experience in Iran after Mosadeq was overthrown.  Given the nature of politics in the Arab world, however, very shortly conflicts between the Ba'ath concept of pan-Arabism and that of Nasser began to loom.  I could only trace this, in part, to the age-old rivalry between the two great river civilizations, still extant today.  Combined with competition among the influential in Iraq, the cycle of intrigue and disaffection resumed.  As its victim, the personable foreign minister was to be murdered after my time.

Because of the government's negotiations with the Kurds, Mosul in northern Iraq's oil fields was off limits to diplomats, but after the coup we could get down to Basra.  I did not leave the country, but there was a family reward.  At Easter, Virginia and an embassy driver flew to Beirut to pick up a car I had ordered from the States.  Virginia and the two big girls took advantage of this and the spring break from school for a memorable trip to the Holy Land, the rock-hewn city of Petra in Jordan, and from Damascus, a drive across the Syrian desert to Baghdad. Symptomatic of the chronic area violence was their getting out of Syria an hour before the border was closed because of internal trouble.

In the spring my old friend, Gordon Mattison, came by traveling in his assignment in charge of a seminar of the Foreign Service Institute (FSI).  His was a major program with Administration push behind it, seeking ways in which we could help friendly governments counter internal subversion and externally inspired revolt.  In passing he mentioned that, although I had not been in Baghdad long, with a new ambassador the thought was I might be changed or want to be changed.  FSI had been alerted to this, and because of my Ph.D. the director had me on a priority list, approved by Mr. Crockett, under secretary for Administration, Loy Henderson's successor.  I asked him to consider that I was happy in Baghdad with interesting work.  The staff generally was rooting that now I would formally be designated as ambassador there, fed by letters  from Washington. While appreciating the wishes, I knew how such things were done, and was more relaxed.

When it became clear that the Ba'ath regime would stay awhile, I had written our assistant secretary on receiving a very complimentary  letter from him.  My reply said that when a new ambassador was named he should feel no hesitancy in shifting me.  The assistant secretary responded that he would keep my ideas in mind, but it was a surprise when the nominee was announced.  It was the director of the Near East office, who had not impressed me in Washington, and I recalled Cavendish Cannon's dictum on the second category of Service ambassadors. After three tours as a deputy, but especially  another proposed with a chief I deemed mediocre, this was unpalatable.  Given this turn, I was prepared when seeing the assistant secretary in  Beirut during a quick Middle East chiefs of mission meeting. I told him, in view of my contacts with the government and diplomatic corps over my period in Baghdad this could prove constricting to an incoming chief of mission, who would naturally want these associations himself. After some compliments I took in stride, the assistant secretary agreed to have me go, despite what I later gathered was some pressure from the nominee for retention.  The incipient ambassador felt uncomfortable going into the post, so I stayed a week after his arrival.  We used the Fourth of July reception as an occasion to introduce him, and after a series of meetings and calls I thought he was fairly launched.

My qualms were confirmed.  By chance I was on the Service personnel evaluation boards when three embassy section chiefs to whom I had accorded excellent ratings, for they had proven themselves under strains, were given poor ratings when the ambassador reviewed their next efficiency reports, written by his deputy.   Jim Akins, later to be ambassador to Saudi Arabia and the leading government authority on international oil, had not gotten along with the new arrival at an earlier posting.   They talked, and Jim decided not to request a transfer.   He ruefully recalls I advised him to cut his losses and seek to leave.

The new assignment was to be FSI after all, as special assistant to its director and coordinator of its mid-career course, and I recalled Gordon's comments.   In Tehran on my departure, the political section had surprised me with a Moslem prayer rug.   Here my diplomatic colleagues of the non-Soviet bloc gave me an inscribed silver tray as a memento.   Protocol act or not, the names I remember. We were homeward bound, and early one morning, despite the hour, the family was surrounded by official Americans as we took the Pan Am plane.   So much had happened within that year, and after this test I felt prepared to handle any diplomatic mission in fair or stormy weather.

Berlin with Charley and
Sunnie Hulick and their
children

The Family - Roy
Lucy, April, Virginia
Janice and Hope

Dean of FSI, with assistant, Walt Chapman, and training course staff officer

# CHAPTER 14

## PRAGMATIC ACADEMIC: WASHINGTON, THE FSI

## July 1963 - June 1966

*President Kennedy was assassinated and President Johnson's Great Society program began. The U.S. and Soviets held underground nuclear tests, Khruschev was deposed, and Brezhnev succeeded him. Mao began the Great Cultural Revolution and detonated China's first atomic bomb. The Vietnam war grew to 42,000 U.S. troops, as the Senate's Tonking Gulf Resolution signaled further escalation. France forced NATO to withdraw its armed forces from France, declaring its own unique participation. Emerging Africa saw the Congo bush war and Mobutu's accession as president, Nkrumah's fall in Ghana, and importantly, a military coup in Nigeria. At the Foreign Service Institute, I was successively special assistant to its director, coordinator of the mid-career course, and dean of the School of Foreign Affairs, charged with the bulk of overseas professional training for civilian officials and some military. Then I was reassigned, following assurances, to the Bureau of African Affairs.*

Since I had not been in Istanbul since 1944, I enjoyed showing my family the changes and remembered sights. Naturally we saw Burton Berry and his home with its magnificent view of the Bosphorus. Later in Germany we stopped in Weisbaden, and Virginia and I flew to Berlin to visit the Hulicks. There the only landmark I could identify was the Brandenburg Gate and the ruined Reichstag. The large empty spaces where bombing debris had been removed and the Berlin Wall are not easily forgotten, one the consequence of the hot, and the other of the cold war. That scabrous wall, eventually to be demolished, was repugnant in its division of a modern city, and its typified conflict between the free and communist worlds.

In New York I headed for Washington and congratulated myself on the brief leave en route, for I started work that afternoon. My predecessor was being hurried overseas by a political ambassador, so this meant about three days overlap. While I had expected it, the director of the Foreign Service Institute (FSI), George Morgan, elaborated on what Gordon had said. Before my name was formally submitted for reassignment, he invoked the priority of the undersecretary for Administration to obtain what he wanted. I was his selection as his special assistant and coordinator of the mid-career course in the School of Foreign Affairs.

The course, lasting twelve weeks, was in the first week of its run when I arrived, but there was a capable staff assistant. It was designed for middle level officers of class 4-5 to broaden their foreign affairs background, to acquaint them with the extent of interagency collaboration, and to spur an interest in executive management. The students averaged half from State and half from other foreign affairs and national security agencies, with readings and guest speakers over the course span, divided into nine parts. The speakers came from in and out of government, but there were some we would have in each course. I retained full notes on two: the brilliant philosopher Joseph Campbell of Sarah Lawrence, whom I got to know, was to be recognized for "The Power of Myth," "The Hero With a Thousand Faces," and "The Masks of God," and thoughtful Ed Wright of our own FSI and a Mideast authority. Both talked on our diverse cultural heritage and approached a foreign culture from an analytical, psychological point of view. Each had two days, and as stimuli were outstanding. Illustratively, the former cultural attache in India earnestly said that he wished he had heard Joe Campbell's talks before his New Delhi posting.

We noted various trends in the U.S. such as civil rights; surveyed development and trade; by panels examined modernization problems in selected countries, and reviewed international communism, its area operations, and possible counter insurgencies. Familiar territory was how American policy was made and implemented. We also had visits to the Pentagon and CIA. I developed a two-day section on negotiations, an indispensable element in diplomacy, and strangely, an innovation. Much can be learned from reading and hearing how others have done it. Thus, we discussed techniques, including those for negotiating with the communists, perennial problems such as Berlin, and the application of game theory to foreign affairs. The final section emphasized operations management for those on the verge of executive responsibilities and interacting with other agencies. Management people gave case studies, an ambassador told how he organized his chancery, and panels analyzed ways to direct American operations. All this in twelve weeks! Successive groups were unanimous in declaring the course benefits, but more notable is what motivated people can learn.

A professor I had long known was lecturing when my staff assistant brought the shocking news that President Kennedy had been assassinated. When I told the group, the speaker voiced our feelings in proposing the session be adjourned, and for days we could not get back into our classroom routine. I had a Tehran memory.

What we were doing in the mid-career course was a small part of a large operation. The FSI was directed by George Morgan and his deputies as the heads of the various schools or training areas. The School of Foreign Affairs concerned itself with professional studies to equip officers for various assignments. I reported to the designated dean as the coordinator of the mid-career course and to George Morgan as his special assistant on separate projects he gave me. There was the School of Languages and Area Studies led by Howard Sollenberger, while my old friend, Ken Landon, popped up as his deputy concerned there with brief and intensified courses on various world regions, and area studies undertaken by officers at universities. The National Interdepartmental Seminar, with strong Administration support, was interagency staffed and devoted to means of assisting in the internal defense of developing countries exposed to subversion.

The Senior Seminar in foreign affairs was, for its State-trained civilians, preferable to the war colleges, and had been so designed in length and scope. Andy Corry, who I got to know well, was in charge and his deputy none other than Lee Metcalf. I could see the cost effectiveness and value of these courses as training tools.

In the varied courses, other agency people equalled those from State. The scope of FSI's work is shown by the fiscal year 1964, ending June 30, when it had over 17,300 students, other agencies supplying slightly more than half. The School of Foreign Affairs handled some 4,600. The School of Languages had the most students, with 9,200, and Area Studies 2,000 more. This considerable plant was housed in a large apartment complex across the river from the Department, and included areas originally intended for garage space, service rooms, and a night club, as well as apartments. Since the mid-career course was in a large interior room, I hung a huge blowup of nighttime Pennsylvania Avenue looking toward the lighted Capitol. It gave us an impression of the great outdoors. Despite the quarters, I was impressed with the dedication and experience applied to the training.

Before the FSI, my ideas on Service training were rudimentary. I had been assigned as a junior officer to the Foreign Service School, then after FSI was set up in 1947 I had taken short courses in cultural anthropology and personnel management. Two years of early morning French impressed me with its language training. The year of the National War College had been a great opportunity. Still, my Service training had been haphazard or on my initiative. Many officers had even less training as part of an obsolescent system that too long was concerned with personnel assignments, and held the outmoded stereotype that all can be learned on the job anyway. In the world we were dealing with and the variety of desirable proficiencies, the minimum advocated span of at least one year training for every ten years service was small enough. Languages were more important, and area studies for specialization in a region was a trend. A big deficiency, I thought, was in the professional tools an officer should have on assignment, particularly in the crucial mid-career levels, where the bulk of officers was concentrated.

Having been immersed in post operations and policy, I overlooked the remarkable changes in professional training. The Institute's message was that specialized training to meet current skills was essential to successful work, for it enabled faster, assured performance. The variety of skills, given America's world role, required regular training, since in the long run it was a budget saver through increased effectiveness. Universities were not the answer for the bulk of training needed, for academics were geared to time periods and approaches not always suited to intensive in-house types of training the officers needed. I favored some paths FSI's School of Foreign Affairs was following, and proposed others.

After looking at our foreign affairs from an FSI angle, it occurred to me how foreign techniques of the U.S. and Russia can draw their tactical analogies from games. The Russians try carefully arranged planning and multiple options derived from chess. We Americans draw upon our football, involving some game planning, but more improvisation. It is no accident that General Patton's mobile tank army in World War II used the code name "Lucky Forward." In embassies,the agency and section heads are combined in the country team, we have bureaucratic end runs, and the ambassador is even termed by some the quarterback.

As my training views evolved, George Morgan decided that he wanted me and the administrative deputy, John Thomas, to work with two of Mr. Crockett's men in studying a program for all mid-level officers; that is, after their early years in the Service and up to the senior stage of the war colleges. To discuss a philosophy of mid-career training, to envision the specialties needed, and to project these took time. Any comparable panel, if not papering its differences, requires a corporate identity as views merge into an agreed program. We did this, and came up with a report and too daring accompanying recommendations. We eliminated the mid-career course and proposed a program management seminar of 16 weeks to prepare officers for coordinating executive responsibilities in State, needed as more agencies participated in foreign affairs. The mid-career course did not have sufficient management scope for what we had in mind. Concurrently we proposed short programs for the various political, economic, commercial, labor, science, and administrative specialties into which Service careers were organized.

After the survey and recommendations of our little panel, George Morgan decided to enlist me to reorganize the School of Foreign Affairs and to press aspects like economic and management training. The former dean was being shifted to FSI's academic relations. Two years were viewed as a normal FSI assignment, so before then I had begun to get nibbles on forthcoming assignments. but it was here George took an initiative. He broached it as a strong personal favor if I would be, as of January 1, dean of the School of Foreign Affairs. If I had been the realistic idealist I sometimes fancied, I might have pressed as to the aftermath, but that would have been ungenerous. Accepted I did, but as he knew, with twinges. George Morgan was complex and a man to be respected; very intelligent and private. Entering the Service after a World War II military stint, he had made an excellent career and proved to be a fine FSI director. Serious, articulate when he chose, personable and honest, he had a human reserve of intellectual pride. When I chaired the review board for FSI faculty efficiency reports, I had been obliged to say that two of his would not achieve a result if he wanted the officers promoted. Showing his breadth, he accepted my comment, and revised and improved them.

My current preoccupation became the effectiveness of the school. Given his skill in management, we did all possible to stress the courses with which John Stutesman, my first Iranian desk officer, was charged. He was the best possible choice; imaginative and a fine officer. My associate dean was near retirement, so when Walt Chapman did, John became my deputy, assisted by a dozen officers as faculty, including capable staff assistants. The School was a composite, and it was important to place related sectors under managers. The Junior Officer Course for new FSOs was in the hands of two capable men. Various orientation courses for officers and secretaries included Fulbright Scholar grantees, going abroad for a year. Administrative courses were under one officer, with assistants. Another handled consular operations, visas and passports. We had an orientation survey for foreign service wives, run by a woman officer and the wife of an FSO that proved very popular. With the help of the Department of Commerce, we gave courses in trade expansion and a refresher for commercial officers. The Labor Department worked with us in a seminar on international labor affairs. There was a short internal defense course and a two week session on communist strategy handled by an FSO Soviet expert. John Stutesman organized our management sector into four courses: personnel operations, basic management, executive and advanced executive studies. We contentedly got funds to take the advanced course to officers, such as DCMs, in a particular geographic region, where they would meet overseas.

We could be innovative, always with Service needs in mind, so one of the most unusual courses we offered was a trailbreaking economics study. It had been developing, but not progressing fast enough, as a 22 week intensive course for mid-level FSOs to give them the equivalent of an undergraduate major in economics. This shook the academics -and we consulted the best - who admitted our crying need in this field could not be met in colleges outside of a year, as a minimum. We needed comparatively few graduate trained economists, but our shortage of those undergraduate-trained was acute. It worked beautifully, and the course became an FSI feature, with the officers, tested after each course, consistently scoring higher than the mean of college economics majors. It was the Service commitment that did it. There was another pioneering effort. The Ford Foundation through George Morgan's proposal had given us a grant to develop a four week course on the impact of science in foreign affairs, of growing importance. After careful study it was given twice in my time under the guidance of a former science attache. It was a success, and Ford was satisfied with our report. With the changes we were making and proposing, our budget became inadequate, but after we made a presentation on the proposed use of added funds to the administrative undersecretary, he heartily approved. It should be emphasized that I found Mr. Crockett consistently broad gauged in support of more training for FSOs, while trying to build FSI as an institution for all foreign affairs agencies.

The Senior Seminar, operating as a separate FSI component and extending over ten months like the war colleges, was the apex of FSI's training system. In foreign affairs it was the finest senior training one could receive, and much honing had gone into its contents. The small student numbers were a natural for a private seminar atmosphere in which the most distinguished speakers could talk informally, and Andy Corry brought it to an excellent pitch before leaving as ambassador to Sierra Leone. A bachelor, former Rhodes Scholar, mining engineer, and professor before the Service, he gave an individual flavor to the Seminar, which my friend, Lee Metcalf as his assistant, further personalized. The war colleges traveled in disciplined groups on their annual spring trips. A member of the Senior Seminar, when this time came, was given a plane ticket to an area he was studying for his year's thesis and took off. Beforehand he arranged with our embassies to see people of interest to him. Certainly it was an adult method the numbers permitted.

An advantage to a Washington assignment is the opportunity to see old Service friends. It certainly was the case with the Metcalfs and the Hulicks. After Lee worked with the Senior Seminar, he took off for Pakistan as a consul general, later becoming a second-time inspector and finally deputy inspector general. Charley, after a most strenuous time in Berlin, was executive secretary of the Foreign Service Board of Examiners, plunging into this and other work without rest. It wore him down. However, he made a great recovery and became consul general in Dusseldorf, West Germany, the industrial heart of the Federal Republic.

Again, I had interesting FSI associates. Among those were Howard Sollenberger, heading the School of Languages and Arab Studies, and my irrepressible friend, Ken Landon. Howard, bilingual in Chinese dialects, had a remarkable operation in varied languages taught under most modern methods, which were a model for universities. Ken's staff gave courses specializing in various world areas. John Thomas, FSI's deputy administrative officer, later an FSO and assistant secretary for Administration, worked with me on the middle level training survey, and I came to admire his knowledge of bureaucracy and his alert mind. These three typified the best among the Department's Civil Service Officers.

At FSI I had the occasion to appraise more closely leaders of the Service I knew. While there were others, I focused upon Charles (Chip) Bohlen and Llewellyn (Tommy) Thompson, Loy Henderson and Robert (Bob) Murphy, as in a sense representing, through my experience, the finest of two generations of the Service.

Aboard the exchange ship I had been impressed by Bohlen's observations and his active, warm personality. We never served together, but I followed his career with the assumption that one of our best was destined for the top. In later associations we came to have a most friendly acquaintance. Our final meeting came when as an acting deputy commandant of the War College, I deliberately named myself his escort officer. From his home and to his agreeable surprise, I was with him for his College day, when he was to receive a plaque for his fifteenth lecture. His accustomed naturalness in privately discussing diverse issues made a stimulating day. (He and Soviet experienced colleagues had just concluded that Khrushchev's memoirs were genuine.) On leaving by our college car, he asserted that he felt in fine shape, for his doctor had given him a clean bill of health. Not long after, cancer like Thompson's, had taken him.

Bohlen recalls in his memoir (Thompson wrote none) Tommy's quiet emphasis of principle. At the time of the Hungarian revolt, Tommy believed we had a moral commitment to help Eastern Europe because of our freedom campaign broadcasts, ancillary to the rollback of communism featured in American politics. His friend, Bohlen, did not think the broadcasts and talk were irrelevant, but believed the revolt arose mainly from internal reasons and public hatred of communism.

Thompson and Bohlen had closely parallel careers as Soviet experts. Knowing Tommy from my Eastern European assignments and recurring meetings, my regard for his quiet and informed style grew. In a later period in African affairs, I was to give a lecture at CIA headquarters. I parked in the great horseshoe, where I met Tommy descending. There were no moving cars or people, and he had something on his mind. As we talked, he finally said doctors had diagnosed his cancer, and he was going to fight his best. We parted, and I was saddened. His memorial service at the National Cathedral had Chip Bohlen as eulogist, when in his human way Chip recounted the only time professional rivalry had arisen between them. Tommy then wrote Bohlen that he would refuse the ambassadorship to Moscow rather than jeopardize their friendship. It was later in Loy Henderson's posthumously edited memoir that I realized the breadth of Thompson's sentiment. Loy had said, "In the Service I always respected officers who gave truth, courage, and professional integrity precedence over ambition for rapid promotion and high position."

Both Loy Henderson and Bob Murphy had dissimilar backgrounds; Bob a midwest Irish Catholic and Loy, an Ozarks/West Methodist minister's son, but were alike in stemming from environments that created fabrics of integrity. They were willing to take positions when clearly needed, and both based these on principle. Bob and Loy's cold war approaches were based upon the lack of integrity they perceived in communism and its threat to free institutions. However, they both enjoyed conviviality and had unforced geniality and wit, although Bob's Celtic nature was the more extroverted. As professionals they had a tough vein that enabled them to survive diplomatic defeats and the balance gracefully to accept its victories. Their knack for making friends, I believe, stemmed from a basic awareness of the solid, reasoned experience they presented. Sometimes they lost.

Murphy in assessing the Soviets urged, as political adviser in Germany, that the United States openly run its supplies overland when the Berlin blockade began, basing this on agreed access rights that a war recovering Stalinist regime would not challenge. Henderson, aware of the ruthless Soviet government, warned a contemporary Administration that a wartime alliance did not mean it would be a trusted postwar partner. Bohlen spoke of Henderson as "a man of the highest character...he always spoke his mind." Further, he "led the quiet struggle in the Administration against the soupy and syrupy attitude toward the Soviet Union." Unquestioning admirers of Soviet wartime success, not appreciating this, saw to it that he was sent as ambassador to Iraq. With time he became a respected area figure and director if its bureau. Again on principle and in American national interest, Loy opposed the creation of Israel from Arab lands, in view of the moral question and the importance of the Arab role in the cold war.

*like general George Marshall,*

It seems that any leading professional diplomat must have submitted his resignation at least once when an event clashed with principle. That they were not alone is a Service compliment. Illustratively, Henderson as undersecretary for Administration received a note from Secretary Dulles, who had a negative report upon an ambassador from a traveling major official, that Loy see to his removal.

Henderson surprised Dulles by sending his own resignation. When Dulles asked why, Henderson said the professional known man under his responsibility had been assigned for a specific mission. If the Secretary wanted to overrule him, he naturally had sent his resignation. Dulles showed good sense by telling Loy to destroy the note.

In evaluating the four men and in realizing they were not alone as Service figures, I appreciated one of the strengths at the time of American foreign policy. It was implemented by men of integrity, who in their careers were truly living.

The FSI years demonstrated how the Foreign Service itself, separately from my own education, was evolving. One needed an open mind and adaptability to keep pace with its changing needs. It was a different game from my early years; less esprit d'corps, more specialized in function, much less individualistic (a legacy of the McCarthy era), and more impersonal and bureaucratized, stemming from size and competition with other foreign affairs related agencies. When I thought of the swaths in their early days cut by some classmates, I could not imagine the current organization troubling itself with patience until we straightened out or meted rough career justice as between good and hardship assignments. When we entered the rules were baseball. Now the game rules were football. Nevertheless, my ever-molting profession had people as its greatest asset. Unlike other agencies which had large appropriations for programs which might conceal personnel mediocrity, State had virtually no funds but the salaries and expenses of its people. They had to be competent and their morale of the highest concern, for the policies and operations which State led and coordinated could not, as the other half of the coin, be separated from personal, professional factors. In sharpening the competence of our officers in the environment described, I urged that we had to start with dedicated men who, with other job alternatives, chose the Foreign Service.

Having worked with and observed the best in the Service, in the FSI I expressed concomitantly my ideas upon promotions and executive responsibility. Too often FSOs become so intent upon promotion that they lose sight of the meaning of increased responsibility, which makes the character and personality of every officer more vulnerable to subordinates in the light of decisions taken and methods of operation. It thus is essential that a senior officer make every effort to retain the respect of his associates. During my FSI assignment I lunched with John Steeves, my War College classmate and then director general of the Foreign Service, at our club. A retired ambassador, seeing him, asked to talk privately. On returning John appeared concerned, saying the man was desperate for any job, being bored with retirement. Since I knew him by reputation, colloquially an operator, I told John not to be concerned, for he would have been better off if he had spent a little time preparing for post-retirement action instead of endless hours angling for his next post.

A new trend, which State encouraged and we pressed in the School, was for advanced degrees and help by the Department through sabbaticals and paid courses at universities. Unfortunately our people needed larger doses of professional training than the Department could afford. Our School expedient therefore, was short, professionally relevant courses given to highly motivated officers. The sole exception, once the twelve week mid-career course ended, was our economics course. The proposed sixteen week management course was lost because of its length as our failure. No one challenged the short ones, requiring less time between assignments, because the professional need was so acute and academia could not do the job. Universities supplied certain long term training, which State's personnel office could accept. Officers opting for area specialization, say Africa, would spend an academic year engaged in courses bearing on that continent. Graduate economic training would last as long. Additionally, a new kind of academic assignment was being essayed. Two or three senior officers were sent to universities as diplomats in residence, there to lecture, to utilize their experience where desired by the institutions, and to talk to various organizations in the district. This experiment grew into a successful component of FSI's work. and once used about ten officers annually.

There were some significant losses, in addition to the management course. A field George Morgan pressed, in which FSI could have made a contribution, was in doing case studies in foreign affairs, tracing particular episodes or problems as they were handled professionally, and deriving insights into diplomatic procedures. This later became common practice for academics and retired Foreign Service organizations. However, we were unable to progress on this, involving as it did the use of classified material and the lack of manpower. Between times I attempted a few studies of this type at Morgan's request, but other work intervened. The earlier neglect of this important aspect, which could have served as a significant tie between FSI as the professional transmission belt and academic circles, was clearly regrettable. For lower mid-level officers I lost in trying to give them something on various methods of reporting, as basic to their profession. Similarly, I could not start a brief course on diplomatic negotiation. Little was then written on the subject. It was not really touched upon in universities, but there were principles to learn or from which one could adapt when confronted by reality. In current FSI schedules, short courses on reporting and negotiation have made the list, and academia has done well with them.

In my second FSI year, hazy assignment prospects became more forthright. Two regional bureaus came up with ideas. I also had an interesting talk over lunch about this time with a ranking official of a geographic bureau. He remembered my work and surprised me by saying that I had been nominated as the area's preference for ambassador.  Naturally I was quite pleased at this demonstrated confidence.  However, before further movement took place, the official was given another important assignment, and the nomination disappeared. Eventually Morgan got his awaited career minister promotion and likewise his embassy, the Ivory Coast.  My transition followed when by October I was serving on the Foreign Service annual promotion panels, known as selection boards. While thus occupied, I was relieved as dean, but retained my designation as special assistant to the FSI acting director, Howard Sollenberger.

Each year an aggregation of officers is called for promotion board duty, and a panel for each class seeks to decide who is worth promoting.  A serious participant cannot complete the assignment without feeling that the process was equitable but that biased judgments of writers of efficiency reports can offer problems for the panels.  A report sometimes tells most about the rater.  In fact, it would have been revealing to have a rater's prepared reports included in his own file for personal evaluation.  This was proposed.  We had a ceremonial start by the Department leadership,  and quickly settled to work.  Each year the procedures varied and every few years the evaluation rating forms were changed, and this is how it was in those times.  There then were two reports on each officer rated.  One, performance evaluation, set forth how he did his work over a year ending in June.  This was unclassified and the rated officer was given a copy.  The second, the development  appraisal report or DAR, was classified, supposed to agree generally with what was said in the other, but got down to cases, and was scantily discussed with the ratee.  We found a number of discrepancies between the two reports.  There, too, as I have mentioned, I was disturbed to see what had been done to some of my evaluated Baghdad officers. My panel colleagues separately examined their records to see if they merited the lowest ten or five percent class rating.  They fortunately found they did not.

My board evaluated FSO-3s, a very large class in a total Foreign Service then of about 3,500, and we were being asked to recommend officers for promotion from what was termed the top mid-level grade into the senior level at 0-2.  The entire procedure of that time was simple logic.  As a first step we had sub-panels of three officers to review the files by specializations.  My economic sub-panel included a senior economic officer and a senior official from the Commerce Department.  We found it meant winnowing what we considered to be the top percentage and the lowest percentage.  We did this methodically, and unsurprisingly gave a numerical rating to each officer after we broke our economic category into conventional 10 percentile groupings.  Armed with lists so earnestly derived, the economic segment (minus an officer) joined the full board of nine chaired by an ambassador, Tony Ross, who was most competent. Other categories treated included political, administrative, consular, specialized functions (like doctors), and information and cultural officers of USIA. This last was an experiment that year. Our combined board included five FSOs and four others. There was the chairman, a political-intelligence officer, a consular man, an administrative officer, and myself. The four included representatives from Commerce, Labor, USIA, and a public member recently retired as vice president of the International Machinists. We found enough interest in our own membership, and came to know and generally respect one another. Our procedures in that era were obvious. In the interest of equity, unless a board member thought otherwise, we accepted the sub-panel minority percent screenings, and concentrated on reading the files, say for several years, on the top and low groups. From these we predictably refined the top and low groups using familiar ten percentiles. The top percentage included those who could be promoted, while at the other end, the lowest percentage could be administratively informed and be on the road to selection out of the Service. Each class had a time in grade limit, and worthy men were caught by this, being in the middle or upper, but unpromoted, category. Each member had one vote and, like the one soldier with the blank cartridge, could understand that his single numbering was not decisive.

Going over the gamut of O-3s showed the richness of the Service. The file reading was fatiguing because of the need to do justice to each officer, and there were hundreds of files to study. Some we found whose records were uniformly brilliant and some who were stimulating as personalities. We enjoyed one who in his post was known for his "social law" that things never reached the stage where they couldn't get worse, now called Murphy's Law. Then there were twins, both up for promotion. Also, we rated a husband and wife; he serving in London and she in Paris, while they met weekends. Truthfully much of the reading was uninspiring, so when we encountered a memorable phrase or characterization Bill Trueheart and I collected them. He found the most amusing gleanings:

"I would be willing to serve with him at another post, but would not request the opportunity."

Limiting Factors -"None unusual to a man of Mr. B's 57 years of age."

"One is not immediately attracted by his appearance, nor is one immediately repelled by it."

"There is nothing negative in the general impression which he creates; in fact, he is substantially above average in this regard."

"I noticed an occasional tendency (usually overcome automatically, always when brought to focus by a supervisor) to react negatively when confronted with a foolish or morally indefensible action to which he had responsibility for responding." (From the section on "Adverse Factors.")

"His emotional stability borders on phlegmatism."

"During the period I have known Mrs. B, she has been primarily involved in the process preceding and following the birth of twin girls."

"He is such a nice guy, so devoid of personal ambition or aggressiveness, and so fundamentally decent, that he will probably never be a Chief of Mission."
"Mr. H does not write as clearly as he thinks. Whether this is the result of long years in government, I am not sure."

Two aspects of our work proved very troublesome: rating information - cultural officers and the lowest percentages. By the time FSOs had reached Class 3, on the way they had been annually screened and those marginal from the integration of departmental officers had been generally selected out. Frankly we did not consider - and so declared in our report - that more than 3 percent deserved the marginal rating connoted by the lowest percentage selection. Even here we found Reserve officers brought in for specialties deemed insufficient in the Service, were more frequent, since they had not been appraised over sufficient time. Information and cultural officers previously had some differences in evaluation technique, and USIA was putting its promotion quotas together with State's, so this was a minor problem. By December our work was done and the lists submitted to higher authority, which would determine where the cutoff line for promotion would be drawn. The promotion lists when they appeared were long and included sufficient USIA personnel. Incidentally, the husband and wife were both promoted.

Helping put Service matters into perspective for me at the time was an NEA ambassador, Ray Hare. I wrote congratulating him on reaching the top of the career ladder by being named to the rank of career ambassador. He replied thoughtfully that he had been thinking of the analogy and was struck that he had nowhere else to go but to fall off. Here was a man of character.

In the new year, still as special assistant to the FSI Director, I was assigned to head task forces on various aspects of career organization of interest to Mr. Crockett. The most interesting was assessing the need for labor specialization and outlining it as a career. Of the four on this task force, I chaired it as the lone non-labor experienced officer. The group was capable, and I believe it came up with a good report, but the Labor Department did not like it because the report sought to draw more labor specialists from within the Service and not through Labor. Anyhow, Mr. Crockett, when I presented it to him, liked the recommendations and bought them for at least limited durability.

A leading Foreign Service officer was involved as committee chairman in a reevaluation of professional training policy, and I worked with him. This went well, so in the early spring he asked me to come with him into the Bureau of African Affairs, where he was to be its assistant secretary. As he phrased it, he wanted me there, and after a year intended to recommend me for an ambassadorship in the area. We were having a personal session, during which he asked what

I wanted out of the Service. I found myself saying how I felt, and it is briefly summarized. The Service had given me much, so whatever happened in my professional future I was the gainer. However, it had become big and impersonal. One could not inevitably expect justice or recognition through merit. If it came, fine, but one had to be a realistic idealist. I would like to be an ambassador as a career cap, but if work an officer did was stimulating and he considered it a progression of his experience, this could be satisfying. I was not alone in discovering there was more to life and the Service than a series of promotion hurdles. If an officer did not find it satisfying, he should move to another profession for which he should be prepared. No one, in fact, should hold a substantive position in government unless it was from dedication and the knowledge that he could leave if he wanted.

The future assistant secretary, I think, found my comments something of a new note. So after thought and despite some ambiguous reports from officials I respected, we struck our agreement and I was to follow him into Africa by June. This was my most fateful career decision.

Stanley statue
in Kinshasa

Ambassador and Mrs. Debrah
in Ghanaian dress

Nigerian Ambassador Martins signs an international agreement. My deputy, Bob Smith, stands behind him.

# CHAPTER 15

# CIVIL WAR IN AFRICA: NIGERIA

# June 1966 - September 1969

*At home the civil rights campaign expanded, as did discontent over Viet-*
*nam. Dr King was assassinated and the rights protest exploded. An*
*American triumph came in the manned moon landing. NATO headquar-*
*ters shifted to Belgium, the U.K. Labor government abandoned bases*
*east of Suez, and the Soviets invaded Czechoslovakia. The Sino-Soviet*
*schism continued, while Mao directed the Cultural Revolution. Japan,*
*quietly developing, became the world's third largest industrial state. In*
*Egypt, Sadat was Nasser's successor, and Col. Qaddafi's coup*
*redirected Libya. The Nigerian civil war became another U.S.*
*preoccupation, in which as State's area director, I chaired an interagen-*
*cy task force as humanitarian relief and that war became international*
*and presidential campaign issues. Assurances of a substantial embassy*
*following the assignment evaporated, and I received a department honor*
*award.*

The early March talk pointed me toward the Bureau of African Affairs.
Thereafter in examining Africa south of the Sahara, in some area of which I
would be working, the more absorbing it became. Here was a politically
emerging continent, which in World War II had only two independent entities,
South Africa and Liberia. The procession started with Ghana in 1957, followed
by a flood of new states in the early sixties. Many lacked infrastructures to make
their new status credible, although there were unproven exceptions like Nigeria.
Tribalism and colonial arbitrary boundaries were invitations to internal strife and
national rivalries that could further splinter these experiments in statehood. For
this reason, the Organization for African Unity (OAU) had one overriding
objective: agreement on the validity of all state proclaimed borders. The fragility
of the new states, originally set by colonial interest, can be understood by an
example. Mount Kilimanjaro is in Tanzania rather than Kenya, because Queen
Victoria decided to give a birthday present to her nephew, the Kaiser, in his colonial area. It is remarkable that the OAU succeeded in its objective.

While doing other work, I prepared for the impending assignment, chiefly
through reading in African area studies at FSI. Fortunately I read rapidly, not

forgetting the unscholarly injunction of an eminent Fletcher/Harvard professor that most scholarly books are not worth full reading, but properly should be "gutted." By the end of May, fully interested, I moved into the Bureau having read most and sometimes gutted about 45 books.

The Africa bureau with its new assistant secretary was accompanied by another Department reorganization which broke the office director components into smaller units, as country directorships. There had been five African offices, but the Secretary wanted more responsible attention given to individual countries, hence the split. It was reasoned senior country directors could move things better. Then each bureau added more deputy assistant secretaries to help coordinate the country directors!  It stemmed from a basic misconception, that work was hindered because of unwieldy vertical organization. There was no trouble in getting a subject and decision through the geographic bureaus.  The problem was horizontal:  clearances by other Department sectors and agencies more or less tangentially involved.  Like most reorganizations, the theory was being applied by those with limited background on the reasons for the original setup.  After our chief held his ground, his bureau had ten offices, including an intact one dealing with general regional affairs, and three deputy assistant secretaries.

Earlier, when dean of the School of Foreign Affairs, the then director of the West Africa office had asked me to come as his deputy, learn the assignment for six months, and move in when he became a deputy assistant secretary.  I told Bill Trimble that I felt committed to Morgan for a while longer.   Our assistant secretary intended to place me as director of Southern African affairs, but with the reorganization he shifted me to be country director of English speaking West Africa (minus the French speaking countries set up under two country directors). My area comprised four countries:   Ghana, Liberia, Nigeria and Sierra Leone. I learned that these were our main interest in West Africa, for France, tended to dominate and subsidize its former colonies, having realistically fragmented them at independence into economically non-viable entities.

Bill Trimble as a deputy assistant secretary generally looked after North and West Africa, while Wayne Fredericks shepherded East and South.   The third deputy, Sam Westerfield, was a pleasant man whose responsibility was general economic questions, with whom I had virtually no business.  Trimble took me in hand during the two weeks I read the files and talked to the operators.  He pressed, and was right, to get me quickly to West Africa and London to meet the British Commonwealth Office people charged with the area.  Also, before my responsibilities after the effective date of the country director setup in July, I should see something of the region.

Armed achingly with variegated shots and aralen tablets (once weekly) against malaria, I left in mid-June. On the Pan Am flight down the west coast of Africa, called the red eye special, we touched down at Monrovia. The international airport for the capital of Liberia had been built in World War II as an air ferry station, and between field and town was the large Firestone rubber plantation with the tapped trees in orderly rows. The Ducor Hotel was run by a capable Swiss. The town, however, was an amalgam of some public buildings, nice homes, and a considerable number of shacks.

From the 1840s, when freed American negroes were colonized there, Liberia had an unusual relationship to the United States. By this time we had a surprising 4,000 Americans, including families, and most in official work. It was the one U.S. foothold in West Africa, and illustratively there was a $370 million (1966) American investment in rubber plantations and iron ore mines, as well as a $21 million Voice Of America radio relay station. For simplicity's sake, the U.S. dollar was Liberia's currency. Our objective, I was told, was to keep Liberia as a partner and be able to operate in and from there. The freed descendants were the ruling class, known as the honorables, and they were headed by a canny politician, President Tubman, who through control of the single True Whig party had been regularly reelected. Although more irascible and unable in his 70s to drink as much Scotch, he held full control. As a benevolent dictator he would temporarily imprison critics, while in official gatherings he could show a sense of humor unusual for an authoritarian. Politically astute, he took steps to bring some tribal elements into the ruling hierarchy. His presidential mansion, both as home and executive offices, looked like a Hilton Hotel. Ben Brown, our ambassador, became a friend, and I stayed with him in the compound at Mamba Point (numerous deadly black mamba snakes were caught there), but because there was much to do locally with our Peace Corps people, military mission, and economic aid officials, I took but one excursion. This was to the Bomi Hills iron mine, an operation using the rails from the old New York City elevated railroad to haul the ore cars to port.

Andy Corry, our ambassador to Sierra Leone, met me in Freetown. The British colony also had its start from the settlement of freed slaves at a large estuary, the biggest on the western coast, used as a way station to India. Freetown, the capital, had a goodly imprint of English institutions and was identified by its immense cottonwood tree at the town square, featured in a book by Graham Greene. On that center we were building a new chancery as our programs and staff were being cut.

In Accra, Ghana, which I first saw during World War II, I was attracted to the energy and humor of the people and to their "high life" music. I stayed with the chargé and he saw that I met everyone, particularly key military leaders of the ruling National Liberation Council(NLC), like General Kotoka, an impressive man later killed, who early that year had overthrown the dictatorship of Nkrumah. The latter had headed the state since independence, and had become progressively extravagant and repressive. The new ruling group made a start in putting the country on a hopeful path, coping with the $1 billion loss Nkrumah had engineered and from the onset of the NLC we tried to assist Ghana and its eight million people to recharge as a state of promise.

There was a British-trained civil service, numerous trained private people, and a good economic potential fostered by supplying program loans and surplus agricultural products and other help. More unusual, the NLC kept an essential unity over three years until the groundwork of a constitution and regular elections permitted a civilian regime. The fabric shredded as the country's eventual downfall, later endemic military control, undercut the promise.

A visiting director of the U.S. Export-Import Bank and I went to the U.S. financed dam on the Volta River, the water inviting in the bright sun. Then I noticed no villages on the dam-created lake, evidence of deadly water borne parasites. We had steadily refused to cancel the dam even at Nkrumah's most anti-American stage, reckoning it a project for the country. This proved wise and, together with the large Kaiser aluminum plant related to the dam, was a foundation we then thought to build our economic relations.

I followed a coastal road and the little charmingly designed and named buses, by all called "mammy wagons" for the women traders, from Accra to Lagos in Nigeria. On the way I spent an enjoyable evening in Lome, Togo, with Ambassador Witman, whom I had long known. He was high on his black deputy, Terry Todman, and I came to share his opinion. Years later Terry became a career ambassador, among ten who achieved this over the period after the grade was established. Then in Lagos my Nigeria spot education began.

Nigeria, one quarter of Black Africa, its most populous state (in 1988 over 100 million people), and one with varied resources, became independent in 1960. While the British had worked toward organizing a federal state, there were serious strains caused by cultural differences and regional and tribal rivalries. The Hausa-Fulani leadership in the Northern Region, the Ibos in the Eastern, and the Yorubas in the Western played the game of odd-man-out, as they shifted alliances in controlling the country. In January the army had ended this, dispensing with Northern dominance, and a military council, Ibo flavored, was running things.

Ambassador Mathews was in charge of our embassy, the only Class 1 mission in the African bureau, and a consulate was in each of the three regions. We had known each other for some years, and at an earlier stage he had wanted me as his minister - DCM. Now, since the new deputy also had not seen the country, Mathews arranged for our joint travel. The christian Ibos, about 60 percent of the eastern people, ran things there and everyone commented on their passion for education and technical abilities. Ibos also were the majority with expertise who ran the government in Lagos. At the same time they were resented, as friendly outsiders said, for arrogance and nepotism, the last endemic in Africa. In the North, a mixture of moslem, animist and christian, the disliked Ibos were the business and government technicians too, since that area was educationally backward, and missionary schools as a policy had been restricted to the East and West. It had only been 30 years since the first Ibo foreign educated (U.S.) doctor had returned home to practice, eventually to be the first president of Nigeria, and this remarkable people had made a major contribution to the country.

We explored the Eastern region from Enugu, its capital, to Calabar on the southeast coast. In Enugu the new embassy counselor and I attended a business man's lunch. Shortly before its end, I had symptoms too familiar from other exotic locales. I succumbed in seclusion and returned to the table, whereupon the counselor showed like symptoms and beat a temporary retreat. It was our joint African baptism. Calabar had been a large slave entrepot in the old days and long had European ties. As evidence, Dr. Hinshaw, a physician from the old Calabar chieftain family, told me that he was its fifth generation to be educated in England. We stayed at the picturesque guest house, built on steel girders with material from England and formerly the British Resident's (Sir Roger Casement), where I slept in the largest bedroom I have ever used, 12 by 15 yards, the old reception room. The next day we found the Peace Corps headquarters after locating some young fellows, typically tossing frisbees. Consistently their informal style fitted in West Africa, where the Corps was doing outstanding work.

The North, half of Nigeria's population and two thirds of the area, was little changed by independence. The region had been permitted by the British to retain traditional emirate rule, in the fashion of the princely states of India, so representative institutions at the local level had not developed as in the south. We talked to people in Kaduna, the regional capital, Zaria, and Kano, finding the emirs of Zaria and Kano to be contrasts, one traditionalist and the other modern. In a noteworthy court setting, surrounded by colorfully gowned retainers, it was a bit disconcerting to find an extra finger in shaking hands with the Emir of Zaria, but his six fingers seemed to be proof of legitimacy. Kano was cosmopolitan and photography his hobby. A feature of his town was the unusual large pyramids covered with green canvas; peanuts in storage, the main crop. It also was remarkable to see the Islamic influence and mosques projected into the "holy north" from the other side of the Sahara, but I was uneasy for the future with the signs of burning in the foreigners quarter of Kano, where there had been riots in May against the Ibos.

The Western region had its capital in Ibadan, the Yoruba center and one of the largest cities in Africa, whose military governor, Colonel Fajuyi, was a confident man. He and his staff of senior civil servants, with whom we lunched, were able to operate more effectively than any group elsewhere in Nigeria and, as our consul said, the staff was pleased it had such a worthy leader.

Of the various figures in Nigeria, I was particularly impressed with one of the ruling council of the Federal Military Government (FMG). Colonel Gowon was a christian from a small tribe in the so-called middle belt area of the Northern region. We had two occasions to talk, but the most satisfying was a time alone and undisturbed after a dinner, thanks to Ambassador Mathews' foresight. Abraham Lincoln, said the colonel, was his hero. He had been with the Nigerian component of the international force that had served in the chaotic Congo, and was determined that Nigerian rivalries would not go that route.

After two weeks in Nigeria, I flew to London, where I met with our people and the Commonwealth Office, which handled affairs with the former African colonies as Commonwealth members. I even saw my old Baghdad colleague, now gratefully the former British ambassador. Mulling over the trip on the Atlantic crossing, I found much in my notes and memories as an indispensable grounding.

Africa was unusual. Aside from the environment, it was infectious to see the vitality and optimism, the extrovert nature of the people. With foreigners they were at ease and never at a loss for words. The great contrast between East and West Africans, I came to suspect, is because in the East they knew the foreigner as a competitor for the land, as in Kenya, hence viewing them with reserve. In the West, given the mosquito ally, they knew the foreigner as non-challenging trader, missionary, and colonial administrator, whom they treated as equals. There were the active bazaars with local handicrafts and textiles; the colorful dress, made more so by the dark people whose complexions had varied shades; the acceptance of physical sexual vigor, seen in beer ads announcing Power, and the mentality of the leaders, as impressive as anywhere. Part of the stimulus, I knew, came from being again part of substantive overseas operations.

It was in Nigeria, among varied aspects of lore, that I met up with Wawa. For reasons all can appreciate who have served in underdeveloped countries, small things have the habit of becoming knotted far more than the norm. An instance: at a car service station, we asked to have a soft tire checked. The attendant found the air hose did not extend to that tire, and, in a compliance of sorts, checked a nearer one. In places like Nigeria, the victim would exclaim, "Wawa," which means 'West Africa wins again'. The superlative is "Wawet," West Africa wins every time!

The Nigeria desk officer, Dave Bolen, had on my return left for the National War College, where I met him at the Officers' Club to swap suggestions. Dave had been a quarter miler on our Olympic relay team, and by drive and ambition had an excellent Service record. He confided that since he was black, he did not want assignments confined to Africa, and eventually hoped to be a chief of mission in Europe. He later became our ambassador to East Germany, a worthwhile assignment.

The country director system was in effect, and returning July 19, I was handling West Africa or AF/W, over a ten day interval of a quietly ticking office clock. Initially we were six officers and five secretaries, with Al Nyren, my deputy, also serving as economic officer, since Nigeria, Liberia, and Ghana were one third of the African states deemed of substantive interest for American economic aid. Bob Smith handled Nigeria with one assistant, and had formerly been our consul at Enugu in the East, proving a crackerjack and mainstay. Bob Sherwood, Liberia-Sierra Leone desk officer, did a fine job, and Ghana affairs were handled by Cy Chalfin, a good one too. Indeed I was fortunate throughout with the calibre of the staff. The next few years, as usual, there were quite a few changes from the original complement. Thankfully I became acquainted with everyone, because from July 29 and for three years we rode the wave of the chronic, major Nigeria crisis.

Our media focus on the present, so our public, taught to relish distractions, has tended to view events in terms of their currency. The environment being described may have the faint whiff and dry tongue of a dustcoated distant struggle. Nevertheless, task forces of varying duration still are a feature in the operations center and White House. Although with more technical organization and people than before, they maintain close agency and national security council staff relations. The problems too, in general design retain familiar features. In Africa, famines in Ethopia bring forth humanitarian energies. In Iran, after Mosadeq we picture the menacing figure of the Ayatollah. In the hemisphere, cold war attention shifts from Cuba to Central America. The parallels go on as new problems with the same strategic causes, like the Persian Gulf crisis, arise. It seems an ordinary precaution to mull over our successes and failures, since to recall my wise acquaintance, Santayana, those who do not remember the mistakes of the past are doomed to repeat them.

The Northern leadership had run the civilian government, which the majority Ibo military regime succeeded. Now on July 29 there was an outburst against the Eastern Ibos and mass killings. The head of the Federal Military Government

(FMG), General Ironsi, was killed while visiting the Western region's outstanding military governor, General Fajuyi, who heroically accepted death after refusing to be separated from his guest. Because he had no significant political or tribal base, General Gowon headed a reconstituted FMG. However, the military governor of the Eastern region, Colonel Ojukwu, began to negotiate autonomously with the FMG, of which he was a member. The Ibos were shocked by the pogrom organized in the North by some old-line politicians bidding to recover influence and to prod Northern elements of the army. Some 30,000 were killed or injured, as throughout Nigeria most Ibos recoiled within their homeland. The military restored order, and negotiations began for reparations and adjusting the relationship between the federal and Eastern regional military governments.

The stakes involved the threatened breakup of Nigeria, again one quarter of all Black Africa, and which our government thought the most promising for economic and political development. One could not ignore its strong effects on the rest of a newly independent Africa, so my life became immersed in the problem. The assistant secretary had been our first ambassador to the country. He was quite concerned in hands on fashion, and we saw each other daily. We quickly established the Nigeria interagency task force to cope with the July-August situation, and later we were to reconstitute it twice again for long periods. The practice was set by the Department for a major crisis. As country director I headed the task force, which drew its resources from wherever useful. We moved to space in the operations center on the seventh floor of the Department and were in business twenty four hours a day. In practice AF/W was the core and Al Nyren was my initial deputy. Meanwhile we left a skeleton staff to handle routine business in our regular offices, and the country officer for Liberia-Sierra Leone acted, a telephone removed from me, in charge of AF/W, with the Ghana desk officer helping him. In subsequent flareups on Nigeria we followed the pattern first set. We drew on officers in the bureau, preferably with Nigerian experience, and counterparts in other agencies such as AID and USIA. There was a watch schedule of officers and secretaries, and while Al acted as general manager, I was responsible for keeping our policy people in State and other major components informed.

Both Democratic and Republican Administrations over time proved to be in policy agreement on Nigeria. In brief because of the country's importance we wanted a single entity of the parts called Nigeria. If this failed, we would have to treat with separate entities like the Eastern region, which came to be called Biafra. Also, both Administrations adopted a logical policy in making the State Deputy Secretary the top policy-operating official in the government for Nigeria. Hence, it was Nicholas Katzenbach for President Johnson and Elliot Richardson for President Nixon, with both of whom we had excellent relations. Ours had formed with Katzenbach when he was newly appointed from being Attorney

General to being our Acting Secretary. Secretary Rusk was at the UN, so on visiting the operations center Katzenbach was curious about us, the first crisis setup he had witnessed, which meant we gave him a briefing. I always found him accessible, soft spoken, and a man I enjoyed working with. Richardson was personable and a quick learner, who I came to like and respect as he followed what had become our continuing policy on Nigeria. One bureaucratic talent of his I envied. At official meetings he made the most artistic and complex doodles I ever saw! Generally mine were mazes and spinning wheels.

With the parameters set, there was an advantage whenever the Nigeria task force was formally operative in our regular offices or in the operations center. As its chairman I sent needful cables without further State or agency clearances. In the operations center I had a dual role, directly responsible to the Deputy Secretary and to the assistant secretary. I phoned the latter nearly every day, met with him frequently, saw the Deputy Secretary's staff, with whom I built a good relationship, daily, and the Deputy Secretary several times weekly.

As a task force in the Operations Center or back in our area offices, we got our messages (called scat copies) off the machines before copies were made for regular distribution, and worked long hours and weekends. When the Nigerian situation merely bubbled, we got our scat copies as our durable secretaries, Evelyn or Beverly, headed to the operations center in response to phone calls. Our outgoing messages, if occasionally of a policy nature, had AF front office clearance or that of the Deputy Secretary (himself or staff).

A most important element was the Congress as domestic heat grew. From our assistant secretary's good suggestion, I built a solid friendship over the years with a perceptive close assistant of Senator Fulbright, the Democratic Chairman of the Senate Foreign Relations Committee. Don Henderson came to be the first I called on the Hill, for I respected his judgment and he our policy objectives. His help was immeasurable. Also Senator Packwood, a Republican, I thoroughly briefed at his request, and he became a staunch supporter. It never occurred to me that these relationships were unusual until I found I was the only country director in the bureau with such ties. Normally this is done by a congressional liaison office, but we required the direct contact.

Nigeria was a complex country, and while the major tribal forces mentioned had essential control in their politically designated regions, there were other tribal and sub-tribal groupings to make their influence felt. During negotiations between Gowon and Ojukwu on the degree of autonomy for the Eastern region, there was the problem of relating this to other regions. Even in the East, 40 percent of the people were not Ibo and were generally unhappy at the prospect of losing the moderating federal hand in their behalf. What the federal side would settle for, the East would not. By the time the latter would, the former wouldn't. The melancholy chronicle, even after the war began, was replete with such slippage. Because of Nigeria's troubles, its burgeoning oil production was delayed. Oil was concentrated along the Mid-West and Eastern sector coasts, but only later did it become the second African oil producer after Libya and a solid American source. The Ibos wanted the swelling oil revenues and so did the FMG, making another muddying factor.

Before the fighting, a year from the onset of the crisis, the FMG reorganized Nigeria into twelve states: six north, three east, one mid-west, one west, and Lagos as a state. The Eastern Ibo heartland was one state, the other two minority tribal areas. While the twelve state constitution was popular with the rest of the country, it failed in Iboland, one of the densely populated parts of Africa and not economically sustaining without the rest of the East.

After the first year, our family was shocked by the sudden death of our daughter April. It was traumatic, for distracting preoccupations had me neglect my family. I thought of retiring from the Service and released the assistant secretary from any commitment for an ambassadorship as he said he wanted when the family had recovered. But as Bob Murphy said, "You never get over the tragedy." Over the next two years, despite Nigeria pressures I strove to be with my family. A Service wife later wrote "although it was a distinct and often privileged life, we were disciplined by our dedication [but] I think those who suffered the most in our lives were our children." Within a year I could tell our chief that the family was reasonably adjusted, but this summer of the 1968 election he advised waiting until 1969, when there could be suitable posts available. There were pressing issues and I agreed to stay.

It is difficult to picture the unrelenting pressures, the long hours of seven day work weeks. As in Bucharest a year passed without leave and there was little in the remainder. I was not bouncing back as fast as before, and instinctively knew I must exercise. Each morning, the only time free, I did a shortened fifteen minutes of calisthenics. Faced by the intensities of the work over an eventual three years it helped, but not fully, for the relentless strains inevitably sapped energy. Once we tried a little home reception, when it looked as if there would be no surprises. I reached home after 9 p.m., the guests gone. Similarly, in a summer we had driven to see Montreal relatives. The first morning I had a phone call from the assistant secretary asking that I quickly return. Leaving an unhappy and bewildered family, I set out by car, arriving in Washington that night. Little indicators hopefully alluded to a more relaxed day. Every Saturday and Sunday our entourage dressed in jacket and slacks, discarding the accepted weekday business suits. The psychological change helped.

In the bureau we followed customary procedures. Every morning after people read the cables our chief had a staff meeting (about half an hour) with his deputies and country directors. Wednesdays there was a large hour meeting, too long and often with boring guest speakers. I had earlier become a staunch supporter of half-hour maximum large staff meetings. Each country director knew his business, but one who impressed me was John Root, a long time North Africa specialist, for I liked his approach and on many things we saw alike. We became friends.

The assistant secretary was a man of drive and nervous energy, a chain smoker, a fine drafter, a mediocre administrator, of great caution, and socially hearty. He and I had our personal relationship stemming from my bureau entry and intimate association over Nigeria. It became apparent his earlier identification with Nigeria as a great hope in Africa and the civil war attention this brought, made him exceedingly cautious and proved my greatest handicap. The warm current of opinion swirled over the years, the heat rose, and on the perimeter he was watchful. Most graphically I saw the problem in March 1969. With that edition of the task force eight months operative, I proposed, consonant with criteria and precedent, the unit be accorded a unit honor citation. As bureau head, he had signed special commendations to their agencies of my other associates, and I wanted my staff to have this on their records. Some of my officers and secretaries had been through every phase with me. When there was no action, I raised it with him. Hesitantly he expressed concern that by singling the task force unit for public commendation this would draw unfavorable emotional attention by those influential and critical of our Nigeria policy. When he knew I clearly disagreed, he assented to sign individual letters, which I drafted, when the task force formally ended. It was not formally dissolved, for he wanted it as long as he remained with AF. When he left, I understood the letters were not sent. I believe I arranged for several in-grade salary increases and a promotion.

Nigeria took 95 percent of my time, and the desk officers for the other AF/W countries were able to carry on well, which gave me a further pride in the Service. Al Nyren left for his next assignment, Bob Smith became my deputy, and capable George Sherry, already with us and former consul at Ibadan, took Bob's old slot. The rotation worked smoothly. When the Ibos, as the state of Biafra, prepared to fight for independence, federal Nigeria was bracing to oppose this for, if it succeeded, Nigeria would fragment. Before the fighting started, in an AF discussion, I had given my view with others. Unless the U.S., at least in conjunction with Britain, did everything within its resources to avoid the warfare threatening some form of federal Nigeria and the search for some security guarantees for the Ibos, we could regret this for American policy. The impending conflict would become a source for international involvement by the great powers that would cause major concern. Our chief had an argument in saying that, with the times and because of Vietnam, congressional antipathy to innocuous measures might be decried as U.S. involvement. We could not act directly. This, of course, would be modified as American humanitarian instincts rose with the continuing war.

At irregular intervals each geographic bureau holds chiefs of mission conferences in the field attended by its assistant secretary and others from Washington. There was one in Tangier for several days, when I saw the town and its casbah again. Next I accompanied our chief to Monrovia, where he was to participate in the dedication of a U.S. financed dam. Liberian society and President Tubman were in form, and the dedication ceremony was memorable for its ritual. I went to Accra for several days, and thereafter to Lagos and London. Such periodic visits and impressions were very useful. Other quick trips were to Lagos and London on special problems arising over Nigeria, but the chronic crisis tended to keep me in Washington. On a visit to London, however, I found Elim O'Shaughnessy as political counselor, and it was a healthy diversion from Africa to have a long lunch with him. With marriage and children, like the rest of us, Elim was a father concerned about their future, notably schooling. Our talk covered the Service, our futures, and posts. It was our last meeting.

After fighting began, we refused to license arms sales to either side. The British sold to the FMG as a Commonwealth government, but no aircraft. The FMG turned to the Russians, who, in selling planes and bombs and heavy land equipment, exploited the windfall to advance their influence in a fresh area. The FMG controlled the sea approaches to Biafra and, after a slow federal offensive occupied the minority states of the east, no access was possible to Biafra except over federal territory. Nevertheless the French, by various means never officially admitted, flew in arms to Biafra by night flights. The Ivory Coast and Gabon, heavily French influenced, were staging areas, and Portugal also allowed arms to be flown to Biafra via its West African possessions. To confuse things, there were South Africans engaged in the transport. The Organization of African Unity (OAU), consistently held to the federal Nigerian side, whereas four African states recognized Biafra: Ivory Coast, Gabon, Tanzania, and Zambia. Indeed it was complex.

A frequent problem is field post subjectivity toward the local country. It is difficult to do, but vital to U.S. interests that the situation be told exactly as it is, without local biases that can distort facts, evaluations, and recommendations. Nigeria was a case in point. It was hard to get our embassy, really not

Ambassador Mathews who suffered for it, to show warts on the FMG. For the first year of the conflict particularly, AF/W found itself in the middle, not agreeing with embassy over-optimism that the FMG would overcome Biafra quickly, and contending with strong pro-Ibo sentiments from other agencies discrediting the embassy's reports. I think AF/W came out about right.

In State it is a crisis when a situation of a major nature can quickly and continuously change with new developments. Our Nigeria task force found itself responding as a fire crew to a series of alarms. Recognizing that the situation had every prospect of being quite prolonged, I proposed to my harried AF/W group that we eke out an extra effort. This would be an outline on possible measures to protect our interests in Nigeria over a four to six months span. We did not have time or energy for a detailed study. We had no model but, blessed with a practical national policy, we outlined the problem, our objectives, assumptions, and key issues; next we sketched three one-page possible scenarios, and, for each in two page tabular form, the principal actors, together with their probable actions. The total came to fourteen legal pages. A fifteenth, from appropriate agencies, assessed the opposing military forces. Only then did we alert the assistant secretary and other task force agency components of the project's scope, when I requested a meeting with him and his other agency counterparts. We circulated the contingency paper in advance and had a several hour session, where I explained its rationale and our most probable choice. It was educational for everyone, so the task force had guidelines, the agencies were not at the mercy of the winds, and it was crowned over time by our scenario choice proving the nearest to reality.

Satisfied we had something, with broader cooperation a second effort for a subsequent six months was prepared, but with mixed success. While we recognized relief aid to Biafran areas was important, we underestimated the distortion of its effects on our operations. In Montreal my first chief had warned of the perils of the nasty combination of oil and politics. If he had been around, I would have told him there was an even worse mix when humanitarian relief was added.

A year of fighting and the isolation of the Biafran controlled area created, by the summer of my second year, a crucial food shortage and starvation there. When Biafra's prospects looked bleak, the French moved in with arms flights. The Ibo regime thus determined to continue the struggle despite widespread starvation, and to use this to excite world sympathy, political support for its cause, and eventual independence. Relief flights into Biafra grew in volume; all at night. To help the suffering on both sides, since there were also large numbers of destitute in federal controlled areas of the East, the International Committee of the Red Cross (ICRC), operated in both areas. The Joint Church Aid, a combine of European and North American religious organizations, was active on the Biafra side. In America it was composed of the Catholic Relief Agency, the U.S. Council of Churches, and the American-Jewish Committee. We parceled our relief effort to both contestants, and the contributions steadily mounted for food commodities and administrative expenses, including ships to Nigeria and aircraft flying supplies to Biafra from foreign offshore islands. By the end of June 1969, the American Government had made available over $63 million in cash, food and transportation, while American private agencies added over $12 million more. It totalled over $75 million or half of the worldwide contribution. The FMG had informed the ICRC that it could fly relief at night to the one Biafran airfield available, but at its own risk. The Joint Church Aid, elements of which were suspected in the early days of perhaps unwittingly mixing ammo boxes with food cargos, the FMG declared an illegal enterprise. Meanwhile Nigerian military technology could not interdict Uli, the Biafra airfield, nor did it have a night fighter capability. The night flights of food (with various aircraft and international crews) and arms continued from every source over FMG airspace. It was an unprecedented international situation.

Relief operations seem to attract a diverse assortment of people and motives. The cause for Biafra caught on in Europe and America, for suffering was widespread. Humanitarian feelings in America were aroused, and the government sought to do everything possible to get food to the starving on both sides through the international organizations. There were many upstanding people whose intentions were of the highest. Then there were other elements, such as opportunists, outright shady characters, and those politically inspired, whose sympathies at best were viewed askance. All sheltered under the relief umbrella.

A Canadian clergyman and a Swedish pilot come to mind as dedicated men. An Englishwoman, who bilked some persons in New York and hastily left the country, was an unsavory type. Politically there were Americans, aside from those sincere ones, who worked for Biafran relief as a hidden step on behalf of Biafran independence. Even those wanting Biafra independent had different intentions. Some unreconstructed whites wanted evidence that African countries outside of South Africa could not advance without white support and should be kept small. The Ibos of Biafra had an active lobby in the U.S. and their enterprise was exceptional. First the issue of christian Ibo versus moslem FMG was tried. This did not hold up because there were more christians in the rest of Nigeria than in Biafra. In fact, three Western Nigeria Catholic bishops protested to the Vatican over what they feared was a pro-Ibo policy. I got to know favorably some of the leading Biafran figures whom Ojukwu sent on assignments. The FMG did the same, and one could only bitterly regret that no way could be found to stop the fighting, which was the only way the massive suffering could be ended. Ingeniously the Ibos managed to win the world propaganda battle, while the Nigerians whittled away at Biafran territory. The strategy was a brief federal push, then prolonged building for the next. In doing this, the federal government finally created on three sides of Biafra the equivalent of three field divisions with their accompanying logistics, a remarkable indigenous achievement not duplicated in Africa's conflicts to this day. After two years of campaigning the Ibos were pressed into an enclave whose population was estimated at from three to four million.

The Ibos rejected any effort to have relief flights use Uli airport during the day. We and others spent lengthy periods trying to concoct formulas which would separate relief flights, which thereby could deliver more, from the night arms airlift, but were unsuccessful. The Ibos opposed any method of delivering relief, whether by land, water route or air, which would remove the essential cover the night relief flights provided the arms lift. The federal side felt that relief was maintaining Ibo morale while actually broadening starvation and prolonging the war, and accordingly was opposed to the humanitarian effort on Biafra's behalf. At one point the FMG was on record with the ICRC for a daylight flight plan generally conceded as reasonable, but Biafra took the flak for a time and that plan was lost in the mist.

In our Congress there were strong proponents of Biafran relief from both parties, such as Senator Kennedy of Massachusetts and Republican Senator Goodell of New York. Both House and Senate had to be kept informed, hearings were held periodically by committees, and the public correspondence was prodigious. In the summer of 1968 the State Department was receiving eleven thousand letters weekly. We handled some, but the bulk of public mail was answered by a section dealing with this and using continually updated form letters we drafted. Campus interest too, was high, so I was among those who talked about the conflict and relief at various universities, such as Michigan State. Finally, the issue was debated in the presidential campaign, and the party candidates made statements.

The African bureau had a unique characteristic in that its activities and U.S. policies were closely attended by the American black leadership. There was an unprecedented and remarkable break between black and white liberal activists over Biafra, for only one black leader came out for Biafran independence. In my recollection it was the only postwar issue that found American liberals divided on racial lines. Black sentiment, looking to the emerging African states as support for the civil rights struggle at home, favored an intact Nigeria rather than one weakened by division. Infrequently I met and dealt with black leaders, later nationally recognized, for information or briefing purposes, and their interest was reflected by black congressmen.

Politically we were active behind the scenes, not taking open leadership, but working with other states, particularly the British Commonwealth, and leading personalities in projects and initiatives designed to end the fighting. This was an intricate and delicate matter, and meant continuing efforts to erect scaffolding when earlier frames collapsed. The subject was too important not to keep trying. Our tactics on this reflected paradoxical American opinion in leading the drive for relief, but not getting publicly out front on peace-seeking. The African states were on record, for example, in opposing outside intervention, while they tried various mediating means, sometimes feeble.   Biafra naturally sought to get American leadership for peace, in order to have this interpreted as a pro-Biafran turn. The United Nations would take no action until it was requested by the OAU, which would never happen. In brief, each day brought a surprise despite hardening experience.   It was a kaleidoscope which could change design as foreign and domestic aspects of politics and relief shifted.

With political and relief elements forming such a serious combination, in July 1968 Deputy Secretary Katzenbach proposed the Nigeria task force be formally reconstituted. This time there was a difference.  I persuaded him that we could operate effectively from the AF/W offices, adjourning to the operations center upstairs for periods as required.  By my chairing the group drawn from all agencies and Department sectors and having frequent meetings to help mesh activities, we were able to coordinate well.  The big issue of relief, the need to organize the American official effort to funnel supplies to the relief agencies, and the indispensable liaison with them were salient features.  My experience stretched into new areas in seeing that our relief measures were consonant with our political objectives of non-direct involvement and non-acceptance of responsibility for the outcome of the war.

As Nigeria pyramided as a center of attention, in the interest of effectiveness by the end of my second year I proposed to the assistant secretary that he appoint a separate country director for it alone.  I would step aside to other work in a reshuffle.  He. however, wanted me to continue to chair the task force arrangement and responded by giving me additional staff, permanent or temporary, as required.  We did much work for Deputy Secretary Katzenbach as the Johnson Administration drew to a close, and one of our special projects was a long November speech wrapping up our Nigerian policy rationale.  When President Nixon took office, our task force hit another high gear.

After President Nixon was elected, domestic pressures mounted from church groups, influential people, and Congress to do more on relief.  The Administration thus decided at the end of February 1969 to appoint a relief coordinator, Clyde Ferguson, designated with the rank of ambassador to dramatize its concern with the problem and to be a focus for it.  He was to concentrate on relief entirely, both at home and overseas, and to draw his resources from AID, while avoiding any political role. In view of the interrelation, this was a difficult responsibility. Nevertheless, Ferguson, when he settled in, through trial and error got a competent staff, did excellently, and we cooperated. This gave me and my associates leeway to concentrate on political aspects such as peace seeking efforts, which in profusion were blossoming and fading. At various times this involved the OAU, African leaders jointly and separately, the Commonwealth Secretariat, the British, and virtually every Western European country from Sweden to Italy, not to omit Canada. Working quietly with receptive states and leaders, we sought to find an acceptable basis to get the disputants talking. It was onerous and exasperating, salvaged only by the objective, as with relief operations. The new President, with the help of national security adviser Kissinger, moved fairly rapidly to appraise our policy at the NSC. President Nixon's conclusion was that while his heart favored Biafra, his head, in understanding the national interest, favored the central government in Lagos. The earlier national policy was intact.

Our long task force continued around a core of five people. Through many hours of day and night, we worked under the glaring tube lights of our familiar sector in the operations center, using cots in sparse sleeping quarters. We acquired a bond of respect and friendship over time. Haven North, a longtime leading figure in its African bureau, was our AID expert, valuable in our general approach, who could tell us or get from his staff all we needed about relief supplies, route capacities, and such essentials. Colonel Dick Kennedy was the Pentagon's man, and also a tower of strength for his incisive and open mind. He later shifted to the White House NSC staff, was chairman of the Nuclear Regulatory Commission, and still later, had two assignments as State ambassador at large, dealing with nuclear non-proliferation and another as State's under secretary for Administration. The NSC staff man for Africa was Roger Morris, who overlapped both Administrations. Roger, barely thirty, was brilliant and a catalyst. Energetic, humorous, and articulate, he later became a biographer and scholar. Bob Smith was indispensable with his knowledge of Nigeria and excellent professional qualities, proven by his final successful assignment as ambassador to Malta. Not a numerologist, I was struck after the fact by the coincidence of groupings of five in several serious periods of my career: Japanese internment, Bucharest cold war activity, and now Nigeria.

The demands on all of us for some stretches were physically exhausting as we fought deadlines and sought to satisfy, not only ourselves, but our chiefs. They were pleased with our varied efforts; an NSC policy draft, U.S. operating alternatives, a lengthy official statement, or a spectrum of other actions. One searching effort was a long survey and policy statement for Deputy Secretary Richardson, representing the Republican Administration, to make before Senator

Kennedy's committee. Both were from Massachusetts. The senator was nettled by finding his questions mainly answered by the statement before he could ask them.

The rest of my West Africa area could be active and have episodes too, but aside from a few instances, these did not coincide with Nigerian surges. Sierra Leone had its coups, while Ghana and Liberia were given official and state visits to Washington, with the preparations and panoply these required. President Johnson's White House reception for President Tubman stands out to me for its Duke Ellington orchestra concert.

Our AF/W field ambassadors were very competent, and this in itself was a great help. Three were career, and there was a political appointee in Ghana, who fortunately was energetic and capable. Still, the care and feeding of ambassadors, particularly political appointees, is a saga in itself. The U.S. remains the only democracy which attempts to use politicians (a high percentage of all ambassadors and at the best posts) for the professional conduct of its diplomacy. All the others can't be wrong. There is a lag in American understanding of world changes, as well as global power shifts, that could create a constricting area for our policy success. Now there is a smaller margin for error, which well intentioned amateurs do not recognize.

My African ambassadors were a diverse group, affable and friendly. Among these, by length of stay the capable Liberian was their dean. We were on good personal terms, and with Bob Sherwood, I helped introduce him and the Ghanaian to major league baseball. The two successive Nigerian ambassadors were enmeshed in their country's fate, and I saw them frequently. Sierra Leone's ambassadors were in a revolving door. Being supplied with funds for this, the ambassadors were socially active, but as usual for FSOs in Washington, our reciprocal activity was limited, even more so because of my uncertain hours.

My own three annual efficiency reports were completed by different deputy assistant secretaries and with varying detail. The second part, of course, was confidential, and the assistant secretary reviewed both of these with general affirmations. The first two successively I thought less career pointed because of my possible retirement and then at an inappropriate period for an embassy nomination, while the bureau head stressed to me his satisfaction over AF/W's spirit and teamwork. Remembering Mr. Herter, my only unvoiced reservation was why in logic the assistant secretary had not done the ratings and a willing Deputy Secretary the review or commentary. This is, of course, bureaucratic, but those efficiency reports were career guideposts.

The new Administration began Africa appointments, and the bureau chief won his. The State committee curiously had not approved my nomination to the White House. Then with another efficiency report, which I thought vague, our chief, preparing to leave, attached his review. However, I was now up for the Ivory Coast, the booming francophone state in West Africa. Then a change of AF signals named my friend, John Root, who was denied earlier and whose French was excellent. Mine was adequate. John, disturbed, told me at lunch he had consulted others on bowing out, feeling that since I had the bureau's most demanding work, this dictated I should have it. I gave my estimate of his abilities and said he should have no thought of refusing. I did not prompt the assistant secretary for clarification, a weary lapse on my part. Still, just before the bureau chief left, at his request I told him of my preferences among the still open missions. I assumed he had congressional problems, exemplified by the earlier Unit citation episode, and wanted a less visible mission for me. He proposed Cameroon, an English-French speaking neighbor of Nigeria. Virgina and I discussed it and agreed; it would be a two year assignment before retirement. Now David Newsom, the new assistant secretary for Africa, was to carry through.

Dave Newsom I had known for some time, and thought it an excellent appointment. He wanted to reorganize the bureau, essentially seeking a return to the office director format and to make me responsible for the fourteen West African countries. On this I gave two plans: (1) two deputies, one of whom would be full time on Nigeria, or (2) a separate office for Nigeria, like my earlier proposal. He chose splitting off Nigeria, making it a special staff, and I breathed in relief. The war was trending toward a Nigerian victory. However, the change for me and our bureau sector came toward the end of August. Thirty-seven months of immersion in Nigeria were ended, and my family cheered. Still called AF/W, my new parish contained the francophone states of the bulge of Africa, together with my three old anglophones (sometimes called saxophones). It was all provisional, awaiting the nomination system. The career nomination route was my preference, but at least one Republican friend, Kim Roosevelt, wrote a strong letter about me to Deputy Secretary Richardson. I had known the Department's ranking career officer, the under secretary for Political Affairs, Alexis Johnson, for many years. I saw him when my name was proposed to the Department's committee, and whenever my name came up, I was reliably told, he was favorable.

Newsom, one Fall day, obviously troubled, told me straight. The committee had turned me down again, and I was to be dropped from consideration. Firmly I said my nomination should not have been his responsibility, and our former chief should have handled my future before he came aboard. On leaving him, I assumed from my selection board experience that the action was a summation of my last AF reports, which, particularly Part 2, must have been pedestrian. As mentioned, my vitality was worn down, and I had not pressed, but it was not easy to accept what I deemed a violation of the professionalism I had built as a career foundation. The previous assistant secretary shortly returned to Washington on consultation. I was frank. Avowing shock, he declared he would call on various officials. Not anticipating any positive result, I do not know whom he saw.

The annual honor awards of the Bureau came about this time. On behalf of the Secretary, before the staff, Dave Newsom announced my receipt of the superior honor award given for my work as chairman of the Nigeria task force. There was a citation and medal. I recognized it as his gentlemanly action. Alex Johnson I called on to thank for his support, of which the grapevine had told me. I had faced by my code the reality of the future. Newsom wanted me to stay with him, and this I would do. The award citation mentioned "professionalism, stamina, and dedication." I could appreciate those.

1971 National War College commandant, deputies, and wives.   Right to left:   Lt. Gen.
McPherson, USAF; Rear Admiral Jackson, USN, and myself

# CHAPTER 16

# INDIAN SUMMER: AFRICA, WASHINGTON & NWC

## September 1969 - June 30, 1972

*In a most active period, protestors held large demonstrations and the press heavily faulted our Vietnam policy. President Nixon declared a "phased withdrawal" and more use of Vietnamese troops. America continued its Apollo moon flights, and U.S. - Soviet treaties prohibited military use of the ocean floor and bacterial weapons. India defeated Pakistan for sub-continent supremacy; the U.K. entered the Common Market after France ended objections; and the U.S. returned Okinawa to Japan. The Sino-Soviet schism endured, as did China's disastrous Cultural Revolution, while the U.S. developed China ties from "ping pong" diplomacy to President Nixon's visit. The Nigerian civil war ended in Biafra's complete defeat, guaranteeing African state boundaries. After being director of a enlarged State AF/W, at the National War College I was department chairman for more than half of its curriculum. The second year I acted for six months as a deputy commandant, a good conclusion to a Foreign Service career.*

My new AF/W was a healthy antidote and an elixir. Ray Perkins, familiar with Africa, was my deputy, while the Liberia-Sierra Leone and Ghana desk officers with their assistants were included, the new element being four francophone desk officers, one of whom handled regional economic matters, and their secretaries. While learning about nine new countries, meeting and corresponding with their ambassadors and ours, and using my French, I appraised the new officers. They had less experience than the anglophone desk men, so I encouraged them to take short FSI courses.

My immediate need was to create cohesion. The francophone side had been through two reorganizations, and there were secretary morale problems. By year's end I think the office was on a reasonable keel, and for this Ray Perkins was a great help. Newsom knew that, while pleased to work with him, I had a career timetable. My long held plan, if after a two year embassy, was to retire at 59, or without one, to retire from Washington at 58. By then my two youngest daughters would separately enter college and be a high school senior. If I were a college professor, that was a good time to move from Washington. Also I wanted to retire before the mandatory retirement age of 60.

Our two most important francophones were Ivory Coast and Guinea. Since independence in 1960, when there were 10,000 French in Ivory Coast, its economy grew with the French, so they now numbered 40,000. We also had aided by being a major backer of a large dam being built. Of the five West African Entente states, Ivory Coast was most influential and its head, Houphouet-Boigny, an African leader. Guinea had broken with France after independence and under Sekou Toure had taken an African Marxist revolutionary way. Like Ivory Coast, it was a one party state, but differed in its totalitarian model. Guinea followed a pragmatic course, but disillusioned with Soviet and Red Chinese aid and political interference, had turned to the West for investment to develop its large mineral resources, notably bauxite. American companies, with U.S. investment guarantees, had been among those responding.

There were seven others: Senegal, led by the poet, Senghor; The Gambia, a river enclave surrounded by Senegal; Mali, controlled by a military junta cool to the communists; Niger with the acute Diori; Upper Volta (now Burkina Faso); Togo, run by military men planning as their buttress a single party, civilian staffed government; and finally, Dahomey (now Benin). It was a never dull aggregation. Since I intended to operate as usual in the new AF/W, it was important to see the area at first hand, so by the New Year I was off, and the trip lasted six weeks. It took me, as well, to Paris and London and to our African chiefs of mission conference at Kinshasa in Zaire, where the Secretary was on an African tour. In Paris the French foreign office people were less forthcoming than expected, but Africa began with Ouagadougou, Upper Volta. Afield the questions affecting the area, which in Washington inexorably took a problem and paper cast, had living and optimistic flesh and blood. The negative aspects - formidable economic problems, disappointing political developments, needed French subsidies - all were known. Talking business with embassy people, foreigners, and local people, I was taken by the vitality, the sights, sounds, and contrasts comprising the familiar field atmosphere I shared.

After ten years of general African independence and changes over my three years, there was a growing realism as the Africans realized that the outside world could not solve their national problems and that economic development could not be rapid because the resources were not readily available. Since then there has been little progess, although regimes were more aware of their limitations, such as francophone economic dependence on French subventions and soft world prices for their few large commodity exports. There was a popular trend toward state control of extractive industries and progressive replacement of foreign technicians and representatives by qualified local people. They would take assistance from wherever it might come, believing that a friend would give aid. At the same time, "African socialism," variously defined, typified national efforts to mobilize resources for development without having a Moscow or Beijing brand. ~~Nation~~

building and national consciousness seemed to be growing, as well as efforts at regional cooperation. Ferment and changing attitudes showed in various ways, and leadership and professional competence in West Africa, despite coups and corruption, for the time being appeared to be holding their own. Despite the socialist aura to development, the greatest economic influence was the European Common Market, whose trade and investment were growing forces. For U.S. policy we could be thankful that the French, despite their divide and rule policy at independence, were so involved in francophone trade and aid. The British too, were thinking of their interests in terms of Common Market association.

The country leaders of the period had different political fates, and I was struck by their diversity: Diori of Niger, who had sought anglophone-francophone cooperation for development; General Lamizana of Upper Volta talking of national austerity, neatly dressed in a threadbare jacket, a hole in a trouser cuff, and with a gold Rolex wristwatch; Stevens of Sierra Leone, receiving us and talking while several unidentified people stood around; General Eyadema of Togo, alert, dapper, and articulate; Senghor of Senegal, the quiet poet-scholar turned politician-leader; and authoritarian Sekou Toure of Guinea, who had the knack in conversation of impressing foreigners.

By now I knew our ambassadors, and they offered me good working programs. John Root and I spent two days of a weekend traveling in Ivory Coast, during which we visited the Bandama Dam site, which eventually would create a lake three times the size of Lake Geneva. Bob Miner (his wife away) and I in Sierra Leone were bachelors together. The former Senegalese ambassador in Washington was acting foreign minister during my Dakar visit, and was most hospitable. The Guineans, into a phase of redressing their balance with the West over the communists, insisted that I stay in government guest quarters, not as comfortable as the embassy residence, but the intent was there. In each country there was the good humor and open nature of the people, and the magnificent sunsets of the tropics.

For some posts I was able to be useful. In Monrovia I was of assistance to the ambassador and DCM. In Conakry, with a newly arrived chargé, I guided the post and the Department on pressing matters between Guinea and ourselves. Sekou Toure was amused when I pointedly said I did not intend to take up one issue with him, a substantive one, after having talked with his ministers. Thereupon I made a detailed resumé of the position given to them.

The Organization of African Unity village at Kinshasa, Zaire, had been built originally by the regime for OAU conferences, and we were the first foreign aggregation to use it. The impressive complex was in excellent order, and John Root and I were in the same well-kept cottage. It was a good conference, with

Secretary Rogers present for two days. There was Brewster Morris, formerly of Montreal, as an ambassador and Dr. Don McIntyre, previously of Baghdad. The Congo river pool retained its overlooking statue of explorer Stanley, hand to hat brim, seeming to say, "I've had the Congo up to here." The monument no longer is there.

On the road again, there was a full day stop I could not resist - Lagos. That January Ojukwu had fled and the Ibos announced their capitulation, so the war was over before I left Washington. On the way I had an outline of developments in meeting Clyde Ferguson. The pro-Biafran people were pressing us to have Nigeria take massive steps in relief, which was bringing great strains to our relations. After all, Nigeria had won and, at most, was open to friendly persuasion. Our people deemed the Nigerian Red Cross slow in handling relief adequately, but the feared massacres and widespread persecution of the Ibos did not materialize. Quickly fraternization began, and Ibos returned to the rest of Nigeria and Lagos. It was a strategic victory for Africa, since Nigeria's national and African international boundaries would remain intact. In Lagos I talked to the embassy people, who were disturbed by Washington domestic pressures as not appreciating Nigerian attitudes, but the visiting Secretary gave the embassy his support, so the comparatively new ambassador and staff were feeling better. Gowon was still the leader, and this guaranteed a moderate course toward the Ibos. The oil was resuming its flow and the future looked promising. I had seen and heard for myself. *Tragically later military elements intervened* -

The last African mission, Bamako, Mali offered a temptation, but there was no time to visit Timbuctu, for an early morning takeoff took me to London, a freezing contrast to a Bamako day at 100 degrees. After talks with the British and visiting a Parliament session on Zimbabwe, I left for Washington with Clyde Ferguson, returning with a firmer sense of the West African environment and what we should be doing.

A personnel matter troubled me. A chargé of a very small embassy I sensed to be very taut, but with his young wife and baby as domestic balances, he seemed to handle the responsibility. Nevertheless when I returned to Washington I made a serious recommendation that he be transferred to a metropolitan post in order to get the assignment isolation out of his system. I assumed it was done after my own transfer, but instead he was sent to a two-man post in Equatorial Guinea. The isolated officer, by now paranoid, killed his associate.

At each place after consulting with the ambassador I wrote my impressions, discussed operating matters, and made action recommendations to my Washington deputy. There was a goodly pile when I returned and checked on what still remained to do. From these and accumulated ideas I drafted a report to Dave

Newsom with regionally applicable recommendations, which he liked. Next I started the men on the initiative of a policy and operations review of West Africa. Our office was meshing nicely and there was a sense of regional purpose. We were seeking more self-help funds to be used as the ambassadors decided, and taking other operations steps.

One day our State deputy commandant at the National War College, my old friend Ambassador J. Wesley (Johnny) Jones, asked me to lunch. He wanted me to join him as chairman of the department of international relations and area studies, a sector responsible for over half of the curriculum and consisting of FSOs, visiting professors, and military officers. Earlier I had declined to be considered as diplomat-in-residence at Bryn Mawr, Haverford, and Swarthmore, since I did not want to move from Washington until retirement. Now things were going well in AF/W, even if there was no letup in the busy bureau pace. Undeniably it was attractive to be in an assignment transitional to academia without operations pressures. I told the ambassador that while very interested, I expected it to be for one year, and that the College might not want this. Also, I would have to discuss it with Virginia and Dave Newsom. Johnny checked with the Commandant and found him agreeable. Virginia was enthusiastic. I talked with Dave and he, with my plans in mind, thought I should take it. I called Johnny.

In the wake of Nigeria, I had decided one thing - the result was not going to affect my outlook, as I had seen occur to others through frustration or adversity. The work with the rest of West Africa undoubtedly aided this resolve, and now the National War College made it a certainty. The College, in some respects, was like coming home; the nearest thing to a repeated friendly post or compatible bureau assignment. The impressive brick and concrete columned building after twenty years was virtually unchanged, aside from the boon of air conditioning, while the familiar lecture auditorium was now named after Eisenhower and the smaller one after Air Force General Arnold. To complete the trinity, the old typing pool, now a lounge and reception area, was inscribed for the first commandant, Admiral Hill.

Many things were the same: ratios of Army, Air Force, Sea Services, and civilians (half State). The students numbered 140, now lieutenant colonels and navy commanders, but still gathered in committees and combined into discussion groups. Thanks to the computer, each of the twelve courses through the ten-month curriculum found the students randomly rotated. The morning lectures again featured experts, followed by a question and answer period, concluding with discussion groups on the daily readings and lectures. The inter-agency faculty acted as group moderators and committee advisers, counseled those from their agencies, and helped, as qualified, with student research papers. Even as before, the university professors, three area specialists, had one year sabbatical assignments from their schools.

This time I paid attention to faculty organization. We were lucky in the commandant and deputies. Air Force Lieutenant General McPherson was a tall, agreeable man who had his views, but controlled the school as a gentleman leader. Rear Admiral Jackson as executive officer channeled the elements reporting to him, much like a deputy chief of mission. He was frank and took suggestions, and we got on well. Johnny Jones, as the deputy for international affairs (DCIA) and the third of the directing group, was lively and keen, and an advertisement for the Foreign Service.

Shortly after my shift to the War College, Virginia had a medical crisis that could have required major brain surgery, avoided by what the top-flight surgeon termed a fantastic development. It was not until Christmas that she resumed a completely normal routine, but we kept crossed fingers for several months. All proved well, and we felt so favored to be in Washington instead of overseas. Fate had created a magnificent good turn of fortune and I had no lingering complaint. Any future plans were in abeyance pending Virginia's complete recovery, but by early spring I resumed academic contacts and writing, and made my availability known into the second college year.

Since the College was primarily for the military and responsible to the Joint Chiefs of Staff, any civilian was judicious in proposing new emphases or innovations. It was not unreasonable, in view of the school's success, to be satisfied with the tested and to firm the curriculum in advance. Johnny and the admiral commented on this, but were receptive to ideas for reasonable change and flexibility. I was grateful the Army was charged with the College budget, for the secretary was an Army colonel, very helpful to me and my department. He thought some paneling would look well in my office, put it in, and it did.

As Johnny said, it was hard to decompress after the action and responsibilities of previous assignments. Over time I came to appreciate this and the pleasurable benefits of regular hours and five day weeks, new to the family. I also met the military fondness for acronyms. My department of international relations and area studies was known as DIRAS and had ten faculty the first year. Of my own DIRAS group, aside from Col. Danford and a Navy Captain, there were two FSO-2s, Bill Witt and Jim Pratt. Jim, a Soviet expert, had been political counselor in Moscow and Bill was from African Affairs. Two CIA men were from the evaluation side, one of whom, Doug Mulholland, years later became State assistant secretary for Intelligence and Research. Of the three university professors, I was closest to Dick Butwell (Southeast Asia), a former colleague of Ken Landon's at American University. It was a competent shop.

Additionally our group led the intensive preparations and operation of the committee area problems related to the three week spring trips abroad. Ah, those trips. Colonel Danford made the arrangements for the two class visits to the United Nations and military installations, as well as coordinating details of committee area problems culminating overseas. Here the class was broken into five parts, faculty included, as it studied American issues related to Latin America, Africa, Europe, the Middle East and South Asia, and East Asia. Each trip group thereafter insisted its overseas experience was the best.

The diversity of student and faculty background and personality made our little oasis a stimulating place. There was at least one quasi-expert in the audience, raising questions and getting into the discussion. Incidentally, the ones frequently questioning were called springbutts, and there were always the sphinxes. We had some great speakers and well-known figures, as well as some ranking people, who sometimes did not come through. I enjoyed Chip Bohlen, Foy Kohler, Dave Newsom, and Jim Akins, who was fine on Mideast oil. Frank Williams, the former ambassador to Ghana, impressed us all with his talk on the black minority at home. When it came to Africa, I spoke on West and Central Africa.

The scheduled momentum of the year made the months pass rapidly. Mornings were full. Afternoons embodied faculty meetings and individual planning discussions, while the students read and researched. I was in touch with the State Department for speakers and information and to meet friends, but gradually I developed an informed detachment toward the figurative sound and fury I had known.

Suddenly we were at the point of the three week overseas trips. The Far East was my choice, for I had known only Japan and some of China. We had a good African bureau contingent that year, so also aboard were former associates like George Sherry (AFW), Bob Melone (Tehran and AF field), and Nancy Rawls (AF field and the only woman student). The head of curriculum development led our sortie, and we had the school adjutant and Dick Butwell. Privately I had talked to Perce Jackson, and contrary to rank protocol, suggested it would be more useful if a military man headed our trip. He was surprised, but agreed to it. Besides, I wanted the temporary freedom from such responsibility.

Honolulu had been urbanized since 1939, and Waikiki was a tourist hotel mass. Pearl Harbor now had the Arizona Memorial and CINCPAC, where Dick Butwell and I teamed up on rooms, while I had a long deferred mai tai on the beach at the Royal Hawaiian. From there, time changes were greatest, and I used my sleeping pills on the long flight to Sydney, Australia. Our plane was of the commodious type that took those Bob Hope entertainment troupes to far away military installations during the Christmas holidays, so we had everything drinkable and eatable aboard, as we sat three abreast, facing friends over folding tables. One table had the world's most continuous, flying poker game. Also, there was plenty of cargo space, generously used by shoppers. Pago Pago, Samoa, gave a breather, and a lovely locale it was. Then came Sydney.

I earlier arranged to meet some old Kobe friends for a buffet dinner the first night there, and Mrs. James had it in her home with two daughters, at one of whose weddings I had ushered. There was Cyril Owen, with whom I'd played rugby, and his wife, Rosemary Winter, a Kobe veteran. It was quite a group. Sydney itself was a jewel with its harbor, the celebrated opera house, and the famed bridge. The fellows were struck by the healthy young women in mini skirts, and could well understand why our Vietnam GIs took their leave there. Our consul general, an old Service colleague, among other things told me that for the volume of such leaves there had been a remarkably low incidence of trouble. Canberra, the capital, differed from Sydney as a product of the latest in city planning. Here the Australians gave us full hospitality and informative briefings, and there were responsive officials, including the embassy's economic counselor, Al Nyren, my first AF/W deputy. I came away with the Australians ranking among the top in my book. Those amazing temples in Bangkok were out of Disneyland, and the complex mixture of modernity came as a surprise. I liked the place. Our embassy handling was mediocre, but I got some informative impressions from a former working colleague in a key spot.

It began to appear that the entire area offered great promise of development and stability once the Vietnam war subsided. Japan had the area a bit apprehensive, since its economic success seemed a disturbing harbinger of political and later, military influence that events would prove in error. Seoul proved one of the best stops. On all sides we got the informed word, notably from the ambassador, whom I had last met in Damascus as vice consul Bill Porter, when he covered for his boss. A highlight was the visit by helicopter and bus to the Demilitarized Zone, with its armistice conference hut. It was sporadically active, as we saw on visiting the lines held by the South Koreans, but the most unusual feature was the peninsula-wide Zone itself, which had become an remarkable wildlife refuge.

I had been looking forward to Japan. The urban area of Tokyo, its traffic swirl, electric trains, and shopping and work multitudes, seemed to have changed only in degree from earlier recall. The interviews and briefings we had, led by Armin Meyer as ambassador, indicated to me that the economic changes everyone talked of had not disrupted the cultural fabric I had known. Everything was expensive, and the group was fortunate with the one military hotel left in Tokyo, where prices were reasonable and the meals good. My old Kobe friend,

Australian Howard Harker and his wife, Joy, were at Kamakura, not far from the Great Buddha. He had retired as Far East director for Imperial Chemical Industries, and confirmed some Japanese impressions and added more insights. As a combat veteran he simply remarked, "In the war the Japanese behaved very badly." At every stop I met more close colleagues and friends who had valuable observations, this quasi-farewell tour making me more conscious of Service years. Now there was a last long leg to Washington.

The one woman in the class, Foreign Service Officer Nancy Rawls, I had met as commercial attache in Monrovia. In the College she made an excellent impression, and I knew she was slated for a top assignment. After our return we had lunch in town, and she was preoccupied. Nancy wanted advice, for she was to be nominated as ambassador to Ivory Coast, succeeding John Root whose tour was ending. Her query was whether, as a woman, she should accept, for she feared there would be Service criticism of the nomination. I responded that she was an outstanding officer. She had to understand the nature of the American political system. It was accepted that all elements of our society should be represented in our diplomacy, and women were long overdue and under represented. She should welcome the nomination, knowing she had the hearty wishes of all her working colleagues. Nancy felt better, and I had to contain a smile over the cameo reappearance of Ivory Coast.

The College's graduation ceremony was different that year. State's Pete Spicer so thoroughly enjoyed the change of scene that over the year he grew a full beard as a sign of a free spirit. Signalling the academic holiday was over, a clean shaven Pete strode toward the podium for his certificate, to the enthusiastic cheers of the entire class.

By August the reconstituted academic crew was aboard. A fresh year began, but a big gap was Johnny's successor. There was much moving of chessmen, but no ambassador as a series of assignments was delayed, so until the State deputy commandant successor arrived, at the request of the Commandant I handled that job as well as my own. Bill Leonhart, our excellent ambassador in Belgrade, who I had known as a junior secretary during the Tito-Stalin rift, was named and eventually came aboard when over half the year had passed. As acting deputy, I had added duties in helping to choose and meet guest speakers, as well as sharing a host role at club lunches.

One of the School's virtues was academic open mindedness, with disparate views presented from the podium and in readings. A prominent dissenter, Daniel Ellsberg, in the previous academic year had a respectful hearing in objecting to our Vietnam policy. Shortly thereafter he released the so-called Pentagon Papers. This policy often surprised academic guest speakers, who confessed to the lack of a like atmosphere on their campuses! Academic interests also impelled me to attend conferences and conventions and to visit universities. Academia, despite the Vietnam political partisanship, became more attractive. The future, if I could see it, would find me as professor at a satisfying small college whose president knew the Foreign Service. With this and beyond would be years of overseas cruises as lecturer and professor to tourists and students, which would become a third career.

Visible customs change over time, and now when I could stop to observe, there were two among others I remarked. No one whistled anymore. It was an everyday cheerful sound in America's environment that had virtually disappeared. A tedious gesture also had taken hold, to stand and applaud any speaker, presumably because you looked foolish if still seated. There were other changes as I looked closely, and understood that such altered behavior slowly affects a culture.

The College environment also helped to put the span of personal and professional years in perspective. Experience is not the only truth, and from mine it was unbalancing to place some normally ambitious people with incomplete development of their private pursuits into policy positions in government. An outlook commendably rational could become erratic in the new environment. Most successful in the transition are those not bent on a reputation, having had satisfying private careers. To me, my two presidential national security assistants are appropriate models.

Once on consultation and a visit to my friend, Bromley Smith, in his basement White House quarters, I was introduced to his chief, an energetic man. Then, as if expecting some revelatory gossip from my recent assignment, he said I should consider him as a Father Confessor and be fully frank. My arching eyebrows matched Brom's. Jim Akins was a watch officer in State's operations center, when he received a White House phone call from a top official, who outlined a course of action he wanted the Department to initiate. Jim confounded him by saying he could not do this because it would backfire. Incensed, the official asked his identity, promising to be heard from. Nothing happened, for on reflection the man probably decided not to look foolish. A newly appointed ranking State official remarked to a small group that we should join him "in having fun" during his tenure. There is a line between dilettante and professional.

I thought seriously of the Foreign Service wives in my time and their indispensable role, as the State Department got two people for the price of one. They had to be the doers in duties the spouses could not shoulder; cooperate with office administrators in details of family living; check education facilities and health precautions; participate in varied social life, and be pleasant to unfamiliar people, while participating in activities that furthered American objectives. Stirring times in Washington or at various posts sometimes left the designated dependent isolated with the children as the officer followed a duty schedule. It was as formidable an array of actions, in their way, as their Service husbands would pursue.

The ever-evolving Foreign Service can be seen by charts in State's Newsletter of May 1991. Half its budget, as usual, is salaries and expenses, with a quarter of this being diplomatic and consular relations, the old core of State's activities. Major portions of the other half of State's budget, as custom, go for UN and foreign buildings programs. Remarked by change are other categories among salaries and expenses, progressively greater than diplomatic and consular relations; diplomatic security, information management (equipment and computers), and general administrative activities. Smaller slices of that fifty percent go for executive direction (8%) and professional training and medical services (3%). One need not question these categories, totalling three quarters, whose meaning may have shifted over time, but it shows the extensive technical backstopping that foreign affairs now require. In less complex days they would be deemed, in the widest sense, administrative supplements to substantive work. Time is creating a new diplomat, able to understand and effectively use the variety of new instruments modern relations show as essential.

There is a revolution in the organizational influences of our foreign policy. Before World War II our policy, for good or ill, was run by the president and the State Department. Foreign policy is now fully political, heavily molded by public polls and congressional committees, and there is constant controversy over our handling of interests. Separate public and private bureaucracies reflect our diverse politics, while State, lacking a constituency, tries to act with national interest. Agency budgets are a source of power. This means that in major American embassies, separate from interactions at home, the departments and agencies represented, such as CIA, AID, and USIA, are numerous while the State Department fields a fraction of such personnel. Since most of these entities have separate mail or code access to Washington as well as separate budgets, it becomes a strenuous task to avoid mixed signals there and to develop a sensible coordination. Accommodation is reached in each embassy in time, but global power shifts can create disturbing policy aftermaths to failure, while disparate domestic voices can grow.

On reviewing my Service career I found, given the state of the world, that it was marked by successive conflicts and crises interspersed by change of pace assignments at regular intervals. Before I was involved in the actions of World War II there had been a first period which gave me the opportunity to learn the Service's basic skills. The vortex of war found me easing into its strains, culminating in the further tragedy of the cold war. This lengthy contest proved to be the core of my Foreign Service experience, as I became familiar with Soviet strategies and tactics. Then I learned and participated in the various means our government used as counter strategies and to train other officers for their worldwide tests. The cold war immersed me, both in bureaucratic and flesh and blood aspects of its trials. Fortune did not always smile on my family and me, but life's eventual satisfactions were undeniable. A final benefit came with this War College assignment and the occasion to assess my role in our unique profession.

Affected by change are aspects of the Foreign Service and their ongoing significance. In the diplomatic entrance of the State Department large plaques commemorate officers who have died while at their duty. Air crashes are not generally listed, unlike shipwrecks and disease in the old days, yet the list grows. In more recent years on a plaque there are a full half dozen of my first name associates killed by terrorists. As many more have escaped bombings. On television news, Chris Chapman, as our minister in Paris was seen by an enterprising cameraman ducking behind a car as a gunman shot at him and then walked away. The Foreign Service Journal of May 1988 reports that diplomats and their facilities are attacked almost as often as our military, with the Service over the past twenty years suffering a violent death every 90 days. Diplomacy, under my eyes, is now a hazardous profession.

Career men tell of colleagues who are left in comparative anonymity. One, of course, is Jack Iams' exploit in uncovering the Soviet missile center. There are others. Consul Walter Orebaugh escaped from house arrest, and over time became leader of an Italian partisan band. He holds America's top civilian award, the Medal of Freedom. Another consul in Tihwa, Chinese Turkestan, Hall Paxton, was cut off by the communists after the Nationalist collapse. He and his wife organized and rode a caravan, complete with camels, over interminable miles and the world's highest mountains, to safety in India. He lies in Isfahan, his last post. Adventure is an ongoing ingredient in Service lives, and I accepted this, having been a vicarious partner and active participant.

My second spring trip of the College came quickly. It was the Middle East and South Asia, mainly because I had a strong desire to see the subcontinent, but also to appraise my old area. Turkey, seen in Istanbul and Ankara, had modernized considerably. Burton Berry was in Europe, but the familiar Istanbul sights, including the consulate, general, were worth revisiting. The porters at Galata bridge were gone, but still in the bazaar. Then in Ankara I spent some comfortable hours with an old Turkish diplomat friend, Turgut Menemencioglu. We had first met in Bucharest, where his wife offered a sizeable puppet, Punch, we always used as a Christmas tree ornament. He was the only foreign diplomat with whom, based on mutual regard, I used to meet at least once yearly when he was ambassador at Washington and at the U.N.¹ We would choose a quiet bar, and over several hours would review the state of the world. Turgut here gave me a more informed perspective than our official briefings.

Tehran was surprising, seeming one big traffic jam, and the embassy was now in its center as the city spread to the mountains. There was a session with the Shah, whom I regretfully sensed was still on stage, but still impressed his audience. Like Tehran, our stops were short, but the group had prepared well for the trip with briefings and interviews, so that maximum benefit was derived from the assorted local contacts that were arranged and the on-site meetings. The subcontinent held two major countries, Pakistan and India. The latter, including Bombay, New Delhi, and a bus trip to Agra for the Taj Mahal, was just too vast and complex. India had defeated Pakistan and was unmistakable leader of South Asia, but its traditions and population morass offered difficult prospects for the future. Pakistan was reeling from its defeat and the loss of East Pakistan as Bangladesh. All depended on peace talks with India, its impressive leader, Bhutto, senior, declared in a satisfying afternoon gathering. Rawalpindi, Islamabad (the capital), and the hill station, Murree, gave further background, where at lunch I met the legendary Air Force general, Chuck Yeager.

Bob Neumann, our ambassador in Kabul, I first knew as a professor when he had come by us in Baghdad. The embassy proved to be a happy crew, Bob competent and unchanged, as he gave us a full picture and saw that we met diverse Afghans. The place to me was comparable to Tehran of twenty years before, yet the sophisticated, out of sight, Soviet dominance was a new dimension, and looked to grow. Atop the world's largest oil pool, we saw Saudi Arabia through Riyadh its capital and the ubiquitous royal family running its ministries. The conservative mentality and Islamic tradition were exemplified in King Faisal's remarks. The Arab-Israeli problem appeared for the time to be under control, and certainly Israel seemed in good shape and confident, as Ambassador Wally Barbour, my old chief, briefed me.

On landing in Washington all of us were tired, but we had consulted the trip doctor at one or more points along the way, thus keeping our walking wounded to a minimum. Thinking on it, while it was stimulating to see the varied sights and to meet many old colleagues, my low-key attitude toward our overseas operations had been reinforced.

The rest of May was the year's windup. It meant concluding academic duties and a checklist of pre-retirement actions. But the Department earlier had requested one final assignment of me as chairman of an 18 member inter-agency committee to reexamine and reset post hardship differential allowance criteria.

Despite the changes, this had not been done in 20 odd years. We looked at hardship categories from health to violence, and set up revised elements and weightings against which all overseas civilian posts would be periodically judged. One of our main participants from the administrative side, whom I earlier knew and came to respect more, years later was killed in Rome by terrorists.

Final College evaluations were made on the students I followed as adviser, and then I did my last Foreign Service efficiency report, on Bill Witt, who had been a support in my department and an asset to the College.

Official College functions were habitual at year's end, and the military did these things very well, even to last day retirement ceremonies for Perce Jackson and myself. I received a College plaque, a Defense Department civilian citation, and my State Department retirement letter from the Secretary. My few remarks did not come easily, but it was good to have my family and Loy Henderson, Lee Metcalf, Bruce Lancaster, and other friends there.

The feeling that I had retired from the Foreign Service came the previous day as I prepared to pack personal effects from my pleasant office. Before starting and while seated at my desk, I took a long look. On the wall opposite my desk was a favorite still painting that in hectic earlier times had been a welcome eye rest. To my left were the open bookshelves with African artifacts, Mideast silver, and books and brochures. On that wall was a silver tray inscribed from the shah, and on a shelf a citation, the Nigerian cooker souvenir. Two autographed photos were there, from Burton Berry and Loy Henderson, the finest field chiefs in my experience. Beside my desk, as usual, was a framed wall map of the United States. I felt seasoned as I thought about what the Service had offered. There would be no nostalgia. Memories were something else.

On my desk was a folder of family photos. Life, I thought, would always give surprises, but for Virginia and me it would be even better. Our daughters were there. Lucy, eventually a Ph.D. in Comparative Literature, would be a college language professor; Janice would become an ordained Episcopal minister, and Hope would have a B.S. in Nursing. Teaching, preaching, and nursing; all forms of social service. Maybe after all, something of the Foreign Service had rubbed off.

It was time to get moving. Under the desk top glass was the world map I would no longer need, with the Foreign Service areas and posts indicated. Then the last of the rules of living from Satchel Paige, the legendary pitcher, came to mind, and I grinned. "Never look back. Something might be gaining on you."

INDEX